AF531522

Fundamentals of Agricultural Extension

NIPA® GENX ELECTRONIC RESOURCES & SOLUTIONS P. LTD.
New Delhi-110 034

About the Editor

Dr Sapna Jarial is an agricultural extensionist with expertise in research for development, extension management and promotion of innovative crop-livestock systems in South Asia and Tropical Africa. Her academic qualifications include a B.Sc. Agriculture from Himachal Pradesh Agricultural University; M.Sc. Dairy Extension from the National Dairy Research Institute, India, and PhD. in Dairy Extension Management from National Dairy Research Institute, Karnal, Haryana with merit. She was a DAAD research fellow at department of Resource Economics Humboldt University Germany. Her research interests include extension advisory services, entrepreneurship, gender in agriculture and innovation. She is an Associate Professor in Agricultural Extension at the Department of Agricultural Economics and Extension, School of Agriculture, Lovely Professional University, Phagwara, Punjab. She has written 5 books, over 35 research and review papers.

Fundamentals of Agricultural Extension

Sapna Jarial
Department of Agricultural Economics and Extension
Lovely Professional University
Phagwara, Punjab

NIPA® GENX ELECTRONIC RESOURCES & SOLUTIONS P. LTD.
New Delhi-110 034

NIPA. GENX ELECTRONIC RESOURCES & SOLUTIONS P. LTD.

101,103, Vikas Surya Plaza, CU Block
L.S.C.Market, Pitam Pura, New Delhi-110 034
Ph : +91 11 27341616, 27341717, 27341718
E-mail: newindiapublishingagency@gmail.com
www: www.nipabooks.com

For customer assistance, please contact
Phone: + 91-11-27 34 17 17
Fax: + 91-11-27 34 16 16

Print ISBN: 978-93-58878-12-7
ebook ISBN: 978-93-58875-63-8

Composed and Designed by NIPA®.

Preface

Extension education is crucial for sustainable development and innovation in global agriculture. "Fundamentals of Agricultural Extension" thoroughly examines this critical topic and is designed to prepare future agriculturists with the necessary information and abilities to understand and impact this ever-changing industry. The book combines in-depth academic analysis and practical advice to examine extension education's impact on agricultural development comprehensively. It covers theory, mind maps, and descriptive questions for student learning. This book originates from the belief that the future of agriculture depends on the successful sharing of information and technology, along with strong community involvement and leadership. The book covers various aspects of extension education, such as organisational structures, Information and Communication Technologies (ICT) applications, rural and community development, extension administration, technology transfer, and communication principles. This book is structured into six units encompassing twenty chapters, meticulously guiding readers in a detailed exploration of agricultural extension.

This document outlines the course outcomes for undergraduate students majoring in BSc Agriculture, Forestry, Horticulture, Fisheries, and Veterinary Sciences, aiming to be both ambitious and fundamental. They are crafted to empower students to critically examine extension education's core principles, assess the impact of ICT tools on community development, and navigate the complexities of technology transfer and innovation diffusion within the agricultural sector. This book explores topics such as the history and system of extension education in India and modern advancements in agricultural extension like cyber extension and market-led strategies, bridging traditional practices with the future of agricultural extension. This work is a toolkit to inspire and empower individuals to promote sustainable and equitable agricultural growth among a new generation of agriculturists. "Fundamentals of Agricultural Extension" serves as a complete academic resource and actively encourages students, educators, and practitioners to address the challenges and opportunities in modern agriculture. This book encourages readers to explore and make a difference by using their knowledge and insights to advance agricultural innovation and development in the 21st century and beyond.

Course outcomes

Examine the concept and fundamental tenets of extension education alongside impactful teaching techniques tailored to farmers' agricultural advancement.

Show the organisational hierarchy of rural development programs that use agricultural extension to improve farming practices.

Evaluate how ICT tools are used to spread technology for community development.

Explore the fundamental concepts of communication and the latest developments in agricultural extension methods.

Examine ideas related to introducing and spreading innovations, strategies for motivating people, and methods for planning and assessing extension programs.

Unit 1: Introduction to Extension Education

History and Extension System in India, Meaning, Definition, Objectives, and Scope of Extension Education, Programme Planning: Meaning, Process, Principles, and Steps in Programme Development

Unit 2: Rural Development and Community Development

Definition, Meaning, and Concept of Rural Development, Principles and Philosophy of Community Development

Unit 3: Rural Leadership and Extension Administration

Concept and Definition of Rural Leadership, Types of Leaders in Rural Context, Meaning and Concept of Extension Administration, Principles and Functions of Extension Administration

Unit 4: Transfer of Technology and Monitoring and Evaluation

Concept and Models of Transfer of Technology, ICT Applications in Transfer of Technology, Capacity Building of Extension Personnel, Training: Classification and Importance, Concept and Definition of Monitoring and Evaluation and Monitoring and Evaluation of Extension Programmes

Unit 5: New Trends in Agriculture Extension and Communication

Privatisation of Extension, Cyber Extension/e-Extension, Market-led Extension and Farmer-led Extension, Expert Systems. Meaning and Definitions of Communication, Principles and Functions of Communication Barriers to Communication.

Unit 6: Diffusion and Adoption and Agriculture Journalism

Diffusion and Adoption of Innovation: Concepts and Meanings, Process and Stages of Adoption, Adopter Categories, Concept and Meaning of Agriculture Journalism and Importance and Role of Agriculture Journalism.

Editor

Contents

1

History and Extension Systems in India

Sapna Jarial

Department of Agricultural Economics and Extension, Lovely Professional University Phagwara, Punjab

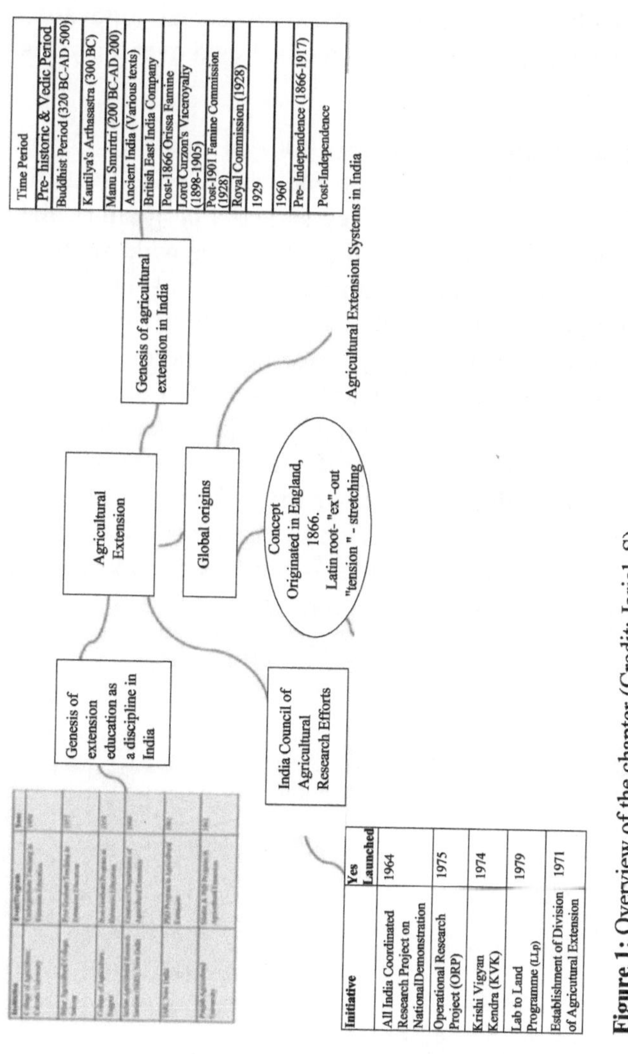

Figure 1: Overview of the chapter (Credit: Jarial, S)

Worldwide, agriculture is the foundation of early human civilization. Humans transitioned from hunting and gathering to farming when they settled near rivers. As a consistent source of food, agriculture aided in human evolution. From then on, the economy has been sustained by agriculture. Among other things, illnesses and natural disasters frequently have an impact on agriculture. Such a state required advisory. This explains the existence of the agricultural extension domain. A social innovation, agricultural extension has been copied, altered, and developed over the years.

The term "extension"

The term "extension" started being used in the 1800s in England. Oxford and Cambridge universities wanted to educate people who lived in industrial cities and could not come to their campuses. They started a programme they called "university extension" in 1867, when they taught a wide range of topics in nearby communities. This concept gained traction fast, and by the 1890s, peripatetic lecturers and travelling teachers were teaching subjects like agriculture. The term "extension" was employed for this type of education over time. (Jones, 1994). The expansion and accomplishment of this effort in Britain had an impact on the start of related initiatives abroad. In the United States, this method became popular and widely used, where there are land-grant colleges focusing on agriculture. There, in many states, comparable out-of-college lectures were becoming established by the 1890s (True, 1900, 1928). These colleges enhanced their curricula to better serve agricultural families. Different terminology is used in different languages for the word extension (Table 1).

Table 1: Extension Terminology in Different Languages

Term	Language	Original Word	Meaning
Extension	Latin	Ex and tensio	Stretching out
	French	Vulgarisation	Extension
	Dutch	Voorlichting	Lighting the path
	Arabic	AI - Ershad	Guidance
	German	Beratung	Advisory work
	Spanish	Capacitation	Training, Capacity Building
	Thai, Lao	Song- Suem	To promote
	Persian	Tarvij & Gostaresh	To promote and to extend
	Indonesian	Penyuluhan	Give illumination in dark (from 'suluh' or 'obor')

The Global Origins

However, the nineteenth century saw the advent of contemporary agricultural extension methods. There was a long, if uneven, tradition of providing farmers with pertinent information and guidance. Around 1800 B.C., the earliest known instance occurred in Mesopotamia, or roughly modern-day Iraq. Archaeologists have discovered ancient clay tablets that contained instructions on how to get rid of rodents and water crops. According to Ahmed (1982), as cited in Bne Saad (1990) these tips are crucial for preventing any potential loss of tax income from farmers.

Additionally, hieroglyphics on a few Egyptian pillars offered instructions on how to save crops and lives from the Nile floods. The emergence of agricultural writings was a major step forward. Only a small number of the original texts from the Phoenician and Greek periods have survived; some were modified by Roman authors. A number of significant Latin works were composed in the midst of second and fourth centuries A.D., often predicated on real-world farming experiences, with the intention of assisting Roman landowners in preserving and enhancing their properties and income.(White, 1970, 1977).

Concurrently, the earliest agricultural records appeared during this era in imperial China, advancement and dissemination systems also emerged. Since the state was primarily dependent its revenue starting in the sixth century B.C. from levies on land, it was concerned that landowners and their tenants should increase their productivity. Without a doubt, the process of providing information and advice and funding relevant agricultural research both began in the late Han Dynasty (25-220 A.D.). Written in 535 A.D., "Essential Techniques/or the Peasantry" is the earliest complete Chinese agricultural treatise that has survived to the present day., aimed to improve estate management by educating landlords how to advise renters. Agricultural treatises and practical handbooks were greatly aided in their dissemination by the efficient local government administrations of the Sung and Yuan Dynasties (960–1368), which also organised and promoted sericulture education, research, and extension work. These endeavours were greatly aided by the invention of woodblock printing. Such efforts continued throughout the succeeding Ming (1368–1644) and Chi'ing (1644–1912) dynasties. The growing population and occasional dangers of starvation prompted these ongoing endeavours, and the government also recognised the importance of well-coordinated extension programmes on agricultural recommendations for the best results. (Bray, 1984; Delman, 1991; Elvin, 1973; Perkins, 1969).

Genesis of Agricultural Extension in India

The development of farming practices and policies in India spans from the pre-historic and Vedic periods, emphasizing agriculture as the economy's foundation with methods like ploughing and sowing, to the post-independence era marked by initiatives like the Community Development Programme and National Extension Service. Significant developments include collective cultivation and irrigation in the Buddhist period, the introduction of plant nutrition and crop classifications in Kautilya's Arthasastra, and soil classification in ancient texts. During the time of the British East India Company, the agricultural economy in rural areas collapsed., resulting in the creation of departments dedicated to agriculture following 1866 famine in Orissa. Lord Curzon's viceroyalty and the post-1901 Famine Commission brought financial support and the start of the Imperial Agricultural Research Institute. The Royal Commission in 1928 emphasized demonstrations and organization, leading to the founding of the Imperial Council of Agricultural Research in 1929 and the first State Agricultural University in 1960. These developments laid the foundation for an organized extension system that continued to evolve post-Independence.

Table 2: Genesis of agricultural extension in India

Time Period	Development/Practice/Policy	Notable Details/ Individuals/Organizations
Pre-historic & Vedic Period	Agriculture as the basis of the economy; principles of ploughing, sowing, harvesting, threshing, and manuring	
Buddhist Period (320 BC-AD 500)	Collective cultivation, irrigation, and field division	Community-based cultivation, village head supervision

Kautilya's Arthasastra (300 BC)	General principles of plant nutrition, main crops, ruler interventions	Mention of Superintendents of Agriculture, crops like sugarcane, paddy, etc.
Manu Smriti (200 BC-AD 200)	Maintenance of proper seed quality; classification of soils	
Ancient India (Various texts)	Classification of soils, agricultural implements, improved practices	Bumivarga, Vanaushadhivarga, Vaisyavarga chapters of Amarakosha, Krisi-Samgraha/Krishi-Parasara
British East India Company	Breakdown of rural agricultural economy	
Post-1866 Orissa Famine	Establishment of central and provincial agriculture departments	Series of famines leading to commissions, Department of Revenue, Agriculture and Commerce (1871), agricultural secretariat (1881)
Lord Curzon's Viceroyalty (1898-1905)	Financial allocation to agriculture, appointment of full-time Directors	Deputy Directors for experimental and extension work
Post-1901 Famine Commission	Establishment of Imperial Agricultural Research Institute, Pusa; link between colleges and districts	Horticulturist and Agronomist positions, Indian Agriculture Service, Government of India Act of 1919
Royal Commission (1928)	Recommendations for demonstrations, coordination, and organization	Director of Agriculture, coordinated research activity, Royal Commission Report (1928)
1929	Establishment of Imperial Council of Agricultural Research (now Indian Council of Agricultural Research - ICAR)	64 ICAR institutions, 63 agricultural universities
1960	First State Agricultural University (SAU) established	Pant Nagar, followed by other SAUs
Pre-Independence (1866-1947)	Foundation of organized extension system	
Post-Independence	Community Development Programme (CDP) in 1952, National Extension Service (NES) in 1953	Organized extension services for rural reconstruction

Indian Council of Agricultural Research Efforts

Indian Council of Agricultural Research (ICAR) has launched several key initiatives to enhance agricultural practices in India. In 1964, the All India Coordinated Research Project on National Demonstration was initiated for nationwide technology transfer in major food crops, notably cereals, achieving 50% more than targeted yields in demonstrations. The Operational Research Project (ORP), though its launch in 1975, focused on disseminating proven technology on a watershed basis, addressing technological, extension, or administrative constraints. Established in 1974, Krishi Vigyan Kendra (KVK) provided need-based, skill-oriented vocational training in agriculture, incorporating the farming system concept without awarding certificates or diplomas. The Lab to Land Programme (LLP), started in 1979, aimed at improving the financial situation of subsistence farmers, marginal farmers, and agricultural labourers without land, particularly from scheduled castes and tribes, through technology transfer, later merging with KVK in 1992. In addition, the State Department of Agriculture received feedback and training support from the newly formed Division of Agricultural Extension in 1971, which had previously been a part of Extension Education. The purpose of this division is to demonstrate cutting-edge technology, perform extension research, and develop methodologies. These initiatives collectively marked significant strides in agricultural development and technology dissemination in India.

Table 3: ICAR efforts for agricultural extension in India

Initiative	Year Launched	Description	Key Principles/Goals
All India Coordinated Research Project on National Demonstration	1964	Major food crops (mainly cereals) technology transfer project nationwide with uniform design and pattern.	Demonstrating technologies to farmers; 50% of demonstrations exceeded targeted yields.
Operational Research Project (ORP)	1975	Designed to disseminate proven technology in a discipline/area to farmers in a watershed, covering a village or cluster of villages and studying barriers to technology spread.	Large-scale demonstration of new technologies; focusing on technological, extension, or administrative constraints.

Krishi Vigyan Kendra (KVK)	1974	Concept designed to impart need-based, skill-oriented vocational training to farmers, extension workers, and self-employment seekers. Based at Pondicherry under Tamil Nadu Agricultural University.	Agricultural production, work-experience training, priority to weaker sections; no certificates/ diplomas awarded; farming system concept.
Lab to Land Programme (LLP)	1979	ICAR launched it to improve the economic situation of small and marginal farmers and landless agricultural labourers, focusing on scheduled castes and tribes, by transferring improved technology.	Economic upliftment, technology transfer; merged with KVK in 1992.
Establishment of Division of Agricultural Extension	1971	ICAR established a section of Extension Education, later strengthened and renamed as Division of Agricultural Extension. ICAR and SAUS also initiated frontline extension.	Conduct extension research, develop methodology, demonstrate latest technologies, provide feedback and training support to State Department of Agriculture

Genesis of Extension Education as a Discipline in India

The genesis of extension education as a distinct academic discipline in India began in the mid-20th century. In 1950, the College of Agriculture at Calcutta University pioneered undergraduate teaching in extension education, marking the start of formal academic courses at the undergraduate level. This was followed by the launch of the first post-graduate teaching program in extension education at Bihar Agricultural College, Sabour, in 1955. Three years later, in 1958, the College of Agriculture in Nagpur initiated its own post-graduate program in the field. A significant milestone was reached in 1960 with the Indian Agricultural Research Institute (IARI) in New Delhi establishing a separate Department of Agricultural Extension, supported by the Ford Foundation and guided by expert advice from J. Paul Leagans. The following year, 1961, was notable for two advancements: IARI introduced the first PhD program in Agricultural Extension, and Punjab Agricultural University started offering both Master's degree and PhD programs in Agricultural Extension, reflecting the growing importance and recognition of this field in the academic and agricultural sectors of India.

Table 4: Extension discipline in India

Institution	Event/Program	Year	Details
College of Agriculture, Calcutta University	Undergraduate Teaching in Extension Education	1950	Start of undergraduate-level teaching in extension education.
Bihar Agricultural College, Sabour	Post-Graduate Teaching in Extension Education	1955	Launch of the first post-graduate teaching program in extension education.
College of Agriculture, Nagpur	Post-Graduate Program in Extension Education	1958	Start of a post-graduate program in extension education.
Indian Agricultural Research Institute (IARI), New Delhi	Creation of Department of Agricultural Extension	1960	Creation of a separate Department of Agricultural Extension with assistance from the Ford Foundation and expert advice from J. Paul Leagans.
IARI, New Delhi	PhD Program in Agricultural Extension	1961	Introduction of the first PhD program in Agricultural Extension.
Punjab Agricultural University	Master & PhD Program in Agricultural Extension	1961	Introduction of both Master's degree and PhD program in Agricultural Extension.

Extension Systems in India

In India, there are five major agricultural extension systems devoted to extension:

i. The central Ministry of Agriculture, including ICAR and Directorate of Extension;

ii. State Departments of Agriculture and Agricultural Universities;

iii. The Departments of Agriculture, Animal Husbandry, Horticulture and Fisheries, as well as the Krishi Vigyan Kendra and, more recently, the Agricultural Technology Management Agency at the district level;

iv. Milk, fruit, cotton, oilseeds, coconut, spice, and other producer cooperatives and federations;

v. NGOs and other civil society organisations.

Shortly after independence, various extension programmes were initiated to achieve food self-sufficiency. The 1947 Grow More Food (GMF) Campaign, the 1952 Community Development Programme (CDP), and the 1953 National Extension Service (NES) are examples. Later, some significant pre-green revolution programmes started location-specific c extension activities. Between

1961 to 1967, these were the Intensive Agricultural District Program (IADP), the Intensive Agricultural Area Program (IAAP), the High Yielding Varieties Program (HYVP), and the Farmer Training Center (FTC). A pilot training and visit (T&V) programme was launched in Rajasthan in 1974 to teach functional competency, modelled after the World Bank's experience (Amateur, 199). National expansion occurred in 1977. The 1984–95 National Agricultural Extension Programme (NAEP) and 1998 National Agricultural Technology Project (NATP) included technology diffusion advances. The district-level autonomous extension agency Agricultural Technology Management Agency (ATMA), established in 2005, was crucial to extension system reform. Meanwhile, the Indian Council of Agricultural Research (ICAR)-led National Agricultural Research and Extension System (NARES) produced several efficient extension programmes.

Krishi Vigyan Kendras (KVKs), ICAR's main extension arm, were founded in 1992.KVKs are the main technology backstop for district agricultural extension operations. The Indian public agricultural extension system has three levels: state, central, and NARES. State departments (agriculture, horticulture, animal husbandry, fisheries, etc) are crucial to the employees and beneficiaries in their states. State agricultural universities give most technological support to state departments. The ATMA functions as a coordinating system of all the agencies involved in a delivery of extension services in the district.

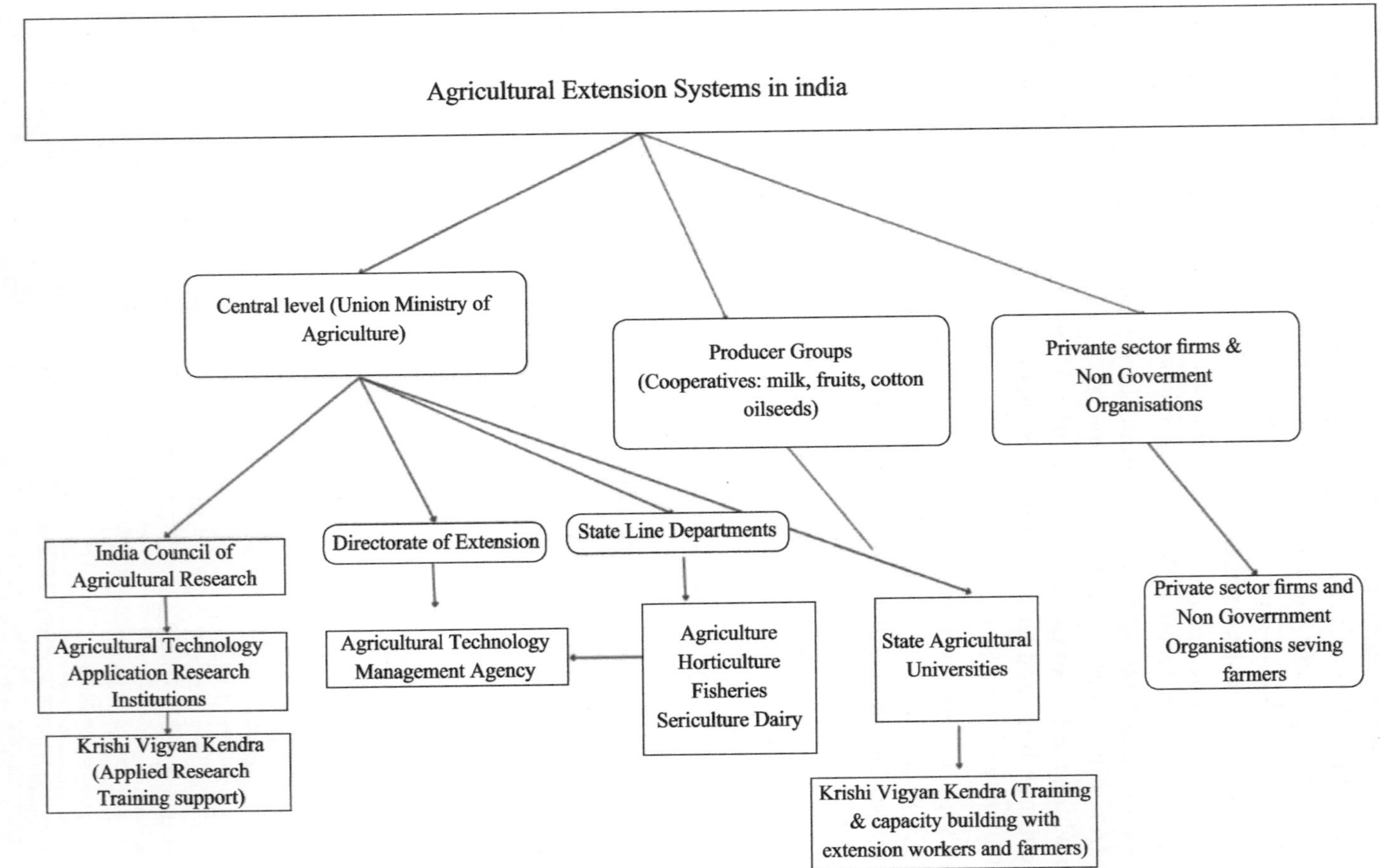

Figure 2: Extension systems in India

The Union Ministry of Agriculture and Farmers Welfare creates and implements national agriculture and allied extension programmes. The Directorate of Extension is the Department of Agriculture and Farmers Welfare's extension hub. Under its scheme "Support to State Extension Programmes for Extension Reforms" (SSEPER) initiated in 2005, it releases grants-in-aid to state governments. The ATMA facilitates the scheme's implementation by urging the formation of farmer groups and agricultural schools with the purpose of boosting agricultural technology.

Furthermore, various commodity boards, such as those for spices, tea, coffee, rubber, coconuts, dairy, and fisheries, operate under various ministries to offer commodity-specific extension services. These services include technical advice, subsidies, training, accreditation of input providers, analytical testing and quality assurance of products, marketing promotion, and more. Provision of extension services is also carried out by other central government entities, such as seed corporations and input manufacturing businesses. The National Food Security Mission, watershed development programmes, technological missions on various crops (including horticulture crops, maize, oilseeds, and pulses), and others all have their own methods of extension. Of late, the Rashtriya Krishi Vikas Yojana (RKVY), funded by the central government, is being implemented through the state governments.

In addition, the National Institute of Agricultural Extension Management (MANAGE) was founded in Hyderabad in 1987 to train senior extension functionaries and develop appropriate extension strategies, with the goal of bolstering the extension system by innovative methodologies and capacity building. Along with four extension education institutes-(EEI) already in operation at Nilokheri, Haryana (1959); Anand, Gujarat (1962); Hyderabad, Andhra Pradesh (1962); and Jorhat, Assam (1987).

The NARES—comprising the ICAR and state agricultural universities (SAUs)—contributes to Indian agriculture in terms of developing location-specific cutting-edge technologies to support the national agri-food system. ICAR reaches out to farmers mainly through KVKs, which are mandated to conduct on-farm trials (OFTs), front-line demonstrations (FLDs) and capacity development programmes (CDPs). ICAR, with a vast network of 731 KVKs all over the country, provides vocational training to primary producers and extension personnel. The activities are monitored zonally by the Agricultural Technology Application Research Institute (ATARI), and there are currently 11 ATARIs. The ICAR has also started Agricultural Technology Information Centres (ATIC) since 2000 in selected ICAR institutes and SAUs to function as a single window system, showcasing or selling technologies and products developed in the institute or university. Direct extension activities by SAUs and ICAR institutes are limited to their immediate territories. Recently, public sector extension agencies have used ICTs more. For instance, mKISAN lets central and state organisations send SMS messages to specific stakeholders in vernacular languages. The idea of institute-level agribusiness incubation (ABI) centres boosted public extension services for agricultural start-ups.

Private Sector Agriculture Extension System

Private sector extension promotes efficient input delivery and need-based farm advisory services, gaining pace. The private sector can offer context-specific services. Consequently, contact farming agreements, public–private partnerships (PPPs), and embedded services are crucial for agricultural extension. Nationwide, an estimated 0.3 million agro-input dealers are active, specializing in distributing agro-machinery, seeds, fertilisers, and pesticides. In contrast, the number of authorised extension worker positions in the country is an estimated 0.15 million, with over 30 per cent being unfilled. They provided information quality, however, presents a difficulty in this context.

In addition to supplying inputs, several organisations have initiated outreach initiatives either independently or in collaboration with other public or civil society stakeholders. The endeavours initiated by ITC, like e-Choupal, Chaupal Sagar, and Chaupal Pradarsan Khet (CPK), provide farmers with access to information about weather and innovative farming practices, collection and storage facilities, and technology demonstrations, respectively. In addition, numerous businesses provide funds in accordance with their corporate social responsibility (CSR) policies.

NGO/Civil Society Extension System

India is home to about 3 million registered non-governmental organisations (NGOs), of which approximately 15,000–20,000 are dedicated to land-based livelihoods and the development of rural areas. (Gulati et al 2018). Prominent among them are- Professional Assistance for Development Action (PRADAN), Bharatiya Agro-Industries Federation (BAIF), Syngenta Foundation, Action for Food Production (AFPRO), and Self-Employed Women's Association (SEWA), among many others. The effective utilisation of social capital has become a significant factor in generating income and alleviating poverty examples are-commodity-based farmers' organisations, farmers' interest groups (FIGs), self-help groups (SHGs), and cooperatives. (Swanson and Samy 2006). The examples include the Maharashtra State Grape Growers' Association, Young Farmers Association Punjab, Organic Farming Association of India (OFAI), and many more. Agriculture cooperatives include approximately 3.75 lakh of the 5.8 lakh functional cooperatives dispersed throughout India; they have 280-million-member farmers. Numerous prosperous cooperatives can be found across various sectors. The following cooperatives have established a significant presence: AMUL in Gujarat, Mother Dairy in North India, OMFED in Odisha, and MILMA in Kerala—all in the milk sector—Indian Farmers Fertiliser Cooperative Limited in the fertiliser sector, National Agricultural Cooperative Marketing Federation of India in the marketing sector, and others.

In conclusion, agricultural extension is pivotal in the evolution of human civilization and has transitioned from early practices near rivers to a sophisticated global system. Originating in the 1800s in England as a "university extension," this concept expanded globally, influencing education and practical applications in agriculture. The term varies across languages, encompassing meanings from 'guidance' to 'training'. In India, agricultural extension evolved through historical developments, from Vedic practices to modern post-independence policies significantly influenced by British rule and research institutions. The Indian Council of Agricultural Research (ICAR) played a crucial role, initiating projects like the All India Coordinated Research Project and Krishi Vigyan Kendra, aimed at enhancing agricultural practices and technology transfer. The academic discipline of extension education in India started in the mid-20th century, with various universities establishing undergraduate and postgraduate programs. India's extension system is diverse, involving government ministries, state departments, universities, NGOs, and the private sector, each contributing to knowledge dissemination and practice. Private sector and civil society organizations complement these efforts, focusing on rural development and efficient farm advisory services. Cooperatives like AMUL significantly contribute to this system, highlighting India's multifaceted nature of agricultural extension. This system represents a blend of historical practices, educational advancements, policy developments, and collaborative efforts across sectors.

Answer the Following Questions

1. How did the concept of agricultural extension evolve from its origins in England in the 1800s to become a global phenomenon, impacting education and practical applications in agriculture?
2. Discuss the historical significance of agricultural extension in India, highlighting key developments from the prehistoric and Vedic periods to post-independence initiatives.
3. What role did the Indian Council of Agricultural Research (ICAR) play in enhancing agricultural practices in India, and what were some of its key initiatives and projects?

4. Describe the pluralistic extension system in India, detailing the involvement of government ministries, agricultural universities, NGOs, the private sector, and cooperatives in knowledge dissemination and practice.
5. How have the private sector and civil society contributed to agricultural extension in India, and what are some examples of their initiatives aimed at rural development and efficient farm advisory services?

2

The Evolution of Agricultural Extension Services in India

Deepak Chand Meena

Department of Agricultural Economics and Extension, Lovely Professional University Phagwara, Punjab

Introduction

It is said that Rome was not built in a day. Similarly, Extension was not master minded by one individual; rather it evolved through hard work of extension professionals around the world over more than a country.

The necessity of a human being is food, for which he must rely on agriculture. The agriculture to achieve its expected growth must depend on several factors which include technology, research and obviously extension. The basic function of agricultural extension is to train, teach and guide farmers. Agricultural extension's primary role is to mentor, instruct, and train farmers. In order to assist people form sound judgements and make wise decisions, the extension entails the deliberate use of information communication (Van Den Ban and Hawkins, 1998). Agricultural extension is emphasised in the World Development Report (2007) as a crucial development intervention for boosting the agricultural sector's growth potential. Technology transfer is accelerated via extension, and connections between farmers and the extension service are crucial. A review in the World Bank of a large portfolio of extension projects pointed out that research-extension linkages were fragile and neither research nor extension was satisfactorily aware of the need to understand the constraints and potentials of the different farming systems as a basis for determining relevant technology and technology development requirements (Purcell and Anderson 1997). The study on agricultural information flow in India by Adhiguru *et al.* (2009) has showed that only 40 per cent farm households access information from one or the other source. The public extension system has been found to be accessed by only 5.7 per cent households. Compared to 12.40 per cent of large farms, just 4.8 per cent of small farmers have access to public extension personnel.

Post-Independence Agricultural Extension Efforts in India		
Project/ Campaign	**Year Started**	**Main Objectives/ Characteristics**
Etawah Pilot Project	1948	Development of rural areas in Etawah, Uttar Pradesh: Principles in included self-help. democracy, integrated approach, and cooperation between goverment and NGOs: introduced the concept of ' multipurpose extension worker'.
Nilokheri Experiment	1948	Founded by S.K. Dey: aimed at rehabilitating displaced persons and later integrated surrounding villages: focused on self- sufficiency, vocational training, and cooperative enterprises.
Grow More Food campaign (GMFC)		India's first attempt to increase food production, leading to the Community Development Programme in 1952; focused on rural development and included various sub- programmes.
National Extension Service	1953	Expansion of Community Develophment Programme; stages included Pre-intensive development, and Post-intensive development, focusing agriculture and community development.
Intensive Agricutural District Programme (IADP)	1960	Aimed to increase agricultural production in selected districts; led to the intensive Agriculture Area Programme and the High Yielding Variety Programme, contributing to the first Green Revolution.

History of Extension work

Era	Region/ Country	Key Development in Extension Work	Notes
Early 1700s	Europre and North America	Emergence of extension work in response to industrial development.	Driven by the need to bring scientific and technological advances to farmers.
1728	Scotland	Establishment of the First agricultural society.	Considered the precursor to modern extension work.
1785	USA	Formation of the first agricultural society in Philadephia.	Early example of structured agricultural extension work.
Late 1800s- Early1900s	India (Post Indepedence)	Voluntary effoets at rural construction by social leaders.	Influenced by recurerent famines and colonial government's focus on law and order.
Post - 1947	India (Pre- Indepedence)	Organized extension work begins influenced by models from the USA.	Shifted from a general to a target group approach over time.

Pre- independence Efforts			
Year	**Effort/ Attempt**	**Place**	**Person/Agency**
1903	Scheme of Rural Reconstruction	Sundarban Bengal	Sir Daniel Hamilton
1920	Gurgaon Experiment	Haryana	F.L. Brayne
1921	Sriniketan Project	West Bengal	Rabindra Nath Tagore
1921	Mathandam Attempt	Kerala	Dr. Spencer Hatch
1923	Sewagram Attempt	Wardha, Gujarat	Mahatma Gandhi
1945	Indian Village Service	Lucknow	T. Mosher & B.N. Gupta
1946	Firka Development Scheme	Madras	T Prakashan
Post-Independence Efforts			
1948	Etawah Pilot Project	Uttar Pradesh	Albert Mayer

Extension Efforts in India After 1970s			
Project/ Campalgn	Year started	Key Features	Observation/ Criticlsins
Traning and visit(T&V) system	1974	World Bank- funded: focused on professionalism, regular farmer visits, constinuous training strong link between research and extensinon	Criticlzed for budgetary issues and lack of adequate farmer interaction. feder and slade (1986) noted its effectiveness in increasing contacts and yields.
Krishi vigyan kendras (KVKs)	1974	Mandale of training farmers, farm women, and youth: known as farmer polytechnics: run by SAUs. ICAR and NGOs.	Focuses on various agricultural aspects. beoefiling a large number of farmers annually.
National Extension service	1953	Focused on community development and agricultural services: multifunctional approach with emphasis on interactive communication	
Intensive Agricultural District Programme (IADP)	1960	Aimed at increasing agricultural production in selected distracts: led to intensive Agriculture Area Programme and high yielding variety programme.	Contributed to the first green Revolution.
Agricultural Technology Management Agency (ATMA)	1999	Part of the National Agricultural technology Project: aimed to integrate various stakeholders in agricultural extension	New guidelines, Issued in 2010 due to implementation discrepander.
Information Communication Technology (ICT) in Extension		Use of cyber extension to provide comprehensive information to farmers.	Suggested as a solution for making extension mare effective.

Figure 1: Overview of the chapter (Credit: Jarial, S)

Extension work started as voluntary service by philanthropists and enlightened people to serve the needs for information and wellbeing of rural people. Cooperative extension service of USA is the first organized extension work in the world, which served as model of adaptation for various countries. The history of extension efforts and technological advancements are closely intertwined. After industrial expansion, there was a demand for extension work in North America and Europe in the early 1700s. Agricultural societies were founded out of the desire to bring scientific and technological advancements to farmers. It is believed that Scotland saw the founding of the first such society in 1728. The first agricultural organisation in the United States was founded in Philadelphia in 1785. The earliest groups to do what were thereafter referred to as "extension" were the agricultural societies. In most countries around the world today, extension work is an integral aspect of the rural development plan.

In India, organized extension work was mostly post-independence phenomenon. The principles and methods of extension were imported from USA. The approach of extension in India has changed with time from general to target group approach. Prior to independence, the alien rule under East India Company was largely concerned with maintenance of law and order rather than development. It is a historical fact that recurrent famines from 1875 to 1901 forced the colonial government to initiate agricultural research and education in the country. However, concern for villages moved social leaders to launch voluntary efforts at rural construction. One can find the resemblance of extension work in these events of pre-independence era.

Growth of Agricultural Extension Education as a Discipline in India

At the College of Agriculture, Calcutta University, the teaching of extension education at the undergraduate level began in 1950. 1955 saw the establishment of the first post-graduate programme at Sabour's Bihar Agricultural College. The post-graduate programme, which was started in 1958 at the College of Nagpur, came next. Furthermore, a significant development in the history of extension education was the establishment of a distinct Division of Agricultural Extension at the Indian Agricultural Research Institute (IARI), New Delhi, with funding from the Ford Foundation and guidance from the renowned Dr. J. Paul Leagans. At IARI, the Ph.D. curriculum in the field of extension was initially offered in 1961. Following suit, in 1961, Punjab Agricultural University in Ludhiana offered master's and doctoral programmes in agricultural extension.

At the College of Agriculture, Calcutta University, the teaching of extension education at the undergraduate level began in 1950. 1955 saw the establishment of the first post-graduate programme at Sabour's Bihar Agricultural College.

The post-graduate programme, which was started in 1958 at the College of Nagpur, came next. Furthermore, a significant development in the history of extension education was the establishment of a distinct Division of Agricultural Extension at the Indian Agricultural Research Institute (IARI), New Delhi, with funding from the Ford Foundation and guidance from the renowned Dr. J. Paul Leagans. At IARI, the Ph.D. curriculum in the field of extension was initially offered in 1961. Following suit, in 1961, Punjab Agricultural University in Ludhiana offered master's and doctoral programmes in agricultural extension.

Conceptual Background

The following words describe the extent and jurisdiction of extension, as declared by the Government of India's National Commission on Agriculture (1976): The process of teaching farmers the technologies of scientific agriculture so they may apply the knowledge for better agriculture and a stronger economy is known as extension and extension education. This includes introducing agricultural education into schools, providing non-formal educational facilities through organised extension services, and educating farmers through non-degree institutional programmes that improve their productive activities by teaching them occupational skills.

There had been intermittent initiatives to promote rural life long before the national extension system was introduced in 1952. Understanding the history of early extension initiatives can be helpful in comprehending how Indian extension systems have evolved. There were two main tendencies in the early extension initiatives. Initially, efforts were made to enhance rural living by private organisations and certain well-meaning individuals. Secondly, efforts were undertaken by the government to start several projects aimed at resolving the issues in agriculture.

Table 1: Pre-independence Efforts

Year	Effort/Attempt	Place	Person/Agency
1903	Scheme of Rural Reconstruction	Sundarban, Bengal	Sir Daniel Hamilton
1920	Gurgaon Experiment	Haryana	F.L. Brayne
1921	Sriniketan Project	West Bengal	Rabindra Nath Tagore
1921	Marthandam Attempt	Kerala	Dr. Spencer Hatch
1923	Sewagram Attempt	Wardha,Gujarat	Mahatma Gandhi
1945	Indian Village Service	Lucknow	T. Mosher & B. N. Gupta
1946	Firka Development Scheme	Madras	T Prakashan
Post-independence Efforts			
1948	Etawah Pilot Project	Uttar Pradesh	Albert Mayer
1948	Nilokheri Experiment	Haryana	S. K. Dey

Pre-independence Efforts

Scheme of Rural Reconstruction (1903)

This experiment continued with cooperative marketing and later offered training to the villagers in cottage industries. Sir David Hamilton has started his experiment in model villages along with cooperatives lines at Sunderban in Bengal.

Gurgaon Experiment (1920)

For disseminating new knowledge among the villagers, F.L. Brayne introduced the concept of '**village guide**' in each village who serve as channels for information from outside. Village guides were appointed to execute films, dramas, folksongs. The programme of introducing improved seeds, implements, methods of cultivation etc. was started. Aim of the project was to improve farming, productivity, reduce expenditure on social and religious functions, health standards etc.

Sriniketan Project (1921)

The Nobel Laureate Rabindra Nath Tagore initiated the effort of rural development at Sriniketan, West Bengal in 1921. The concept of **'Brati Balika'** was introduced under this project. Tagore believed in both self-help and mutual help and was one of the first to recognize the need for a change in the outlook of villagers as a precondition for improvement. Activities like demonstration on scientific methods of agriculture, training of youths, adult education etc. were important aspects of the work aimed to make a group of villages self-reliant. The project at Sriniketan was closely guided by Mr. Leonard Elmhirst.

Marthandam Attempt (1921)

Marthandam attempt was initiated by Dr. Spencer Hatch under the support of Young Man Christian Association (YMCA) in the year 1921. This project was started with the idea of establishing demonstration centres during a rural area to provide income generating activities. Self-help was the working principle with expert guidance. At Marthandam (Kerala), Dr. Hatch started a multipurpose cooperative with poultry, bee-keeping, seeds, animal husbandry and other projects. The aim of this attempt was complete development of rural people in spiritual, mental, physical, social, and economic fields.

Sewagram Attempt (1923)

Mahatma Gandhi considered the village to be the essence of Indian life. Gandhiji emphasized the role of the people themselves in constructive programmes.

He argued that self-help was the first step towards moral advancement. He also emphasized the need for decentralized production & equal distribution of wealth and self-sufficiency of Indian villages. He started a number of movements which have spread throughout India, such as the All-India Village Industries Organization, and the Harijan Sewak Sangh.

Indian Village Service (1945)

Indian Village Service was founded in 1945 in Lucknow by A.T. Mosher of New York and Shri B.N. Gupta to help village people realise the best in their own villages by empowering them to effectively aid others as well as themselves through the development of individuals, volunteer leaders, and local agencies.

Firka Development Scheme (1946)

Initiated in 1946, the Firka development programme was a government sponsored initiative in Madras. The goal of this initiative was to set up the villages for a happier, more wealthy, and richer life where each villager would have the chance to grow as a person and as a part of a cohesive society. The key components of this strategy included the delivery of water, the establishment of panchayats, the creation of cooperatives, programmes for sanitation, and the improvement of livestock, irrigation, and agriculture to make the region self-sufficient.

Extension after 1947

Post-independence Efforts

Etawah Pilot Project (1948)

Albert Mayer launched the Etawah pilot project in 1948 with the goal of developing the rural districts of Uttar Pradesh's Etawah District. Self-help, democracy, an integrated strategy, feeling the needs of the people, meticulous planning and achievable goals, an institutional approach, and collaboration between governmental and non-governmental organisations were the project's guiding principles. Under this initiative, the idea of a "**multipurpose extension worker**" was tested for the first time. The curriculum demonstrated advancements in agriculture and created local leadership.

Nilokheri Experiment (1948)

S.K. Dey, was the founder of the Nilokheri Experiment in 1948. It was originally started to rehabilitate 7000 displaced persons from Pakistan after the Independence and later integrated with the 100 surrounding villages. The scheme called "**Mazdoor Manzil**" aimed at self-sufficiency for the rural cum urban township in all the essential requirements of life. Rights for education and medical care for the sick were also guaranteed. Under this programme, the main activities were a vocational training centre run on co-operative lines where people were given vocational training of their choice to run their co-operative enterprises; and the colony had its own dairy, poultry, piggery, printing press, engineering workshops, tannery, and bone-meal factory.

Grow More Food Campaign (GMFC)

India's first organised effort to boost food production was the Grow More Food Campaign (GMFC). This made it possible for the Community Development Programme to start in 1952. The program's overall goal was to help rural residents grow by increasing their self-confidence. Following the launch of the Community Development Programme, S.K. Dey, the then-minister for Panchayati Raj and community development, declared that the fight against poverty, illness, and illiteracy had begun on October 2, 1952. The plan placed a strong emphasis on issues including agricultural production, minor irrigation, applied nutrition, well construction, and rural manpower. According to Taylor *et al.* (1965), the program's failure was attributed to the challenge of finding and training enough people to fill all necessary positions and sufficiently staff the several local locations where it had been implemented. The improvement of its work at the village level was their recommended cure.

National Extension Service

To expand the scope of the Community Development Programme, the National Extension Service was established on October 2, 1953.During the Pre-intensive development stage, there was a need to raise public awareness of the value of agriculture and spark interest in the development project. Enough money was set aside during the intensive development stage to cover expenses for three years, allowing for the establishment of each block development. Amounts were set aside for each block's agricultural demonstration. The offices and house were finished during the post-intensive development phase. The 1950s and 1960s saw the institutionalisation of numerous national extension services, with an emphasis on community development and participatory communication. Extension agents were also overburdened with duties, and agricultural services served multiple purposes during this time.

Intensive Agricultural District Programme (IADP)

To boost agricultural output, the Intensive Agricultural District Programme (IADP) was launched in 1960. It was implemented in seven national districts. The Centre Government launched the Intensive Agriculture Area Programme in 114 districts across the nation in 1964–1965, spurred on by the District Program's success. Protecting and cultivating the chosen crops at the block, district, and state levels was promoted. In 1966, the government launched the High Yielding Variety Programme (HYVP) to boost crop productivity. This focused effort led to the first Green Revolution.

Extension after 1970's

The 1970s saw the rise of Training and Visit (T&V) extension networks and integrated approaches to rural development. In 1974, the T&V system was launched as a project supported by the World Bank. Professionalism was identified by Benor and Baxter (1984) as the T&V system's primary attribute. There is only one line of command that controls the extension service. A Village Extension Worker (VEW) makes routine farm visits. Regular workshops were conducted by the Subject Matter Experts, who also provided recommendations to Village Extension Workers (VEWs) and Agricultural Extension Officers (AEOs). The system provides regular and ongoing training for the extension staff. Under the T&V system, extension agents had regular, lively contact with farmers, and workshops were held to increase output.

Roger Slade and Gershon Feder (1986) examined a few important theories about the implications of T&V extension. The findings, which are based on data from India, demonstrate that T&V significantly raises the quantity of interactions that occur between extension agents and farmers, and that the percentage of farmers reached rises with the duration of the T&V system. It was discovered that extension agents are a valuable resource for information about novel farming techniques, especially when those techniques are costly and sophisticated. The report demonstrates how, in one location the subject of a thorough investigation, T&V significantly increased the yields of a major crop. The T&V system had straightforward principles and a strong connection between extension and research. Due to the shortcomings of the T&V budgetary crisis in developing nations and dispersed farmers, the system was unable to produce the desired outcomes.

The Krishi Vigyan Kendras were founded in 1974 with the goal of implementing the Mohan Singh Mehta Committee's recommendations by providing training to farm men, women, and adolescents. They take part in the transfer of technology even if the initial focus was on human resource development. Because this organisation assists farmers through frontline demonstrations, on-farm trainings, etc., the KVKs are also known as Farmer Poly techniques. The KVKs are district-level establishments managed by non-governmental organisations (NGOs), Indian Council for Agricultural Research (ICAR), and State Agricultural Universities. At KVKs, thousands of farmers receive training each year in fields like crop husbandry, horticulture, animal husbandry and training, fishing, and careers that lead to self-employment. The Trainers'

Training Centres system involved a lot of staff work, except for agricultural production, which largely excluded other farmers. Very little emphasis was placed on extension methods and more on technology in the T&V system. Another issue was the insufficient communication between contact farmers and other farms. (2014) Barman *et al.* The Bank's reluctance to acknowledge that the model was unsuitable for the circumstances of numerous of its client nations was the most unfortunate aspect of this experience to share. To train KVK scientists and subject matter experts, subject-specific training centres, or TTCs, are being established. In 1980, the farming system approach to research and extension (FSRE) was prioritised in the extension. A stronger bond between scientists and farmers promoted the development of location-specific technologies. The National Agricultural Extension Project was also launched in 1983 to close the gap between extension and research. The National Agricultural Technology Project's (NATP) Innovation in Technology Dissemination (ITD) component saw the establishment of the Agricultural Technology Management Agency (ATMA) in 1999.

The programme links all participants, including the Department of Agriculture, Animal Husbandry, Fisheries, KVKs, representatives of farmer associations, and non-governmental organisations. In June 2010, new rules were released by the government due to disparities in the way ATMA was implemented. "The majority of farmers in India do not have access to any source of information, despite the variety of agricultural extension approaches that operate in parallel and occasionally duplicate one another" (Glendenning, et al 2010). In India, various organisations collaborate with one another. Given the vast number of farmers that need to be served by extension organisations, India developed an extension pluralism policy. The nation's National Agricultural Research System (NARS), which includes ICAR and SAUs, has produced a vast amount of information for farmers. Notwithstanding these endeavours, numerous issues persist.

In conclusion, agricultural extension, integral to the advancement of agriculture, has evolved through contributions from professionals worldwide for over a century. Central to human needs, agriculture relies on technology, research, and extension. Agricultural extension's primary role is to educate and guide farmers, facilitating technology transfer and addressing the diverse needs of farming systems. Historical evidence shows extension work beginning as voluntary service, notably in the U.S. with the cooperative extension service, and evolving in tandem with technological developments. In India, post-independence efforts mark the organized beginning of extension work, influenced by principles and methods from the U.S. Calcutta University started teaching extension education in 1950. Calcutta University started teaching extension education in 1950, expanding to postgraduate levels and other universities. The National Dairy Research Institute advanced dairy extension research and education. Efforts at rural reconstruction pre-independence included notable initiatives like the Gurgaon Experiment and the Sriniketan Project. Post-independence, projects like the Etawah Pilot Project and the Grow More Food Campaign furthered rural development. The T&V system, KVK, and ATMA advanced extension methods. Despite various approaches, challenges remain in reaching all farmers. The role of Information Communication Technology (ICT) is emphasized for effective extension, suggesting a need for coordinated efforts from the government and various stakeholders to ensure technology transfer and the true realization of the extension's potential.

Answer the Following Questions

1. Describe the historical evolution of agricultural extension work, highlighting its origins, key initiatives, and significant milestones, particularly in India.
2. How does the Training and Visit (T&V) extension system function, and what were its main attributes and challenges, as identified by scholars such as Benor and Baxter (1984) and Roger Slade and Gershon Feder (1986)?
3. Explain the significance of the Grow More Food Campaign (GMFC) in India's agricultural development efforts post-independence. What were the primary goals of this campaign, and what challenges did it face?

3

Introduction to Extension Education

Nikita Khoisnam

Department of Agricultural Economics and Extension, Lovely Professional University Phagwara, Punjab

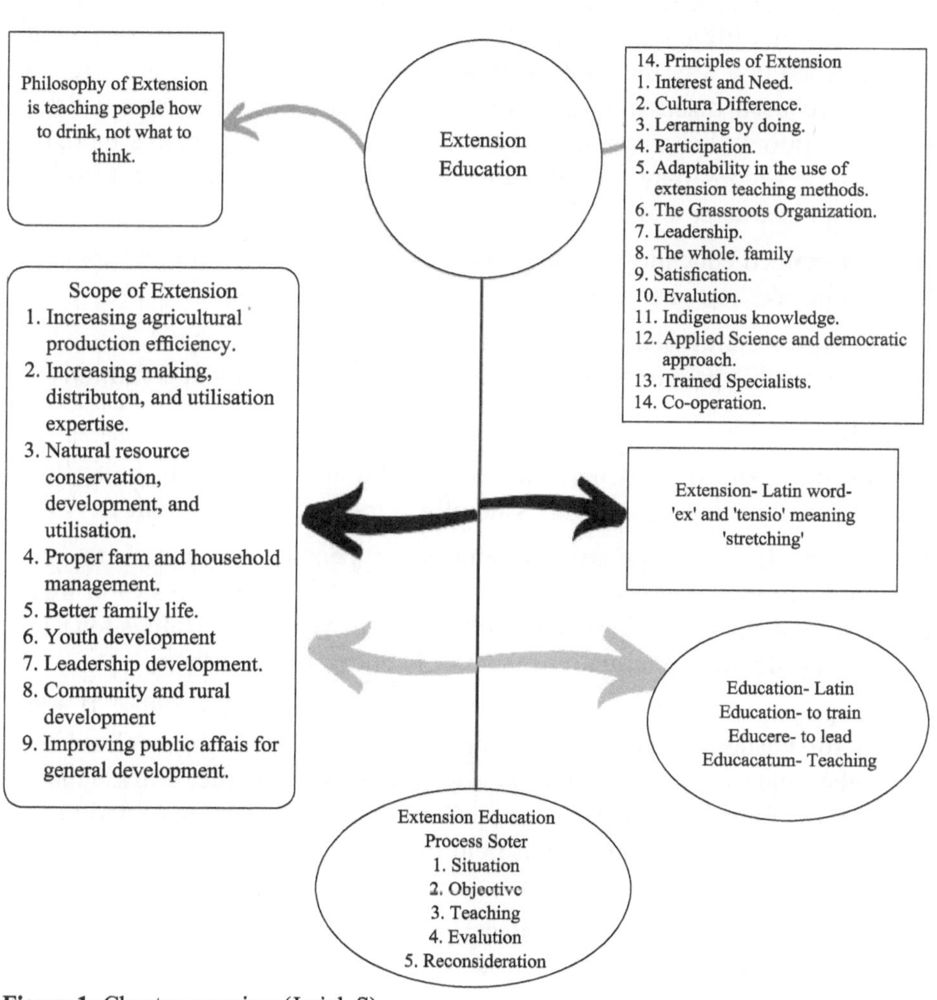

Figure 1: Chapter overview (Jarial, S)

Concept of Education

Education is derived from the Latin terms Educare (Educere) and Educatum. The word "educare" means to train, nourish, or shape. "Educere" means "to lead froth, to pull out." The Latin term "Educatum" refers to the act of teaching. "Shiksha" and "Vidya" are two significant Sanskrit words that stand out as equivalents of English education. Shiksha is a word derived from "Shah," which means "to control or discipline." The term "Vidhya" is derived from the word "Vidh," which means "knowledge." During the ancient schooling period, the most essential aspects of human personality were discipline and knowledge.

Education is the process by which knowledge (things known), attitude (things felt), and skills (things done), in all (or) some (or all) of human behaviour, are produced in a way that is desired. We can classify teaching, training, and research-focused discussion as education methods. Education can occur in formal or informal settings, and any event that impacts a person's thoughts, feelings, or actions may be termed education. Education can occur both in front of an instructor and independently.

Webster defined education as the process of teaching to develop the student's knowledge, skill, or character.

"Sociologist Rodney Stark declares that Education is the cheapest, most rapid and most reliable path to economic advancement under present conditions"

Keywords

Extension: 'Extension' is derived from the Latin roots, 'ex' meaning 'out' and 'tensio' meaning 'stretching'. Literally, it means 'stretching out'.

Education: It is the process of enhancing people's capacities to react appropriately to situations. Or, to put it simply, it is the process of bringing about desired changes in knowledge (things known), attitude (things felt), and skill (things done), either in all of them or in one or more of them.

Philosophy: The word "Philosophy" has a wide range of meanings. It is the search for wisdom, a collection of general rules or guidelines related to a particular study area. Philosophy is a way of looking at life, knowledge, or any of these things from various perspectives. It is a collection of underlying rules and regulations for a certain field of knowledge, activities, etc., like a philosophy of life or extension work.

Principles: Principles are generalised guidelines which form the basis for decisions and actions in a consistent way.

Types of Education

There are mainly three types of education, namely, Informal, Non-formal and Formal. Coombs and Ahmed (1974) drew a distinctive description between these three types and are given as follows.

a) **Informal Education**: Is the life-long process by which every individual develops knowledge, skills, attitudes, and insights through daily encounters and exposure to the environment at home, work, and play, among other things.

b) **Non-formal Education**: Is an organised, systematic educational activity that takes place beyond the formal system to deliver specific types of learning to specific subsets of the population, including adults & children. Programs like these include adult education, vocational education, functional literacy, continuing education, extension education, etc.

c) **Formal Education**: Is a highly institutionalised, chronologically graded, and hierarchically structured education that begins with primary school and continues until university.

Table 1. Difference between Formal, Non-Formal and Informal

Sl. No.	Criteria	Formal Education	Non-formal education/ Extension Education/ Adult Education	Informal Education
1.	Concerned with	Children's and youth's educational development, preparing them for the future.	Actual life situations of adults and youth.	Incidental learning
2.	Attendance	Is compulsory	Participation is voluntary	No need
3.	Learners	Are more homogeneous with regards to age, educational qualification, experience, expertise, interests, and requirements	Is more diverse regarding to age, educational qualification, experience, knowledge, interests, and requirements, which vary with value systems, cultural background, and so on.	Individual learning process.
4.	Preconceived ideas.	Learners do not typically have any predetermined notions.	Learners typically have preconceived assumptions and ideas based on their prior experiences. experiences.	There may or may not be predetermined notions.
5.	Curriculum	Fixed and has predetermined subjects. Students must adapt to the education provided.	There is no set curriculum, and it is adaptable to fit the different needs and desires of farmers.	On the spot learning.

6.	Teaching	Is more formal, with classrooms, assigned textbooks, and exams	Is more formal, with classrooms, mandated textbooks, and examinations	No teacher (self-learning)
7.	Mode of instruction	Vertical- from teacher to learner. More instructional in nature.	Horizontal. Teacher-student collaboration on learning	Self-instructions.
8.	Method of learning	The theory is followed by the practice.	It begins with practice and progresses to theory.	Self-learning.
9.	Teacher	Is older and more experienced than the learners	They could be younger and less experienced than the learners	No teacher.
10.	Knowledge flow	Vertical in nature	Horizontal in nature	No direction.
11.	Evaluation	More formal in the form of marks, grades etc.	More informal evaluation	Self-evaluation.
12.	Approach	Deductive	Inductive	Self-Approach
13.	Degrees and diplomas	Degrees and diplomas will be awarded	No degrees or diplomas are granted, but as this non-formal education evolves, certificates may be awarded to recognize acquired skills.	No degrees or diplomas provided
14.	Orientation	Board-based and general in nature	Specific to situation	Spot orientation
15.	Nature of Education	It aims at developing learners physical and mental faculties	This seeks to increase learners' knowledge, attitudes, and skills in a certain subject.	Spot learning
16.	Duration	It is time bound programme	Free from regimentation, participatory in nature	No time
17.	Place of teaching	Learning takes place within the four walls o the institution	Learning in real life situations-in villages and fields.	Learning takes place in practical Situation
18.	Need orientation	It follows a set schedule and does not adapt to the demands of the students.	It is determined by the people's wants and the availability of resources.	Depends on the individual conditions
19.	Problem solving	Problems of the student are solved by the teacher	Problems of the people are solved by the people	Problems can be solved by Themselves

Definitions of Extension

According to D Ensminger (1961) – "Extension is a programme and a process of helping village people to help themselves, increase their production and to raise their general standard of living".

According to B Rambhai (1958) – "Extension is a two- way channel; it brings scientific information to the village people and also takes the problems of the village people to the scientific institution for a solution. It is a continuous educational process in which both learner and teacher contribute and receive".

According to HW Butt (1961) – "Extension is the increased dissemination of useful knowledge for improving rural life".

According to Van den Ban and Hawkins (2002) – "Extension involves the conscious use of communication of information to help people form sound opinions and make good decisions".

According to Ray (2011) – "Extension may be defined as the science of developing people's capability for sustainable improvement in their quality of life. Therefore, the main aim of the Extension is human resource development".

Definitions of Extension Education

According to Paul Leagans (1971) – "Extension education is an applied social science consisting of relevant content derived from physical, biological and social sciences and, in its process, synthesized into a body of knowledge, concepts, principles and procedures oriented to provide non-credit out of school education largely for adults".

According to Reddy (1993) – "Extension education is a science that deals with the creation, transmission & application of knowledge designed to bring about planned changes in the behaviour-complex of people, to helping them live better by learning the ways of improving their vocations, enterprises & institutions".

According to Singh (1994) – "Extension education is a science that brings about desirable changes in the behaviour of the concerned persons through educational methods to improve their general standard of living with their efforts. It deals with the designs & strategies for the transfer of technology to the concerned persons. In other words, what is taught to the farmers is not Extension Education, though its knowledge is applied for the effective & efficient communication of various change programmes".

According to Ensminger (1957) – "Extension is education, and its purpose is to change attitudes and practices of the people with whom the work is to be done".

According to Leagans (1961) – "Extension education is teaching rural people how to live better by learning ways to improve their farms, home and community institutions".

According to National Commission on Agriculture (1976)- "Extension as an out of -school education and service for the members of the farm family and others directly or indirectly engaged in farm production to enable them to adopt improved practices in production, management, conservation and marketing. Several authors defined extension in various ways emphasising the importance of one or the other aspect of extension".

According to O.P. Dahama (1973) – "Extension education is defined as an educational process to provide knowledge to the rural people about improved practices in a convincing manner and help them to decide within their specific local conditions".

According to Y. C. Sanoria (1986) – "Agricultural Extension is a professional method of non-formal education aimed at inducing behavioural changes in the farmers to increase their income through increased production and productivity by establishing firm linkages with research for solving farmer's problems, ensuring adequate and timely supply of inputs and using proven methods of communication for speeding of the process of diffusion and adoption of innovations."

Concepts of Extension Education

Concept: Concepts and principles are referred to as the "building blocks of discipline." They form the fundamental structure of a subject, making their complete grasp essential to truly comprehend and appreciate the substance and value of a discipline.

Concept	**Description**
1. Extension Work	Extension work, through education and service, helps people improve their socio-economic situation, enabling better decision-making. It encourages behaviours that lead to effective production and marketing, preservation of natural resources, increased livelihood security, improved health, and more fulfilling family and community life. It is site-specific and open to outside criticism, aiming to empower people to take charge of their development by developing their capacities. This includes the Extension Education process (teaching and learning), organization, administration, supervision, financing, and overall development programs.

2. Extension Service	Extension services, operating under various development departments (e.g., agriculture, animal husbandry, etc.), focus on transferring new technologies or innovations and providing advice on better methods, as well as communicating development constraints as feedback for solution creation. They act as a conduit between researchers, development professionals, and the public, collaborating with other departments, credit institutions, NGOs, and international organizations to maximize efforts and effects. Extension service, therefore, emphasizes service in the extension work, using the extension educational process to fulfill its mission and mandate for welfare and development.
3. Extension Job	The role of extension in agriculture and home science is critical in helping individuals make better use of their resources in the face of changing social and economic landscapes. This involves aiding those involved in farming and homemaking to adapt and thrive.
4. Extension Educational Process	The extension educational process focuses on working with people's immediate needs and interests to provide more employment opportunities, increase socioeconomic status, improve household management, and hasten the welfare of rural people. It's an integral part of extension work, emphasizing the development of capacities and the effective delivery of services to meet the immediate and long-term needs of the community.

Scope of Extension Education

The Extension appears to have an endless scope in instances where there is a need to raise awareness among individuals and change their behaviour by educating and informing them. "Kelsey and Hearne (1967) established nine areas of programme emphasis that show the extent of agricultural extension".

Scope

1. Increasing agricultural production efficiency.
2. Increasing marketing, distribution, and utilisation expertise.
3. Natural resource conservation, development, and utilisation.
4. Proper farm and household management.
5. Better family life.
6. Youth development
7. Leadership development.
8. Community and rural development
9. Improving public affairs for general development.

This acronym, "Growth", represents the overarching goals of the Extension in a way that is both meaningful and easy to remember, reflecting its commitment to enhancing agricultural practices, conserving resources, and improving lives within communities.

"Growth"

1. G for Growth (encompassing agricultural production efficiency and general development)
2. R for Resources (natural resource conservation, development and utilisation)
3. O for Outreach (increasing marketing, distribution and utilisation expertise)
4. W for Welfare (better family life, youth and leadership development)
5. T for Transformation (community and rural development)
6. H for Harmony (improving public affairs for general development)

Objectives

1. To improve the rural people's level of living by assisting them in making the best use of their resources.
2. Assist in the formulation and execution of family and village programmes to increase output in various occupations.
3. To create improved family living conditions.

Specific Objectives

1. To provide knowledge and assistance in improving farm management and increasing farm income.
2. To encourage farmers to raise their own food, eat healthy, and live healthy lives.
3. To improve people's social, recreational, intellectual, and spiritual lives.
4. To assist rural families in gaining a better understanding of the village's SWOT analysis.
5. To provide new possibilities to enable rural people to develop their talents and leadership.
6. Developing a sense of rural residents' love of society and patriotism through the development of civil civic awareness.
7. To train young people from rural areas for development work.

The major objectives of Extension may also be categorised as follows -

1. Material production and income growth
2. Educational-Change people's perspectives or develop the individual
3. Community Cultural and Social Development

Philosophy of Extension

The search for wisdom, a group of underlying guidelines or rules of a subject of knowledge, is referred to as philosophy. It is the philosophy of a certain discipline which would provide the concepts or rules for shaping or moulding the activities or programmes related to that discipline.

The philosophy of extension education has been interpreted in a variety of ways by various authors, some of which are included below:

According to Kelsey and Hearne (1967)

The basic philosophy of extension education is to teach people how to think, not what to think. Extension's specific job is furnishing the inspiration, supplying specific advice and technical help, and counselling to see that the people as individuals, families, groups and communities that work together as a unit to solve their problems. Extension workers assist individuals in growing as individuals and achieving exceptional personal well-being.

According to Mildred Horton (1952)

1. In a democracy, the individual is supreme
2. In a civilization's basic unit is its home
3. The family is the human race's original training group
4. Man and land (nature) must work together as the cornerstone of any long-lasting civilization.

For a memorable acronym that encapsulates the principles outlined by Mildred Horton in 1952, focusing on democracy, the importance of home, family as a foundational training group, and the relationship between man and land, we can derive: "DHF Cornerstone"

- D for Democracy (the individual is supreme)
- H for Home (civilization's basic unit)
- F for Family (the human race's original training group)
- Cornerstone representing the essential relationship between Man and Land (nature) as pivotal for a lasting civilization.
- This acronym, "DHF Cornerstone", succinctly captures the essence of Horton's principles, emphasizing the fundamental elements crucial for sustaining civilization: democracy, home, and family, with the man-land relationship being the cornerstone of enduring progress and harmony.

According to Ensminger (1957)

1. Extension as an educational process i.e changing attitudes, knowledge and skills of the people.

2. Extension is teaching people what to want and ways to achieve i.e working with men and women, young people, boys and girls to answer their needs and wants.
3. Extension is helping people to help themselves.
4. Extension is "Learning by doing" and "seeing is believing".
5. Extension is development of individuals, their leaders, their society, and their world.
6. Extension is working together to expand the welfare and happiness of people
7. Extension is working in harmony with the culture of the people
8. Extension is a living relationship, respect and trust for each other
9. Extension is a two-way channel
10. Extension is a continuous educational process.

The acronym, **"Teach Grow"**, effectively summarizes the essence of Ensminger's vision for Extension, highlighting its role in education, empowerment, and community development, fostering a continuous learning and growth process within a framework of respect, trust, and cooperation.

T for Teaching (changing attitudes, knowledge, skills, and teaching people what to want and how to achieve it)

E for Empowerment (helping people to help themselves)

A for Action (learning by doing and seeing is believing)

C for Continuous (a continuous educational process)

H for Harmony (working in harmony with the culture of the people and living in relationship, respect, and trust for each other)

G for Growth (development of individuals, their leaders, their society, and their world)

R for Relationships (living relationship, respect, and trust for each other)

O for Outreach (working together to expand welfare and happiness)

W for Wisdom (a two-way channel of communication and learning)

According to Dahama (1965)

1. Self-assistance
2. Most valuable resources are the people
3. It is a cooperative effort
4. Democracy is the foundation of it

5. It involves a knowledge and experience that is two-way
6. It is based on creating interest by seeing and doing
7. Voluntary, co-operative participation in programmes
8. Persuasion and public education
9. The programme is built around people's attitudes and values
10. The process never ends.

The acronym, **"People Grow",** succinctly captures Dahama's principles for Extension, emphasizing the core elements of people-centric development, engagement, continuous learning, and the democratic, cooperative spirit that underpins the process.

- P for People (most valuable resources are the people, and the programme is built around people's attitudes and values)
- E for Engagement (creating interest by seeing and doing)
- for Ongoing (the process never ends)
- P for Persuasion (persuasion and public education)
- L for Learning (involves a knowledge and experience that is two-way)
- E for Empowerment (self-assistance)
- G for Growth (it is a cooperative effort, implying development and growth)
- R for Resources (voluntary, cooperative participation in programmes)
- for Openness (democracy is the foundation of it)
- W for Wisdom (insight from continuous learning and adaptation)

Functions of Extension

The primary function of extension education, or any sort of education, is to create desired changes in KASA (knowledge, attitude, skill and action).

Changes may be made in their knowledge, skill, attitude, understanding, objective, action & confidence. To that end, extension workers must constantly seek new knowledge in order to improve the effectiveness of their work.

The extension system encompasses all public, commercial, and non-governmental development institutions that transfer, mobilise, and educate people, as opposed to a service or a single institution that generally simply gives advice. It is helpful to think of extension as both a system and the collection of tasks carried out by that system to encourage voluntary change among people for development, according to a review of numerous attempts to define or characterise extension.

Extension Functions Include

1. Technology transfer in different paths towards sustainability development.
2. Transferring management to motivate and organise development actions by all communities.
3. Transferring educational and human resource capacity and
4. Building up the capabilities of all parties involved, managing the market, gathering input, and negotiating prices for goods and services.

Extension Education Process

A successful extension educational programme includes five crucial and interconnected steps. This extension educational process notion is merely meant to clarify the processes required in carrying out a planned educational effort. It does not imply that these processes are in any way distinct from one another. Extensive experience reveals that planning, teaching, and evaluation occur in variable degrees throughout all phases of extension operations. The order of actions is discussed on the basis of concept developed by Leagans (1967).

There are five steps are included in extension education process {SOTER}

1. Situation
2. Objective
3. Teaching
4. Evaluation
5. Reconsideration

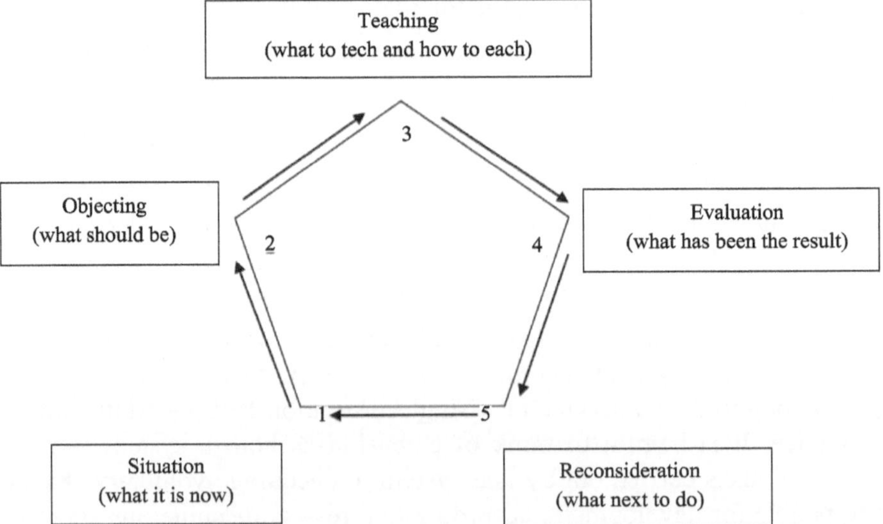

Figure 1: Extension Education Process

First step

The first step includes gathering facts and analysing the problem. Individuals and their enterprises, along with the financial, social, cultural, technological, and physical settings in which they reside and operate can be acquired by conducting an appropriate survey and building rapport with the folks.

The responses will be reviewed in collaboration with the locals to identify the challenges and resources accessible in the community. For example, following a community survey and data analysis, the problem was identified as a farm family's poor income from their crop-producing firm.

Second step

The next step is to decide on realistic goals that the community can achieve. Residents should be included in the selection of a limited number of objectives. The goals should be defined and obvious, and when completed, they should bring satisfaction to the community. The desired behavioural changes in people, as well as economic and social outcomes, should be stated in the objectives.

In the example, the issue was noted as having low enterprise income from crop production. A thorough investigation into the data indicated that the poor revenue was caused by low crop yield, which was attributed to using locally grown seeds with low yield potential, using limited fertiliser, and the lack of crop protection measures. Considering the community's capacity and competency, as well as the resources' accessibility, the goal was set to rise crop yield by 20% within a specific time frame. It was expected that the higher production would result in increased income, which would improve family welfare.

Third step

The third step is teaching, which involves choosing the lessons' subject matter and the instructional strategies and tools to use. In addition to research findings of practical and financial value to the community, it demands the selection and integration of appropriate teaching aids and methods.

As teaching content, technologies, for example, the use of HYV seeds, fertiliser application, and plant protection chemicals, were chosen considering the issues noted in the specific example. Teaching methods included result demonstration, method demonstration, farmer training, and farm publications, while teaching aids included a tape recorder and slides.

Fourth step

The fourth step is to evaluate the teaching, which involves analysing how well the goals have been achieved. A re-survey is recommended to objectively evaluate the outcomes of an educational programme. It is important to collect proof of altered behaviour, which will not only provide a measure of success but will also highlight any shortcomings.

In this case, a re-survey after a specified amount of time revealed that crop yield had improved by 10%. As a result, it indicated that there was a 10% difference in crop production compared to the previously set target (objective) of 20%. The re-survey also revealed two significant shortcomings in carrying out the extension educational programme, namely a lack of effective water management and farmers' inability to use fertiliser and plant protection chemicals as recommended due to a lack of funds.

Fifth step

The fifth step is to reconsider the entire extension education programme in the context of the evaluation's findings. Except for new problems or situations that emerge, the problems identified during the evaluation process may serve as the starting point for the upcoming stage of the educational extension programme. Following a re-consideration of the evaluation results with the people, the following educational goals were regenerated.

They were, for example, training farmers on how to manage their water resources properly and setting up water management demonstrations. For production credit to be obtained in time to buy essential inputs, people were told to contact their local banks. Thus, people will move from an unfavourable to a favourable situation because of the ongoing process of extension education.

Principles of Extension

Principles are generalised rules that serve as the foundation for continuous decision and activity. These ideas have already been valid in producing results under diverse contexts and circumstances. To work with rural people, we must understand these ideas. Some of these principles linked to extended education are listed below: (Mondal, 2021)

1. Principle of Interest and Need.
2. Principle of Cultural Difference.
3. Principle of Learning by doing.
4. Principle of Participation.
5. Principle of Adaptability in the Use of Extension Teaching Methods.
6. The Grassroots Principle of Organization.
7. Principle of Leadership.
8. The Whole-family Principle.

9. Principle of Satisfaction.
10. Principle of Evaluation.
11. Principles of Indigenous knowledge.
12. Principle of Applied Science and Democratic Approach.
13. Principle of Trained Specialists.
14. Principle of Co-operation.

Table 2: Principles of Extension

Principle	Description	Example
Interest and Need	Extension work should be based on people's needs and interests, varying across different regions.	Establishing a market for milk if villagers are raising dairy cows for profit.
Cultural Difference	Extension work must respect cultural contexts and be carried out in accordance with prevalent culture.	Avoiding pig breeding in Muslim communities where it is culturally unacceptable.
Learning by Doing	Encourages hands-on learning and active participation in extension activities.	Teaching farmers to use sprayers and demonstrating increased yield after spraying.
Participation	Extension should enable people to help themselves, promoting participation and experience.	Voluntary collaboration in extension programmes, like the success of Amul in India.
Adaptability in Teaching Methods	Extension programmes should be adaptable and use multiple methods suitable for different audiences.	Using a combination of methods like literature for literates and radio for those with access.
Grassroots Organization	Extension work should be community-based and tailored to local environments.	Implementing three-tiered Panchayat Raj Institution for grassroots organization in extension.
Leadership	Utilizing local leadership in extension work to assist in implementing activities.	Using local opinion leaders to efficiently spread new ideas.
Whole-family	Extension work involves the entire family, focusing on family units in farming communities.	International Year of Family Farming Campaign focused on individual farm homes.
Satisfaction	The success of extension teaching is measured by the satisfaction of learning new skills or changing behavior.	Bangladesh Grameen Bank's success due to the satisfaction of beneficiaries from the microfinance scheme.

Evaluation	Regular evaluation of extension programmes to measure effectiveness and make necessary adjustments.	Corrective action taken if a programme deviates from its intended path.
Indigenous Knowledge	Recognizing and integrating indigenous knowledge systems in extension programmes.	Building extension programmes that respect and include local indigenous knowledge.
Applied Science and Democratic Approach	Extension education based on democratic principles and practical application of scientific ideas.	Farmers given options to adopt new methods based on their practical experiences.
Trained Specialists	Utilizing specialists for training farmers due to the rapidly evolving nature of agriculture and related fields.	Employing specialists to provide the latest and best practices to farmers.
Co-operation	Extension as a collaborative effort, emphasizing learning by doing and collective improvement.	Farmers encouraged to learn new methods through hands-on experience and seeing results firsthand.

Extension Teaching Methods

Definition

Extension Teaching Methods are devices that are used to set up a situation and conditions in which, between the teacher and the students, effective conversation can take place. Extension teaching methods are designed to carry out a variety of objectives, including providing effective communication so that the learner can see, hear, and accomplish the things that need to be learned. In addition, to provides stimulation and motivation that leads to desirable psychological and physical activity on the part of the learner. As a result, it can be stated that the fundamental purpose of extension teaching methods is to awaken learners' enthusiasm and curiosity so that they can develop their skills and knowledge to a certain amount to lead to sustainable living. (Extension Teaching Methods, n.d.).

According to Leagans (1961), "Extension teaching methods are the devices used to create situations in which communication can take place between the instructor and the learner".

Objectives of the Extension Teaching

The main objectives of the extension teaching have been stated as follows: (Home Science, 2005).

1. The fundamental objective is the development of the people. There are people whose intellectual abilities are not fully developed; they either

leave school early or do not pursue higher education or enrol in colleges and universities. These people engage in vocational training programmes and develop their abilities to improve their living situations and achieve something in their lives. This will enable them to find employment and support themselves.

2. To provide information and aid in enabling people to work more productively and effectively. Several professions have demanded that demand that people improve their talents and abilities to the point where they should carry out their activities and jobs properly, including plumbing, electricians, carpentry, welding, and the creation of handicrafts and artwork. In addition, people must productively conduct their operations when performing construction work or any other type of task requiring the use of technology or other resources.
3. To improve opportunities for engagement and assist people in becoming more used to the outside world. Regardless of their status or background, every person is a part of the community and must interact and deal with others who are not part of it to meet all his needs and expectations. An individual requires support from other people, including his family, friends, and members of the society, to function properly and to carry out all his duties. An individual cannot exist alone and cannot perform all his activities and functions on his own.
4. To give people new possibilities to better their level of living and develop their skills and talents. People from underprivileged, marginalised, and socioeconomically disadvantaged backgrounds can have underdeveloped educational skills, poor educational levels, or no schooling at all. To raise their standard of living, it is crucial for them to develop their abilities and talents. These people develop their abilities throughout a range of fields, which may even include creative abilities.
5. To develop individuals into productive members of society. Through extension education and extension teaching methods, people do improve their skills, knowledge, and capabilities; they make every attempt to become self-sufficient. Every person works to provide for himself and his family, but it's crucial that they also set a goal to contribute to the country's progress as productive citizens. Therefore, promoting social welfare is regarded as one of every citizen's most significant objectives.
6. To encourage improvements in the social, cultural, recreational, intellectual, and spiritual aspects of the goal of extension education and extension teaching methods is to foster a variety of qualities and aspects in students, including the ability to be social, communicate effectively with others, recognise cultural values, ethics, and norms, as

well as to concentrate on intellectual, intellectual, leisure, rational, and religious aspects. To be able to support oneself, one must have sufficient knowledge on these topics.

Classification of Extension Teaching Methods

Extension teaching methods are categorised as individual methods, group methods and mass methods. Each of these strategies has benefits and drawbacks. The main aim of the extension agent is to select a particular method or collective of methods according to the situation needs. Different classifications of extension teaching methods are given below:

One way to categorise extension methods is by their use and nature of contact in relation to interpersonal, group, and mass communication. They are categorised into the following categories based on the nature of contact:

Individual contact methods- Extension methods under this category allow for face-to-face or person-to-person communication between rural people and extension experts. These methods effectively teach new skills and build trust between farmers and extension personnel.

Group contact methods- In this category, rural people or farmers are contacted in groups of 20 to 25 people. These groups are usually organised around a shared interest. These methods also require face-to-face interaction with people and allow for sharing ideas, discussions about difficulties, and technical recommendations. The future course of action is, therefore, determined.

Mass contact methods- An extension specialist must approach many people to disseminate information and assist them in using it. Mass-contact approaches easily accomplish this. These strategies are more effective at quickly making people aware of new technologies.

a) According to the use

S.No.	Individual Methods	Group Methods	Mass Methods
1	Farm and home visit	Result demonstration	Farm publication
2	Farmer's call	Method demonstration	Mass meeting
3	Personal letter	Group meeting	Campaign
4	Adaptive or Minikit trial	Small group training	Exhibition
5	Farm clinic	Field day or Farmer's day	Newspaper
6	Flag method	Study tour	Radio, TV, Mobile (SMS)

b) According to the form

S.No.	Written	Spoken	Visual or objectives	Spoken and visual
1	Bulletins	General & special meetings	Result demonstrations	Method demonstration meeting
2	Leaflets, folders, news articles	Farm & home visit	Demonstration plots	Meeting and result demonstration
3	Personal letters	Official calls	Motion pictures or movies, charts	Meetings involving motion pictures, charts, and other visual aids
4	Circular letters	Telephone calls, radio	Slides & filmstrips, models, exhibits	Television

(Mondal, 2021)

The following is an overview of some of the most frequent extension methods utilised by extension professionals:

The following is a brief description of some of the most frequent extension methods utilised by extension professionals:

i. **Farm and home visit** - A farm and home visit is when an extension expert has direct or face-to-face interaction with the farmer or members of his family. These visits involve the exchange or discussion of information. The visits could be used to become familiar with the farmers' difficulties. These visits allow for two-way conversation.

ii. **Method demonstration** - This method is used to show the technique of doing things or carrying out new practices e.g. clean milk production, paneer making, ghee making, etc. This method is usually used for groups of people.

iii. **Result demonstration** - Result demonstration is meant to prove the advantages of recommended practices and to demonstrate their applicability to the local conditions. It is conducted by a farmer under the direct supervision of an extension professional. It is designed to teach others, in addition to the person who conducts the demonstration. It helps the farmers to learn by seeing & doing. This method can be used to show the superiority of practices, such as dahi culture, value addition, hygienic handling of animals, etc.

iv. **Group discussion** - All the farmers cannot be contacted by extension professionals individually because of their large number. It is convenient & feasible to contact them in groups. This method is commonly known as group discussion. It is used to encourage & stimulate people to learn more about the problems that concern the community through discussion.

It is a good method of involving the local people in developing local leadership & in deciding on a plan of action in a democratic way.

v. **Exhibition** - An exhibition is a systematic display of information, actual specimens, models, posters, photographs, charts, etc., in a logical sequence. It is organised to arouse the interest of the clientele in the things displayed. It is one of the best media for reaching many people, especially illiterate & semi-literate people. Exhibitions are used for a wide range of topics, such as planning a model village, showing high-yielding breeds of cattle and buffaloes, new agricultural implements, and the best products of village industries.

vi. **Campaign** - Campaign is used to focus the attention of the people on a particular problem, e.g. milk adulteration, vaccination and prevention of animal diseases, tick control etc. Through this method, maximum number of farmers can be reached in the shortest possible time. It builds up community confidence and involves the people emotionally in a programme.

vii. **Field tour** - Conducted tours for farmers are used to convince them and to provide them with an opportunity to see the results of new practices and products, skills, etc. and to give them an idea regarding the suitability & application of these things in their own area. Such tours may also be arranged to enable the rural people to visit places & institutions (connected with the problems of rural life), such as research institutions, training institutions, agricultural universities, model villages, areas of advanced developments, leading private farms, exhibitions, and agricultural & cattle fairs/dairy mela.

viii. **Print media** - Newspapers, magazines, bulletins, leaflets, folders, pamphlets and wall news sheets are another set of mass media for communicating information to a large number of literate people. They are used for communicating general & specific information on a programme of technology or practice. Small folders, leaflets & pamphlets are used to give specific recommendations about a practice, such as clean milk production, vaccination schedule, detection of milk adulterants, etc.

ix. **Radio** - It is one of the most powerful media of communication. It is a mass medium of communication and can reach many people at any given time involving the least expense. Extension professionals use the radio for communicating information on new methods & techniques, giving timely information about the control of animal diseases such as foot & mouth disease (FMD), animal pests, weather, market news, etc. For this purpose, talks, group discussions, folk songs, dialogues & dramas are usually broadcast. There are radio programmes broadcast by All India Radio (AIR), FM (frequency-modulated) radio, community radio, etc.

x. **Television** - It combines both audio & visual impact and is very suitable for the dissemination of agriculture & dairy information. It is more useful in teaching to do a specific job. A beginning has been made in India for using this medium for development programmes and it is expected that its use will become more extensive in the coming years. At present, along with the Government-owned channel (Doordarshan), several other private channels are telecasting various kinds of entertainment and developmental programmes to reach the viewers.

xi. **Leaflet** - A leaflet is a single sheet of paper used to present information on only one developmental idea in a concise manner, using simple language.

xii. **Folder** - A folder is a single piece of paper folded once or twice, and, when opened, the material is presented in sequence.

xiii. **Pamphlet** - A pamphlet is an unbound single sheet of paper that is printed on both sides, printed in colours with action photographs, giving full information about a topic in greater length than in folders or leaflets.

xiv. **Bulletin** - A bulletin is a publication of around 20 pages, with the primary objective of giving complete information which the intended readers can apply to their own situation.

xv. **Booklet** - When the extension material exceeds 20 pages and is less than 50 pages, it is called a booklet.

Conclusion

The main objective of teaching extension is to direct the rural people for their individual growth and development; to provide knowledge and guidance to enable them to work more productively and efficiently; to assist in becoming familiar with the outside world and to provide better opportunities for interaction; to open new opportunities for developing skills and talents and improving their standard of living; and to make people self-sufficient and productive. Extension teaching methods, viz. individual contact methods, group contact methods, and mass contact methods, are extensively utilised to provide knowledge and information to individuals, whether on an individual or group basis.

Answer the following questions

1. How does Informal Education differ from Formal and Non-formal Education in terms of its approach to learning and the role of the teacher? Compare and contrast the teaching methods, curriculum, and evaluation processes in these three types of education.
2. Discuss the role of Extension Education in rural development, considering its scope, objectives, and functions. How does Extension Education contribute to enhancing agricultural practices, improving livelihoods, and fostering community empowerment? Provide examples to illustrate your points.
3. Explore the principles underlying Extension Education, emphasizing their significance in guiding the planning, implementation, and evaluation of extension programs. How do principles such as learning by doing, cultural sensitivity, and adaptability influence the design and effectiveness of extension initiatives? Provide real-world instances where these principles have been successfully applied.
4. What are the primary objectives of extension teaching methods, and how do they contribute to sustainable living and community development?
5. How do extension teaching methods vary in their classification and utilization, and how do they cater to individual, group, and mass communication needs in agricultural and rural development contexts.

4

Teaching and Learning in Extension

Nikita Khoisnam

Assistant Professor, Department of Agricultural Economics and Extension
Lovely Professional University, Phagwara, Punjab

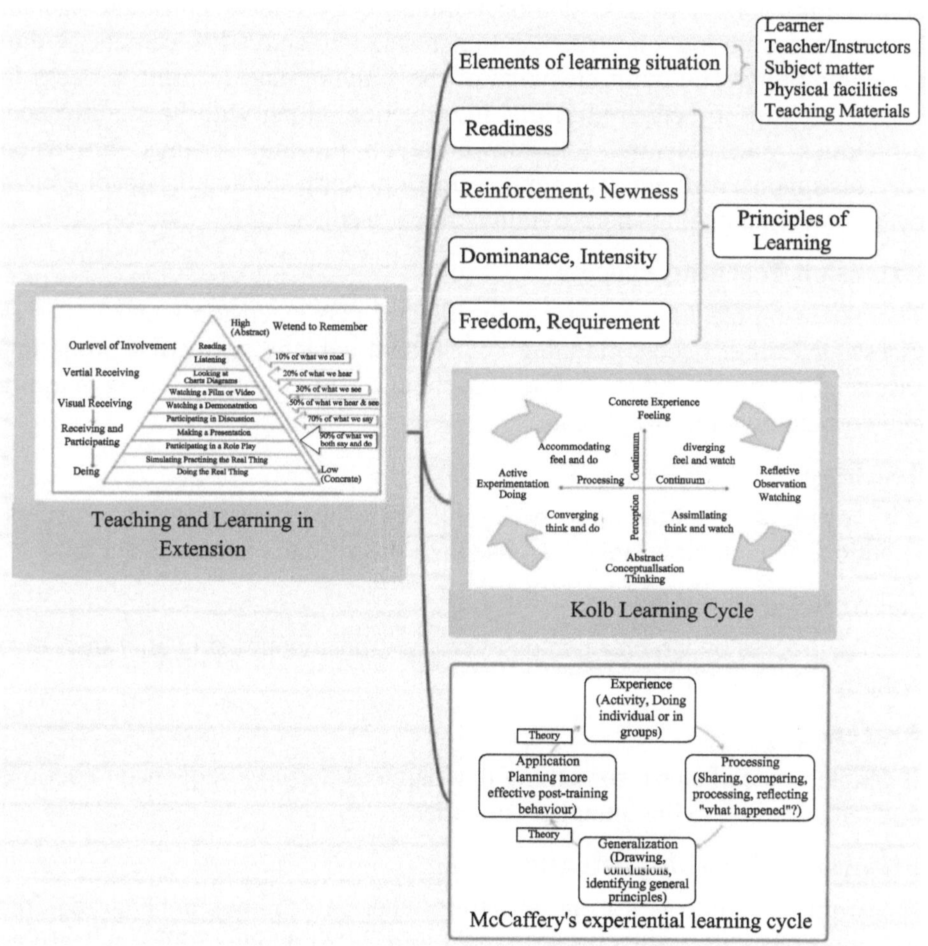

Figure 1: Overview of the chapter (Credit: Jarial, S)

Introduction

The definition of the teaching-learning process, also known as the education process, is a methodical, planned sequence of events that both the teacher and the student follow in order to accomplish the goals of teaching and learning. In primary education, values education is taught through games. Extension services are vital to the global rural and agricultural communities because they spread knowledge, offer useful skills, and encourage sustainable practices. The teaching and learning process, a dynamic exchange between extension agents and community members with the goal of enabling people to better their lives and livelihoods, is at the centre of these extension efforts. The process in question comprises a diverse array of activities, ranging from conducting workshops and demonstrations to individual consultations, all aimed at promoting constructive transformation and advancement within the community. The main elements of the teaching and learning process in extension work are covered in this introduction, along with its significance, difficulties, and potential for transformation in rural settings. Extension services support resilient communities and long-term sustainable development by empowering people and providing effective education.

Extension Teaching Process

The extension teaching process is an integral part extension which involves assessing learner needs, planning educational content, delivering programs, assessing progress, and evaluating effectiveness to promote lifelong learning and community empowerment.

Teaching

It is the process of setting up scenarios that bring the key lessons to the learners' attention, pique their curiosity, arouse their desire, and encourage action.

Learning

It is the process by which a person alters their behaviour using only their own willpower and abilities.

Process

It denotes a set of steps, something that happens during a sequence of actions or events leading to the intended outcome.

Elements of Learning Situation

A learning situation is a state or setting where all the components required to support learning are present. According to Abdullai (2002), a learning environment consists of all the components required to encourage learning.

These components are listed below:

- Learner (community/development beneficiaries)
- Teacher/ Instructors (extension and development worker)
- Subject matter (community-useful development ideas)
- Physical facilities (suitable setting)
- Teaching Materials (textbook material).

The extension and development worker's job as an instructor is to control the other four components to ensure that the students have a successful learning process. The following are the circumstances that allow for effective learning to occur: Leagans (1961).

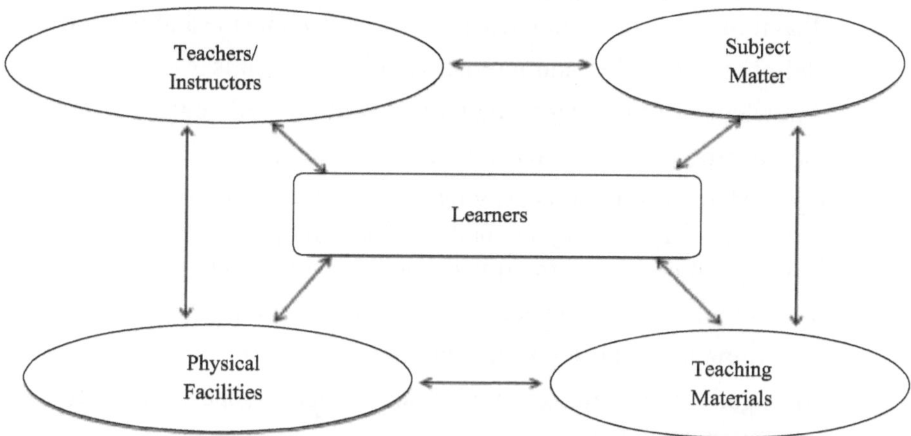

Figure 2: Elements of learning situation

1. Learners - In the learning process, the learner takes centre stage, as the primary goal is to facilitate their learning. Consequently, the other elements serve as means to this end. Learners' acquisition of knowledge depends on several factors:
   - Their need for information
   - Personal interests
   - Level of ambition
   - Comprehension levels
   - Capacity to attribute intended meanings
   - Utilization of acquired information.
2. Teacher/ Instructors - The standard of the learning environment that the instructor creates will determine the quality of the learning. An extension

and development worker or instructor who is successful will take into account the following crucial factors:

- choosing educational opportunities that meet both the needs of the community as a whole and the learners' skills and requirements.
- proficiency with extension techniques and tools.
- knowledge of the needs and capabilities of learners.
- capacity to respond to students' attitudes, feelings, and emotions in a suitable manner
- the capacity to promote students' involvement in the learning environment
- the capacity to set up and oversee the learning environment in a way that minimises or eliminates distractions both inside and outside of it.
- calmness, sincerity, and interpersonal relationships
- knowledge of the subject matter and well-defined goals
- democratic leadership and effective communication

3. Subject Matter (contents) - Any teaching and learning process's content is referred to as its subject matter. If the subject matter satisfies the following requirements, the transfer will be simple and successful:
    - based on factual evidence, legitimate and accurate
    - appropriate in real-world development scenarios
    - arranged in accordance with the learner's needs, interests, and comprehension level
    - suitable and on time
    - significant and connected to particular learning goals
4. Teaching Materials - Without the help of suitable teaching methods and aids, the subject matter cannot be effectively transferred to learners. Proper selection and skilful handling of teaching aids facilitate the creation of a desirable learning situation. Therefore, the teaching methods and aids should be:
    - simple and easy to handle
    - appropriate for the topic at hand
    - easily accessible
    - in good operating order
    - varied, adaptable, and tailored to the students' needs and the learning environment.

5. Physical Facilities - The location, lighting, ventilation, seating arrangements, and other physical amenities must satisfy both the teacher and the students. It is the duty of the instructor to guarantee that the necessary physical spaces are available for producing high-quality scenario for learning.

Criteria for Effective Learning in Extension

The main goal of education is to change human behaviour for more beneficial and productive ends. Acquiring knowledge, skills, attitudes, and other things is part of learning; retention to stop transfer and reversion, to apply it to actual circumstances. The following are necessary for effective learning:

1. Learning must have purpose and relevance- Objectives should be clear and meaningful to learners, addressing topics that are important and desired by a significant portion of the group. These objectives should be achievable through the available educational resources, within the participants' physical and economic constraints, and aligned with their social conditions and learning capacities.
2. Effective learning involves active engagement of the senses- Humans receive messages through five senses: sight, hearing, touch, taste, and smell. In extension education, learning primarily occurs through seeing, hearing, and doing. Therefore, learning experiences should be centered around practical activities, allowing farmers to learn by actively engaging their senses.
3. Learning should emphasize problem-solving and fulfilment- Skills acquired through learning should enable farmers to tackle challenges and improve their quality of life progressively. The learning process should empower individuals to overcome obstacles and find satisfaction in their achievements.
4. Learning must lead to practical comprehension- Simply acquiring knowledge is insufficient; it must be comprehended and applicable in real-life situations. Effective learning ensures that participants understand and can effectively apply the knowledge gained to solve practical problems they encounter.

How do Extension Programs Facilitate Learning?

Learning occurs through the utilization of our five physical senses: sight, sound, touch, taste, and smell. When farmers alter their behavior through their own actions, they engage in activities that involve one or more of these senses for specific purposes.

There are seven primary methods by which individuals learn:

1. Conditioning involves forming an association between a stimulus and a response. Example is Pavlov conditioned dogs to dribble at the sound of a bell.
2. Trial and Error is a process where individuals discover solutions to problems through repeated attempts. However, this method can be time-consuming and inefficient due to unsuccessful efforts.
3. Problem-solving utilizes past learning experiences to address challenges, involving higher mental processes like reasoning and hypothesis testing.
4. Training, akin to conditioning, is beneficial for developing skills, habits, and attitudes. It often employs rewards and punishments to reinforce success and failure, respectively.
5. Insight Learning leads to sudden realizations or solutions, often resulting in a sense of relief. Despite the breakthrough, the learner may not fully comprehend the mechanics of the solution.
6. Imitation involves mimicking behaviors or patterns without extensive reasoning. People readily adopt opinions and beliefs expressed by leaders or found in literature.
7. Memorization entails committing information to memory without necessarily understanding it fully. This method focuses on memorizing details verbatim.

Principles of Learning in Extension

The following fundamental learning concepts are expected of you as an extension and development professional and can be used in your work .

1. **Principles of readiness** - The readiness principle in extension education highlights how crucial it is to make sure that learners are ready and eager to participate in the activities and content that is being offered to them. When learners have a goal and a clear reason for learning something, they are more committed to their learning and advance more quickly than when they are not motivated. Hence, it is important to investigate the learners' perceived needs in order to assist them in concentrating their attention on the issues preventing the fulfilment of those needs. Farmers will be keen to learn and put the control measures on paddy blast into practice in the event of a serious blast attack.
2. **Principle of reinforcement** - It indicates that the most lasting experiences are those that are practiced the most. It has been demonstrated that when learners engage in meaningful practice and review, they learn more effectively and retain the material longer. Only when the practice

is followed by encouraging feedback does it lead to improvement. A response turns into a habit after being given repeatedly. A man becomes perfect via practice. For instance, demonstrating a method gives the farmer the chance to engage in self-activity, or learning by doing.

3. **Principle of effect** - This theory is predicated on the idea that a learner's behaviour is directly related to their motivation. When learning is associated with a negative emotion, it is weakened; learning is strengthened when it is desirable, enjoyable, and pleasant. Whatever the setting, instruction should be purposeful and include components that have a positive impact on students and make them feel satisfied. For instance, replacing high yielding paddy varieties with hybrid rice, which provides a higher yield and income, satisfies farmers.
4. **Principle of dominance** - First, new knowledge leaves a lasting, powerful impression on the mind that is hard to overcome. It can be challenging to teach the right techniques to a student who has picked up a bad one. As a result, the learner's initial encounter should be fruitful, useful, and establish the groundwork for all subsequent experiences. For instance, it is currently challenging to persuade farmers to employ biocontrol techniques to manage pests because the majority of them are dependent on the use of chemicals for plant protection.
5. **Principle of newness** - According to this theory, people remember things that they have learned most recently. Another term for this would be the timing principle. The learner will be helped to complete the task successfully the closer the learning period is to the real time of needing to apply it. The principle of newness often dictates the order in which learners should receive their learning experiences because information that is learned last is typically remembered the best. For instance, farmers get ready to learn more about the new high-yielding varieties during the cropping season.
6. **Principle of intensity** - More attention will be paid if the material is taught well. It means that a learner will retain more information from the original than from a copy. When a learner performs tasks instead of just reading about them, they are more likely to understand them better. When a learner actively participates, learning is more effective.
7. **Principle of freedom** - It is best to learn things freely. Because learning is an active process, learners need to be granted freedom—freedom to choose, to act, and to accept the consequences of their actions. Without independence, learners might not be very interested in learning. For instance, farmers should be free to choose their own vocation; they

should not be coerced into doing a job that goes against their religious beliefs.

8. **Principle of requirement** - As per the law of requirements, "we must have something to accomplish or do something. It can be aptitude, ability, or anything that could aid in knowledge acquisition. Farmers, for instance, should be aware of the effective use of loans when they choose to make use of them. A few more learning principles that are applicable in extension, in addition to the previously mentioned principles, can be found in literature. These principles include those of environment, sense of self-activity, association, transfer, disassociation, attitude, motivation, rewards, and clarity of objectives, satisfaction, participation, and learning progress. Extension-related learning must lead to farmers' functional improvements.

Learning Acquisition Pattern

Training programmes need to make the most of learning by creating engaging experiences that follow adult learning principles. Sheal (1989) adapted Edgar Dale's "Cone of Experience," which shows how participation and engagement connect to learning. It demonstrates various learning methods between reading and real-world application, increasing learning as one descends the cone. Research shows that engaging multiple senses enhances learning, with sight being the most effective. The Cone of Experience, with its ten stages, starting from concrete experiences at the bottom emphasizes sensory involvement over difficulty, promoting meaningful learning through interconnected experiences.

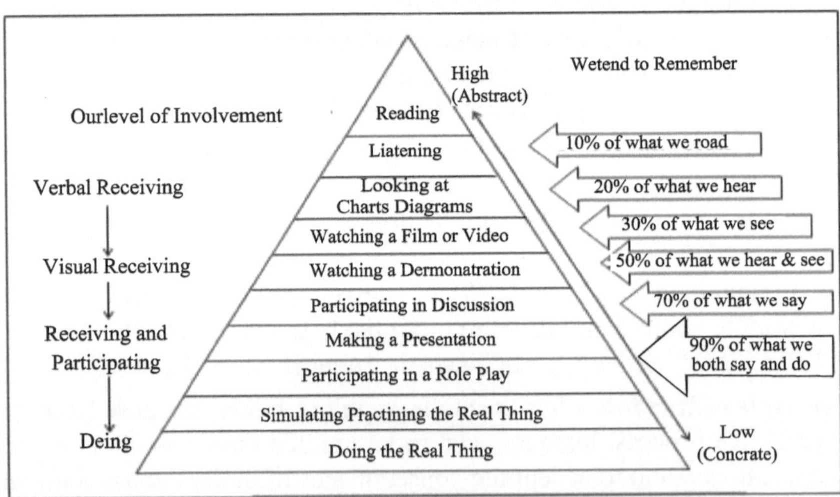

Figure 2: Edgar Dale's Cone of Experience as modified by Sheal, 1989 (Action, Participation and Learning)

Experiential Learning

The meaning and comprehension of the material to be learned are acquired through the mental and physical reactions one has when seeing, hearing, or doing the things to be learned. The emotional and/or physical responses a learner has when exposed to the material in order to comprehend it and acquire new insights that help them tackle problems in the future.

The learners' first-hand experiences play an essential role in achieving desired learning objectives. There is a growing inclination towards experiential training programs aimed at fostering behavioral change in learners. Experiential learning, a learner-centered approach, allows learners to take ownership of their learning process and collaborate with instructors. Specifically, it involves learning through reflection on practical experiences. The level of learner participation is whether high or low, and the content guided by instructors, determined by learners' needs, denote the degree of learner involvement. Different terms such as "learning-by-doing" or "trial and error learning" describe the process of learning from experience. Modern theories of experiential learning have been developed to explain this approach. Experiential learning offers significant teaching benefits, as effective teaching is essential for motivating learners to absorb knowledge. Hence, experiential learning necessitates providing guidance to learners to optimize learning outcomes.

Learning Experience Characteristics

- The goals should be achieved as a result of an effective learning experience.
- It ought to result in the important content's development.
- It ought to support the curiosity and aspiration for increased or improved education.

David Kolb's Experiential Learning Cycle

A typical learning cycle where a learner "touches all the bases" represents the four stages of the Kolb experiential learning style theory:

1. Concrete Experience: A situation is experienced for the first time, or an old experience is interpreted in a different way.
2. Reflective Observation (of the novel encounter): Any discrepancies between experience and understanding are especially significant.
3. Abstract Conceptualization: Reflection gives rise to either a brand-new concept or a modification of an existing abstract idea.
4. Active Experimentation: The learner applies the concepts to the environment to observe the outcomes.

A person is said to be learning effectively when they move through a cycle of four stages:

1. Having a concrete experience
2. Observing and reflecting on that experience
3. Forming abstract concepts (analysis) and generalisations (conclusions); and
4. Using those concepts to test hypotheses in subsequent situations, leading to new experiences.

Kolb (1974) stated that learning is an integrated process in which each step builds upon and reinforces the one before it. Even though anyone can start the cycle at any time and follow it logically through to the end, learning is only truly effective when a student can finish all four model stages. Therefore, none of the cycle stages are effective as a stand-alone learning process.

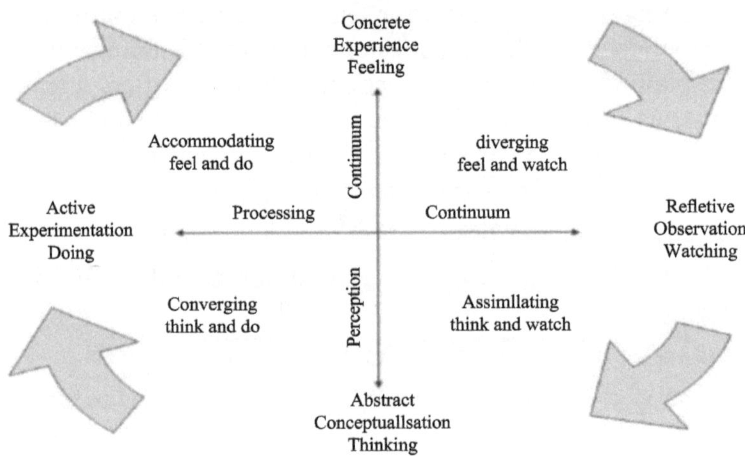

Figure 3: David Kolb Learning Cycle (Azad and Singh, 2017)

Learning from experience is key. Effective learning involves activities that let learners reflect on what they've done, gain insights, and use those insights practically. The ELC model (Figure 4) below explains how adults learn new skills step by step-

- Experience phase: During the Experience phase, participants are hands-on, doing various activities like listening to lectures, engaging in case studies, role-playing, simulating scenarios, playing games, watching films, viewing slideshows, practicing skills, or preparing equipment.
- Process phase: In the Process phase, the teacher or trainer assists participants in remembering and discussing their experiences from the

previous phase. Participants share what they enjoyed or didn't enjoy, what was easy or challenging, and how they felt about it. They talk about their thoughts and feelings, both intellectually and emotionally, either individually or in groups.

- Generalization phase: In the Generalization phase, participants make conclusions and generalizations based on their experiences from the initial phases. Questions about the learning experience aid in forming these generalizations. The teacher or trainer then shifts the discussion from immediate experiences to broader learning concepts.
- Application phase: During the Application phase, participants use the insights and conclusions they've reached to start integrating their learning into their daily routines. The teacher or trainer assists them in considering what actions they'll take once the learning session concludes, with a focus on practical applications at home or work.

Technical information is also included in the ELC, known as theory, and can be introduced before the experience phase. The trainer might use traditional methods to provide this information, followed by hands-on experience. Throughout the ELC process, participants are encouraged to think creatively, and the trainer prompts their thinking with relevant questions at each stage. This approach is beneficial for skill training as it involves participants in practical skill practice, allowing them to draw their own conclusions and identify real-world applications.

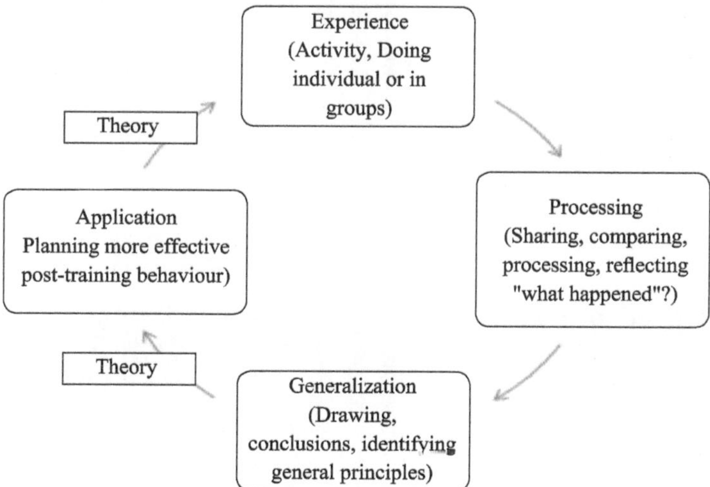

Figure 4: McCaffery's experiential learning cycle. Source: McCaffery James A. 1986. Independent effectiveness: A reconsideration of cross-cultural orientation and training. International Journal of Intercultural Relations, 10(2): 159–78.

Theories of Learning in Extension (Thorndike, 1932)

1. Trial and Error Theory or Connectionism Theory

Thorndike's pioneering research on Animal Intelligence in 1898 introduced the first miniature Trial and Error learning, also known as Connectionism, was proposed by American psychologist E.L. Thorndike. This theory suggests that learning involves forming and strengthening connections between situations and responses. According to Thorndike, learners make attempts, encounter errors, and refine their responses through successive trials, leading to gradual learning. For example, acquiring typing skills often involves trial and error. In one experiment, a hungry cat was placed in a puzzle box with a plate of fish outside. To access the fish, the cat had to figure out how to open the box door by pulling a loop or pressing a lever. Initially, the cat made random movements inside the box, trying different ineffective responses. However, with repeated trials, the cat accidentally pulled the loop, successfully opening the door and accessing the fish. With continued practice, the cat reduced the time taken to pull the loop, demonstrating improved response efficiency over time. This experiment illustrates Thorndike's principle of trial and error learning, where repeated attempts lead to the acquisition of specific behaviors or skills.

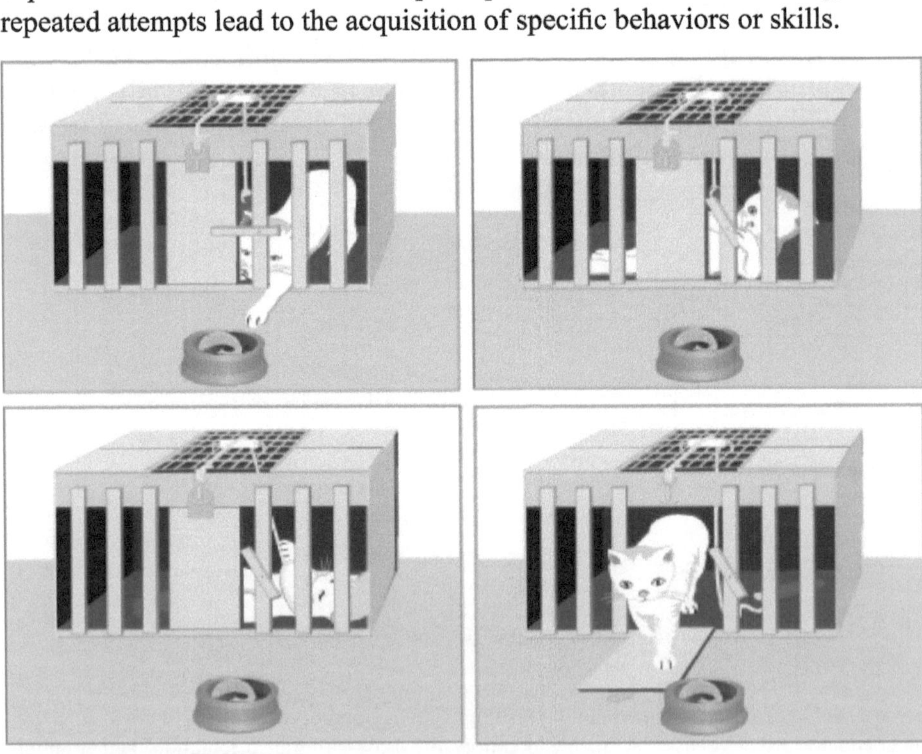

Figure 5: Thorndike's principle of trial and error learning

2. Conditioned Response Theory or Classical conditioned Theory

Conditioning is about changing a natural response by replacing a natural stimulus with an artificial one, which forms a new connection between the artificial stimulus and the natural response. This concept is fundamental to conditioned response learning, as explained by Ivan Pavlov, a Russian doctor and psychologist.

During the early 20th century, Pavlov observed a fascinating phenomenon while studying the digestive system of dogs: the dogs began to salivate upon seeing the lab technicians who typically fed them, even in the absence of food. Pavlov recognized this as a learned response, where the dogs associated the technicians' presence with the imminent delivery of food.

To investigate further, Pavlov conducted experiments where dogs were exposed to a sound preceding the presentation of food. Through repeated pairings of the sound and food, the dogs learned to associate the sound with the forthcoming food, leading to salivation upon hearing the sound alone.

In this classical conditioning paradigm, the unconditioned stimulus (US), such as food, triggers the unconditioned response (UR), like salivation. The neutral stimulus, known as the conditioned stimulus (CS), becomes associated with the US through repeated pairings, eventually eliciting a similar response as the US.

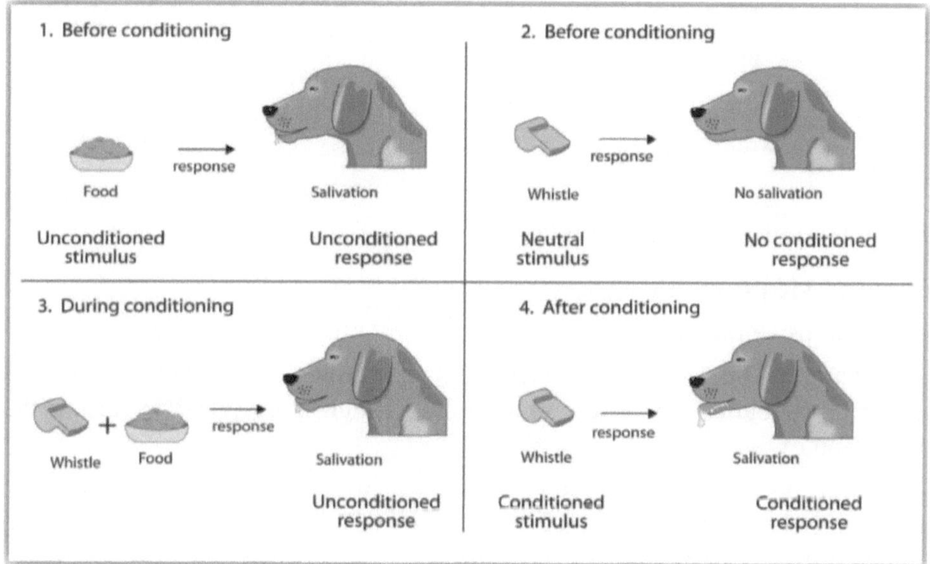

Figure 6: Conditioned Response Theory

3. Learning by Insight Theory

This theory, known as the Gestalt Theory of Learning, stems from the German word "Gestalt," which signifies a whole, total pattern, configuration, or form. Gestalt psychologists diverge from the notion that correct problem solutions are gradually learned through Trial-and-Error. Instead, they reject the reduction of human behavior into numerous specific elements, advocating for the analysis of functional relationships among these elements to determine their meaning. Gestalt psychologists emphasize the configuration of experience rather than its division into elements. For instance, the perception of a person is seen as a configuration resulting from the physical relationships among various body parts such as legs, arms, head, eyes, and ears. Key figures associated with the Gestalt school include Ehrenfels, Wertheimer, Köhler, and Koffka.

Figure 7: Learning by Insight Theory

What is Meant by Extension Teaching?

Different psychologists provided differing definitions of teaching:

According to H.C Morrison "Teaching is an intimate contact between a more mature personality, and a less mature one, which is designed to further the education of the latter".

According to Edmund Amidon "Teaching is an interactive process primarily involving classroom talk, which takes place between teacher and pupil, and occurs during certain definable activities".

According to T.F. Greens "Teaching is a task of a teacher, which is performed for the development of a child".

Effective Teaching Procedure in Extension Work

For effective teaching in extension work, it's important to consider the following procedures:

- Ensure everyone can see: Make sure exhibits and materials are arranged in a way that doesn't block anyone's view. Participants should have a clear view of what's being taught (Yahaya, 2003).
- Speak clearly: Speak clearly so that everyone can understand. Adults understand spoken words better than written words. Make sure all participants can see you when you speak. Engage with the audience directly.
- Start with current needs: Always begin by addressing the present needs and problems of the farmers.
- Present logically: Present your ideas in a logical sequence, focusing on one idea or theme at a time. Whether written or spoken, one sentence or idea at a time is ideal.
- Use practical examples: Use practical devices to illustrate the relationship between ideas.
- Repeat important points: Repeat key ideas to reinforce understanding.
- Create a comfortable environment: Ensure the physical environment is comfortable and conducive to learning.
- Summarize: Wrap up your presentation with a summary of the key points.

Characteristics of Extension Teaching (Laogu, 2005)

If the extension worker is aware of a few teaching techniques, they will aid the learner in understanding the lessons he is trying to impart. Among them are:

1. Specific, well-defined objectives are necessary for extension teaching. To put it simply, a teaching objective is the phrase used to express the final desired end product. Every intentional teacher should be viewed as having clear goals in mind.
2. For maximum impact, extension teaching typically calls for the use of multiple presentation techniques. There is no extension method that can influence everyone it touches or reach all of the people.
3. Extension teaching requires cffective learning experiences. A person's mental or physical reaction when they see, hear, or do the things that they need to learn in order to understand and interpret the content is called a learning experience.

4. Learning scenarios that incorporate the following components should be offered through extension teaching: Effective learning environments include: a) a teacher who participates in the learning group to offer good stimulation and guidance of learning activities; b) learners who are appropriately motivated and aware of their learning needs; and c) the proper use of teaching aids to identify learning experiences.
5. Careful results evaluation is necessary for extension teaching and should direct future initiatives. Extension educators should consistently assess data in a precise and impartial way, using the results to guide their future work.
6. When teaching extension, new materials should be connected to existing knowledge. It is the extension instructor's responsibility to learn, to assess the students' level of understanding, and to appropriately prepare them for new knowledge.
7. With regard to the subject matter (topic) that needs to be learned, extension teaching needs to achieve specific types of educational changes. Changes in knowledge, such as the kinds of seeds to plant and how much fertiliser to apply; changes in skills and abilities, such as mental skills like problem-solving.

Significance of Teaching Process in Extension Work

The teaching process characteristics mentioned above have implications for effective extension work, which can be outlined as follows:

1. Utilize equipment that ensures clear visibility for all audience members.
2. Adults generally comprehend spoken language better than written text, regardless of presentation speed.
3. Begin by addressing the current interests, needs, or issues of the group.
4. Introduce topics systematically, presenting them in a logical sequence, one step at a time.
5. Utilize practical devices to demonstrate the relationships between ideas and materials.
6. Reinforce key ideas by repeating them frequently to the group.
7. Create comfortable and visually appealing physical environments.
8. Aim to foster a sense of accomplishment and eagerness for further learning among participants.
9. Provide a comprehensive summary of the content, outlining what was covered, achieved, and what remains to be addressed.

Steps in Extension Teaching

Extension agents are tasked with approaching extension teaching in a deliberate and systematic fashion. They must lead farmers, farm women, and rural youth through an organized training process, step by step, while also serving as motivators and facilitators. While the specific methods may vary depending on the circumstances, there are foundational steps in extension teaching outlined by Wilson and Gallup (1955). These steps provide a framework for effective communication and education in agricultural extension, helping agents to effectively impart knowledge and skills to their audience.

Step 1 - Capturing the Learner's ATTENTION

Those who participate in extension teaching are first exposed to novel concepts and methods. In the initial phase of extension teaching, people are introduced to new ideas and practices. It's important for them to learn about these new things because it's the start of making changes. If people don't pay attention to the changes that are suggested, they won't realize there's a problem to fix or a need to fulfill. To get people interested, extension workers can use different ways like radio, TV, shows, and talking to them directly through meetings or with the help of local leaders. The main goal of the extension worker is to get people interested in new and better ideas. Farmers should know about ways to improve their practices. According to research findings, people's attention is drawn to different senses in the following extents (Reddy, 1998): Seeing (87%), Hearing (7%), Smell (3.5%), Touch (1.5%) and Taste (1%). "Seeing is believing" is a well-known philosophy in extension. Therefore, the two main senses that are used to draw attention and promote learning are sight and hearing.

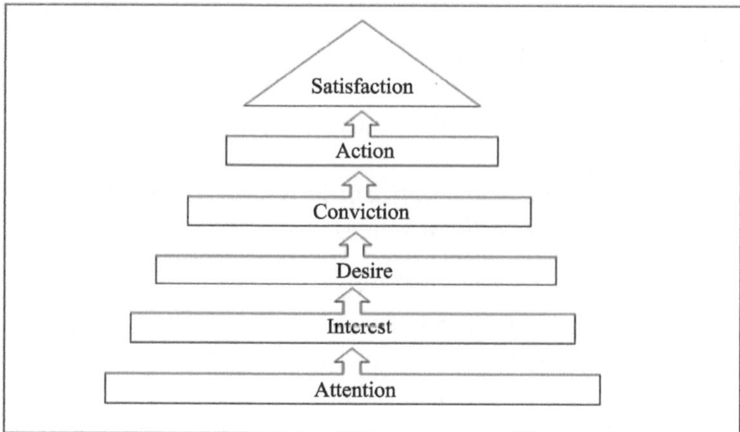

Figure 8: Steps in Extension Teaching

Step 2- Stimulating the Learner's INTEREST

The subsequent step involves igniting people's curiosity once they've grasped the new concept. This can be accomplished by offering them additional, easily understandable information on the topic. It's essential to focus on one concept relevant to their needs at a time. The extension agent can achieve this through personal discussions, engagements with local leaders, agricultural publications, radio broadcasts, television programs, etc. Once attention is captured, the educator can tap into the individual's basic needs or desires and pique their interest in further exploring the idea. Subsequently, the extension worker elucidates how the concept will benefit the farmer, ensuring the message is presented in an engaging manner.

Step 3- Inducing the Learner's DESIRE for Information

It involves motivating people to make a change and altering their current behaviour. In this phase, it is crucial to emphasise the advantages of the novel concept or methodology. At this point, it's important to attend demonstrations, read farm publications, have one-on-one conversations with the extension agent, and participate in group discussions. The learner must remain interested in the concept or improved practice out of desire until that interest develops into a powerful motivation.The extension worker explains to the farmer that the learner sees how the action applies to their own situation and feels confident in their ability to do it.

Step 4- CONVINCING the Learner for Action

At this point, you have to convince people firmly that the novel concept or approach would benefit them personally. They receive sufficient explanations of the concept and its operation. This is the time when field days or farmers' days, slide shows, one-on-one talks with the extension agent, and training become extremely important. Following desire is conviction, or the state in which a person is certain that a novel concept or behaviour will satisfy their needs and is totally convinced of its applicability to their own circumstances. The learner understands what needs to be done and how to do it in this step. They also make sure the student feels confident in their abilities and knows how the action relates to their own circumstances.

Step 5- Prompting ACTION by the Learner

This phase involves implementing the novel concept or procedure. It entails putting together modest demonstrations in actual settings with the required materials. This enables students to obtain first-hand experience. It's critical to collect evidence of change, such as rises in employment, income, or yield. At this point, it's critical to provide demonstrations, have direct communication with the extension agent, supply the required materials, and guarantee essential services. Turning conviction into action is essential for success. It's the extension worker's job to make it easy for farmers to take action. If a new control measure involves action, the recommended tools or chemicals should be readily available to farmers. If action doesn't happen quickly after the desire, the new idea may fade away. Therefore, this phase should never be overlooked.

Step 6- Ensuring that the Learner Achieves SATISFACTION from his Action

Extension initiatives need to produce positive results in order for long-lasting change to occur. Enhanced productivity, increased income, better health, and other factors can all lead to satisfaction. Feeling satisfied reinforces learning and builds confidence, which then motivates further change. To maintain the new behavior, it's important to provide ongoing, relevant information about the practice until the change itself feels necessary. This is the final result of the process. Follow-up by the extension worker helps farmers assess their progress and strengths. Feeling satisfied encourages them to continue their actions with even greater satisfaction. Satisfaction is what drives further learning. "A satisfied customer is the best advertisement" also applies to the extension worker. These six steps often blend together and lose their distinctiveness. However, they are all based on motivation.

Advantages of Extension Teaching

1. Stimulating and Guiding Learning Activities: By providing structured guidance and support, extension teaching stimulates and directs learning activities toward specific goals. This helps individuals stay focused and motivated throughout the learning process.
2. Specifying Desired Changes in Behavior: Extension teaching helps to clearly define the desired changes in the behavior of people. By identifying specific behavioral outcomes, it enables individuals to understand what is expected of them and how they can achieve those changes.
3. Assisting Clients in Understanding Ideas: Extension agents help clients gain a deeper understanding of the ideas being communicated. Through clear explanations, demonstrations, and practical examples, they ensure that clients comprehend the concepts being presented and are able to apply them effectively in their own contexts.

Limitation of Extension Teaching

1. Time-Intensive Preparations: Extension teaching often demands significant time and effort for preparation. Developing lesson plans, gathering resources, and organizing instructional materials can be time-consuming tasks for extension agents. This can pose challenges, particularly when there are limited resources or when agents are responsible for covering a wide range of topics.
2. Individual Differences: Another limitation is the presence of diverse individual differences among the clientele. People have varying levels of education, backgrounds, and learning styles, which can make it challenging to cater to everyone's needs effectively. Extension agents may struggle to tailor their teaching methods to accommodate these differences, leading to potential gaps in understanding among some learners.
3. Lack of Attention: Not all clientele, particularly farmers, may be fully attentive to the teaching process. Factors such as busy schedules, competing priorities, or disinterest in certain topics can contribute to a lack of engagement. This poses a significant obstacle for extension agents who rely on the active participation and receptiveness of their audience to ensure effective learning outcomes.

Conclusion

In rural and agricultural areas, the teaching and learning process in extension is essential for knowledge distribution, skill development, and the encouragement of positive behavioural changes in clients. Extension agents have the ability to enable people to overcome obstacles, embrace new habits, and improve their quality of life by providing them with individualised learning experiences and efficient teaching techniques. But the effectiveness of extension initiatives depends on overcoming a number of obstacles, including time-consuming planning, addressing individual differences, and guaranteeing that students are paying attention. Extension professionals can optimise the outcomes of their educational interventions by consistently modifying their teaching strategies, utilising inventive approaches, and giving priority to the needs and interests of their target audience. Ultimately, extension programmes support resilience, prosperity, and sustainable development in communities by encouraging a culture of lifelong learning and knowledge sharing.

Answer the Following Questions

1. Describe the essential components of a learning situation in extension work and explain how these components interact to support the learning process.
2. Summarize the principles of learning in extension, highlighting how these principles contribute to effective knowledge acquisition and behaviour change among learners.
3. Explain how the experiential learning cycle can be applied in extension teaching to enhance practical comprehension and skill application among learners. Provide examples of activities that could be used at each stage of the cycle.
4. Analyze the challenges and limitations of extension teaching, considering factors such as individual differences, time-intensive preparations, and learner engagement. Discuss strategies that extension agents can employ to address these challenges.
5. Critically evaluate the significance of the teaching process in extension work for achieving sustainable development in rural and agricultural communities. Reflect on the potential impact of well-executed extension teaching on community resilience and long-term development.

5

Extension Programme Planning

Nikita Khoisnam

Department of Agricultural Economics and Extension, Lovely Professional University Phagwara, Punjab

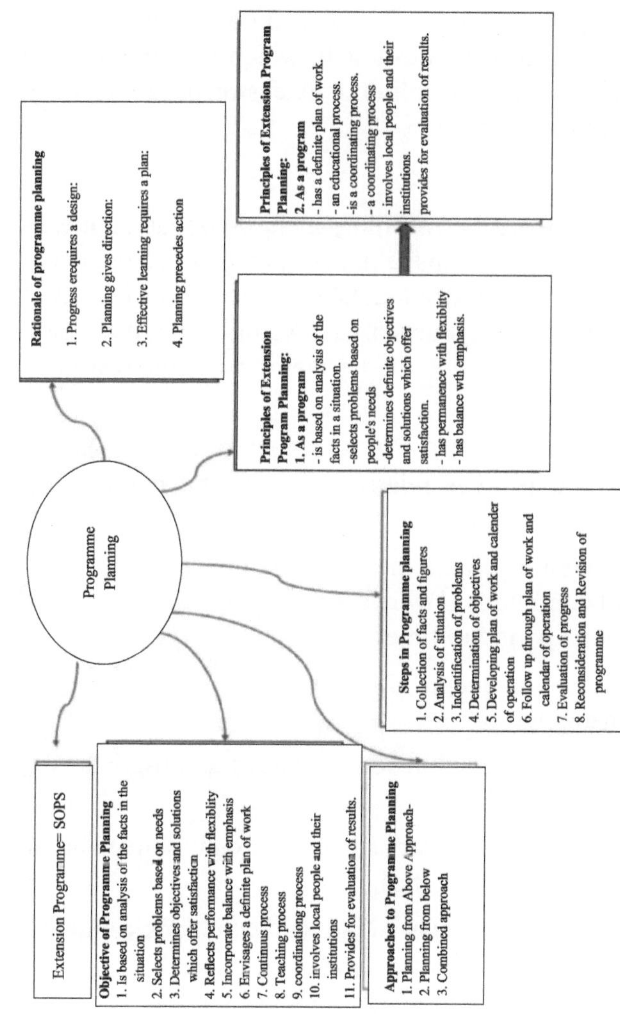

Figure 1: Overview of the chapter (Credit: Jarial, S)

Introduction

Planning is a "dynamic act of reflecting about, thinking about, and choosing among various options regarding the goals and objectives and the route to journey i.e. educational experience, we should follow to reach those destinations" (Forest and Baker, 1994). It offers opportunity to people to "participate" and "contribute" in the process. Therefore, it is understood that "planning extension programs has become an increasingly accepted practice among national authorities" (Maalouf, in Rivera, 1987, p. 116 as cited by Cristovao *et al.,* 1997).

The first step in any systematic attempt to promote rural development is to prepare useful programmes based on people needs. The development of such programmes, require planning which harmonize with the local needs as the people see them and with the national interests with which the country as a whole is concerned, is an important responsibility of extension personnel at all levels national, state, district, block & village.

Extension Programme

The word ‹programme› has several distinct meanings in the dictionary. It means a proclamation, a prospectus, a list of events, a plan of procedure, a course of action prepared or announced before hand, a logical sequence of operations to be performed in solving a problem. When used by an organization, it means a prospectus or a statement issued to promote understanding and interest in an enterprise.

According to Kelsey and Hearne (1949) - It is a statement of situation, objectives, problems and solutions. It is relatively permanent but requires constant revision.

- **Situation-** It is a statement of affairs that includes the cultural, social, economic and physical conditions in which a particular group of people find themselves at a given period of time.
- **Problem-** It is a condition that people after study, with or without help, have decided needs changing.
- **Solution-** It is a course of proposed action to change an unsatisfactory condition to one is more satisfying.
- **Objectives/Aims-** They are generalized and broad statement of directions with respect to given activities.

  Eg: Extension Worker's aim is to improve farmers' economic condition.

- **Goal-** It is the distance in any given direction one expects to go during a given period of time. Extension Programme is relatively permanent but requires constant revision.

  Example: To raise paddy yield by 20 Q/ha. in the current year.

According to Leagans (1961) - It is a set of clearly defined, consciously conceived objectives or ends, derived from an adequate analysis of the situation, which are to be achieved through extension teaching activity.

According to Forest and Baker (1994) - It is a set of purposeful, planned and interrelated experiences to reach our educational objectives and to solve problems.

According to Israel, Harder and Brodeur (2011) - It is a comprehensive set of activities that are intended to bring about a sequence of outcomes among targeted clients.

According to US Department of Agriculture (1956) - It is arrives at cooperatively by the local people and the extension staff and includes a statement of:

a) the situation
b) the problems that are part of the local situation
c) the objectives and goals of the local people in relation to these problems and
d) the recommendations or solutions to reach these objectives on a long-time basis or on a short time basis.

According to Lawrence (1962) – It is the process whereby the people in the country, through their leaders, plan their extension program where the end result is a written program statement. It includes all activities and undertakings of a county extension services which includes:

a) Program planning process
b) written program statement
c) plan of work
d) program execution
e) results and
f) evaluation.

According to Oakley and Garforth, 1985 - An extension program is a written statement which contains the following four elements:

a) Objectives which the agent expects to be achieved in the area within a specified period of time,

b) Means of achieving the objectives
c) Resources that are needed to fulfill the program and
d) Work plan or the schedule of extension activities that will lead to the fulfillment of the program.

Assumptions on Extension Planning

The concept of extension planning is based on a number of assumptions. Boyle (1965) has listed the following assumptions in this regard:

- Planning change is a necessary prerequisite to effective social progress for people and communities.
- The most desirable change is predetermined and democratically achieved.
- Extension education programmes, if properly planned and implemented, can make a significant contribution to planned change.
- It is possible to select, organize and administer a programme that will contribute to the social and economic progress of people.
- People and communities need the guidance, leadership and help of extension educators to solve their problems in a planned and systematic way.

Definitions of Extension Programme Planning

Programme planning is the process of making decisions about the direction and intensity of extension-education efforts of extension-service to bring about social, economic and technological changes. It involves multiple steps including the identification of a problem, selection of desired outcomes, assessment of available resources, implementation and evaluation of the program. In other words it is a procedure of working with the people to recognize unsatisfactory situations or problems and to determine possible solutions.

On the other hand, extension program planning is viewed as a process through which representatives of the people are intensively involved with extension personnel and other professional people in four activities (Boyle, 1965):

1. Studying Facts and Trends
2. Identifying problems and opportunities based on these facts and trends
3. Making decisions about problems and opportunities that should be given priority and
4. Establishing objectives or recommendations for future economic and social development of a community through educational programs.

Other literature defined extension program planning as the process of determining developing and executing programmes. It is a continuous process, where by farm people, with the guidance and leadership of extension personnel attempt to determine, analyse and solve local problems. In this, there are three characteristics-

a) What needs to be done

b) When it should be done

c) How it should be done (Musgraw, 1962).

In addition, Olson (1962) described it as an organized and purposeful process, initiated and guided by agent, to involve a particular group of people in the process of studying their interests, needs and problems, deciding upon and planning education and other actions to change their situation in desired ways and making commitments regarding the role and responsibilities of the participants.

It is an organised and purposeful process initiated and guided by the agent, to involve a particular group of people in the process of studying their interests, needs and other problems, deciding upon and planning education and other actions to change their situation in desired ways and making commitments regarding the role and responsibilities of the participants (J.L. Compton).

It is process of working with the people in an effort to recognise the unsatisfactory situation problem and determine possible solution or objectives or goals. Programme planning may be on the long range or on an annual basis (S.L. Intobia, L.L. Somani, J.P. Lakhera).

Therefore, in the definitions presented above, it implies that extension program planning is a social process involving decisions to determine the target group of peoples' needs, problems, opportunities, resources, and priorities to further understand and involvement of extension educationists and community representatives.

Objectives of Extension Programme Planning

The general objective of an extension programme is to influence people to transform their life in better way. The assumption is that there is a need for change and make people aware of this, if they are not and to develop their needs.

Important objectives of having a programme planning as per Kelsey and Hearne (1966) are as follows:

a) To ensure careful consideration of what is to be done and why.

b) To furnish a guide against which to judge all new proposals.

c) To establish objectives toward which progress can be measured and evaluated.
d) To have a means of choosing the important (deep rooted) from incidental (less important) problems; and the permanent from the temporary changes.
e) To develop a common understanding about the means and ends between functionaries and organizations.
f) To ensure continuity during changes of personnel.
g) To help develop leadership.
h) To avoid wastage of time & money and promote efficiency.
i) To justify expenditure and to ensure flow of funds.
j) To have a statement in written form for public use.

Kelsey and Hearne (1949) mentioned the following rationale for a planned extension program. Therefore, a sound extension program planning:

1. Is based on analysis of the facts in the situation
2. Selects problems based on needs
3. Determines objectives and solutions which offer satisfaction
4. Reflects performance with flexibility
5. Incorporate balance with emphasis
6. Envisages a definite plan of work
7. Is a continuous process
8. Is a teaching process
9. Is a coordinating process
10. Involves local people and their institutions and
11. It provides for evaluation of results.

It is observed that planning program is an integral part of the development process and ensures better and efficient utilization of resources, accountability and human development.

Meanwhile, other rationales of program planning are the following:

1. **Progress requires a design:** As design is established through the education of extension workers who will make a plan of action for progressive and careful planning.
2. **Planning gives direction:** Planning is one of the most important tasks in extension that has five factors to consider: purpose, needs, learning environment, sources of information and requirements.

3. **Effective learning requires a plan:** Successful extension learning requires an objective to achieve. This must be developed from the extension professionals and the group of people concerned.

4. **Planning precedes action:** It is mentioned that the result of action depends on how you answer the questions involved in the planning process. These questions are the following:

   a) What information do farm men and women need most?

   b) Which king of information shall be extended

   c) What information shall be extended first?

   d) How much time shall be devoted to this line of work?

   e) How much effort shall be devoted to this line of work?

Principles of Extension Program Planning

Sandhu (1965) identified a set of principles that maybe applied in developing countries. The discussion will be divided into two parts: as a program and as a process.

1. As a Program

a) Extension program planning is based on analysis of the facts in a situation.

- It is important to take into account the factors or aspects in lands, crops, economic trends, social structure, economic status, tradition and culture should be considered as facts.
- As this principle believes in "Extension knows, if need be, the surer way is to effect cultural change by the slow but certain process of education."

b) Extension program planning selects problems based on people's needs.

- Extension program must meet the felt needs of the people (Brunner, 1945).
- It is very significant to identify problems highlighting the needs of the target group of people.
- Extension workers must adopt the subject matter and teaching strategy based on the learning level of the target group of peoples' needs and interests.

c) Extension program planning determines definite objectives and solutions which offer satisfaction.

- The objectives and proposed solution in the work plan must be flexible as the how the changes evolved from planning to implementation of extension program.

d) Extension program planning has permanence with flexibility.

- A program should be prepared with long-term goals in mind but must be flexible enough to meet the changing needs and interests of the people.

e) Extension program planning has balance with emphasis.

- In planning, comprehensibility of understanding the target group of peoples' needs and interests matter.
- Efficient distribution of time and effort to solve a particular needs and problems must be carried out to the extension professionals' attention.

2. As a Process

a) Extension program planning has a definite plan of work.

- Good organization and careful planning for action is the key to outline a procedure based on the efficiency of its execution in the entire program.
- Plan of work will be further discussed in the stages involved in extension program planning.

b) Extension program planning is an educational process.

- Participation to surveys, interviews and other methodologies is part of the educational process in planning.
- As an extension planner, they must perceive the following activities as a learning process: gaining knowledge, finding facts, recognizing problems, stating problems and proposing possible solutions.

c) Extension program planning is a coordinating process.

- It is part of the planning process for extension professionals to cooperate and coordinate with interested leaders, groups and other agencies to work together for an integrated program.

d) Extension program planning is a continuous process.

- Extension in a changing society must adjust and plan for the future by keeping the choice of the target group of people, being flexible to new problems, working with people in seeking practical solutions and keeping abreast of technological and social change (Sutton, 1961).

e) Extension program planning involves local people and their institutions.

- Aside from the partners and agencies involved in the process, it is inevitable to involve local people and let them participate in the program planning process.

f) Extension program planning provides for evaluation of results.

- Extension program planning and evaluation go together (Matthews, 1962).
- Evaluation is important to know and decide whether the program objectives during the planning process are achieved.

Scope and Importance of Programme Planning

The following roles of programme planning in the process of development indicate its scope.

1. To ensure careful consideration of what is to be done and why.
2. To furnish a guide against how to judge all new proposals.
3. To establish objectives towards which progress can be measured and evaluated.
4. Helps in discovering and planning the ways for action.
5. It prepares the basis for feature course of action.
6. Facilitates decision making for the future.
7. Identification of most significant needs.
8. Identifies the gap between the present situation and the desired situation.
9. Assists in formulation of objectives.
10. Promotes active involvement of local leaders.

Approaches in Planning Extension Program

After discussing the principles, assumptions and rationale behind planning extension program, the most important aspect in planning are the approaches involved in it. All organizations working for agricultural development have their own procedures for planning. When considering the planning of extension programs, there are three different approaches that can be distinguished: planning from above, planning from below and the combination of both approaches.

1. Planning from Above Approach

This approach is also known as top-down or blueprint planning and centralized approach. It is a conventional way of developing a program wherein the agent is simply expected to implement plans made at national level. It is the government institutions holding the mandate of an extension program that strictly follows the policy of the national government. Therefore, this approach is best utilized in the transfer of technology. One good example is the case of disseminating artificial insemination for dairy cattle to improve the best breeding practices. The dissemination policy came from the National Dairy Authority (NDA) of the Department of Agriculture (national level) down to local level and different dairy cooperatives.

According to Dusseldorp and Zijderveld (1991), this approach has clearly defined and generally accepted objectives; detailed and précised knowledge of the process to be implemented in order to reach the objectives; has political will to use available power and resources; and has a predetermined timetable and resources.

Nevertheless, this approach has advantages and disadvantages. Its' advantages are it facilitates management, monitoring and evaluation tasks smoothly because of defined activities and well-identified chain of responsibilities and duties. While its' disadvantages are it does take into account the aspect of socio-cultural environment. It is agency-centered and programs are based on institutional policies and philosophy. It is rigid and assumes high level of stability. Thus, it does not acknowledge the changing needs of the people.

2. Planning from Below Approach

This approach is also known as decentralized, bottom-up, and participatory planning process. It characterized the farmers together with extension agents make plans for developing local agriculture on the basis of local needs and potential, and then make requests for specific assistance from national and regional authorities. This approach is commonly used by non-government institutions (NGO) and private agencies.

According to Bergdall (1993), Dusseldorp & Zijderveid (1991) and Korten (1991), the guiding principle behind is the participatory approach in which the ultimate goal of the program is to increase the power of the local actors. It is possible by planning and implementing their own improvements where development is long a term process and personnel should acts as partners/ facilitators rather than experts. In addition, participation in local actors is stressed and have more time on needs identification and project preparation with the active involvement of the intended beneficiaries.

Similar to the first approach, this approach has advantages and disadvantages too. Its' advantage are it is open and process-centered, embraces error as a learning factor and leads to programs and project with an emergent nature.

However, its' disadvantages are activities start without predefined objectives that led to confusion for the participants and recipients of extension intervention; the success is dependent among the local actors, thus, its very difficult if they will not participate well. Lastly, the overall practice of this of this approach is in contrast with the conventional that may result to complications to the relationships among funding agencies.

3. Combination of the Two Approaches

Successful extension programs should include both planning approaches: combination of bottom-up and top-down. National policies and program provide a framework that guide an agent plans the local programs and establish priorities which local level follows.

Steps in Extension Programme Planning

Programme planning basically a step by step adventure. It is an continuous cycle of eight steps that indicate the programme determination and programme implementation in extension education. The steps are-

1. Collection of facts and figures
2. Analysis of situation
3. Identification of problems
4. Determination of objectives /goals
5. Developing plan of work and calendar of operation
6. Follow up through plan of work and calendar of operation
7. Evaluation of progress
8. Reconsideration and Revision of programme

Figure 1: Steps in Extension Programme Planning

1. **Collection of facts-** Pertinent data may be collected from the available records and by survey of the area with the help of schedule developed for the purpose. Information relating to, their enterprises, levels of technology, facilities and constraints, values etc., relevant to programme building may be collected. Information may also be collected from Panchayats, Cooperatives and other organizations working in the area. Collection of lengthy and time consuming data may be avoided unless essential, as in many cases these are not properly analyzed or utilized, and may lead to wastage of time.

The programme planning process is explained with an example. There is a village where the farmers are poor and something is to be done to improve their economic condition. We conduct a survey of the village and collect information on the number of farm families, their occupations, land-use pattern, utilization of water resources, facilities for marketing, availability of inputs and credit, their attitude towards various enterprises, the strength of extension service in the area etc.

Collection of reliable data is the basic requirement of good planning. Extension worker must collect and interpret authentic information for the use of community leaders. He should make bench mark survey from where people start the process of programme planning.

From available records

Information relating to

- Major crops grown by the farmers in that area
- What methods they are using in their farm
- How these methods are to be corrected
- People (Population, farm families, occupation, transport, drinking water, medical facilities, social classes, local leaders)
- Their enterprises
- Level of technology
- Facilities and constraints, values etc.
- Resources (Irrigation, drainage)

Method of collecting

- Collected from village panchayats revenue records, local newspapers and personal visits. Reports from local leaders
- Discussions and meetings with local famers

2. **Analysis the situation-** After collecting all local information, these facts should be transacted into familiar language so that it can be used for development of individuals or committees. After analyzing ball these problems the solution should be considered.
3. **Identification of problems-** Interpreting the data after good analysis helps identify the problems correctly. These facts raise the interest of the people. There may be many problems, but only the urgent and significant ones which may be solved with the available resources and within the limits of the time should only be selected.

   Example: Low-income level of farmers, employment and nutrition of families.
4. **Determination of objectives and goals-** The objectives are then determined on the basis of the significant needs identified. The objectives should be direct and stated in clear terms. In the present example, the objectives then become to increase the levels of income, employment and nutrition of the farm families in the village.

To make the objectives realistic and actionable, there is need to state them in terms of specific goals. In the determination of goals it may be necessary to again go through the data and information analyzed; to find out what could actually be done in the existing situation, with the available resources and time, which will be compatible and with which the people shall cooperate. It is necessary to discuss with the local people and local institutions, which shall also legitimize the whole programme planning process.

In the example, it is found that the village has a number of ponds with ample water throughout the year. They were used mainly for domestic purposes and not for irrigation as the fields were away. There appeared to be a good scope of introducing the technology of duck-cum- fish-farming in the village. The goals were then finalized after checking up cultural compatibility with the farmers, technical compatibility with the scientists and financial compatibility with the banks and Govt. departments. The goals were set up as follows-

- To raise the yield of fish to 4000 Kg/ha/year by resorting to composite fish culture in about one- third of the ponds in the first year and covering all the ponds in a period of three years.
- To introduce Khaki Campbell duck rearing in about one-fourth of the ponds in the first year and covering all the ponds in a period of four years, to obtain 240 eggs per female bird per year.

  The generation of additional income and employment, and the availability of additional protein food for the participating farm families per year were calculated and found to be satisfactory both by the farmers and the extension worker. The Panchayat was informed of the programmes to which it agreed.

5. **Developing plan of work and calendar of operations-** Plan of work is definite outline of procedures for solving the different problems of the programme. It should have the following five questions-

- What different things and jobs need to be done to accomplish objectives?
- How best to do each of specific jobs?
- Who will be responsible for planning, preparing and execution?
- When each specific part of plan including meeting to be held and executed?
- Why things need to be done?

As mentioned above the plan of work should be in written form and shall indicate who shall do what job i.e. what the change agent system and the client system shall do; which institutions, organizations, service departments shall be involved; what will be the financial requirements and how they shall be met; what arrangements shall be made for marketing of the produce, training of the farmers and so on. The plan should have all the essential details and no important point should be left out.

The calendar of operations shall be prepared on the basis of the plan of work and shall specify when a particular work shall be done, preferably mentioning date and time; how much quantify of different inputs, including credit shall be required and when they must be made available; when, where and for how many days the farmers shall be trained, who are the specialists to be involved in training and preparing the hand outs, when the publications shall be ready for distribution etc. That is, the calendar of operations shall specifically state how and when all the significant activities shall be performed. This should be at least for one season or for a period of one year. In that case, they may be termed as "seasonal plan" or "annual plan".

In the example, the plan of work and calendar of operations shall be developed for composite fish culture and duck rearing on the basis of scientific recommendations. In view of the integrated operation of two different technologies, belonging to two different disciplines of fishery and livestock, some special care need to be taken in developing the plan of work and calendar of operations. Some advance planning and action is also needed for critical inputs like mohua oilcake, desired number and species of fish fries and day old female ducklings, as these are most probably to be pronounced from outside.

6. **Follow through plan of work and calendar of operations-** This is not a routine type of work as many people may think. Training of farmers, communication of information, conducting method demonstrations, making regular visits and monitoring are some of the important functions the extension worker shall perform at this stage. The work shall include solving unforeseen problems and taking corrective steps where needed.

The performance of the extension worker and the organizational support he receives at this stage may make the difference between success or failure of a programme. Obtaining feedback information as to what is happening to the farmers after introduction of new technology is extremely important at this stage.

In the present context, composite fish culture and rearing of Khaki Campbell ducks are new items of technology, and the extension worker shall ensure that all the recommendations are known and precisely applied under expert supervision. It is important at this stage to know how the farmers are responding to the new technologies, what their reactions are, and what problems they are facing in putting the recommendations into practice.

7. **Evaluation of progress-** Evaluation is the process of determining the extent to which we have been able to attain our objectives. It should be a continuous process not only to measure the end result but also

to ensure that all steps are correctly followed. It may be formal or informal, depending on the importance of the programme and also on the availability of trained man-power, funds, facilities and time. Evaluation helps to locate strong and weak points in any programme or plan. Programme evaluation involves the following three essential steps-

a) Setting up of some standards or criteria in relation to the objectives
b) Collection of information
c) Making the judgement, and drawing some unbiased and valid conclusions.

Importance of evaluation:

a) Evaluation of any programme during and after the execution is essential to judge whether the programme is moving in the right direction or not.
b) Negative factor or any difficulty or impeding problem should be removed.
c) Positive factor of the programme should be accelerated
d) Evaluation should be made jointly by the extension worker and local or concerning organisations

Through: Records, prepared documents, reports, discussions with concerned persons

- Before starting of programme
- During the execution of programme
- After the completion of programme

Evaluation helps in:

a) To establish a bench mark
b) Shows how far our plans have progressed
c) Shows whether we are proceeding in the right direction. Proof of omissions, recommended changes suggests new directions.
d) Indicate the effectiveness of the programme
e) Helps to locate strong and weak points in any work or plan
f) Improves skills in working with the people
g) Helps to determine priorities for activities in the plan of work
h) Brings confidence and satisfaction to our work.

8. **Reconsideration and revision of the programme-** On the basis of the results of evaluation, the programme should be reconsidered and revised if needed. This reconsideration should be done not only with the participants; but also with the scientists, extension managers and local bodied like panchayats etc.

Reconsideration shall help in making necessary corrections and modifications in the programme. In reconsideration, emphasis should be on the removal of technical defects if any, and how to obtain more cooperation and involvement of the participants and various organizations. The purpose of such an exercise is to make the extension programme more effective, so that it can attain the objectives and bring satisfaction to the people within the limits of time. The crucial point in the success of programme planning is proper blending of local experience with relevant results of research. The direct and indirect consequences of the technological innovations must be recognized in planning and implementation of technological change.

Conclusion

If the extension programmes are prepared and executed in accordance with the programme planning principles, the goals and objectives will be met, along with the results, and the extension programme will be successful. Regardless of the type of clients or the society they may support, there are some programme planning ideas that are universal. The objectives of the programme must therefore be kept in mind at all times when developing extension programmes and ensuring that they are efficiently implemented.

Answer the following questions

1. What is the significance of extension program planning in rural development, and how does it ensure alignment with local needs and national interests?
2. Compare and contrast the "planning from above" and "planning from below" approaches in extension program planning, highlighting their advantages, disadvantages, and suitability for different contexts.
3. Describe the steps involved in extension program planning, emphasizing the importance of each step in ensuring effective implementation and evaluation of extension programs.

6

Rural Development

Vipal Bhagat and Sapna Jarial

Department of Agricultural Economics and Extension, Lovely Professional University Phagwara, Punjab

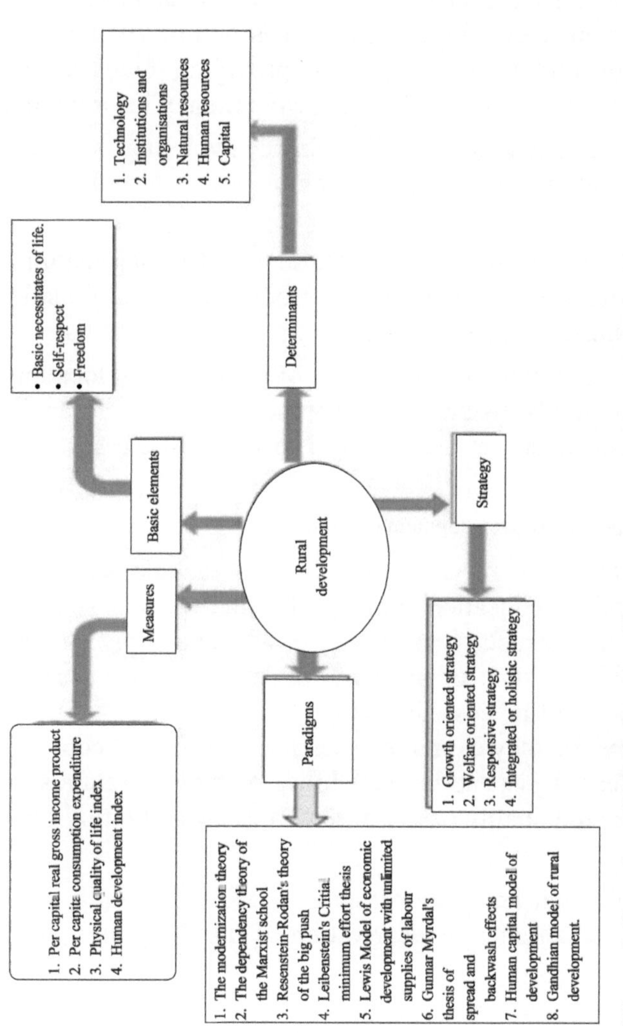

Figure 1: Overview of the Chapter Rural Development (Credit: Jarial,S)

Rural Development Concept

Rural development falls under the wider concept of "Development," a goal universally valued by individuals, families, communities, and countries around the globe, regardless of its definition.

Rural development encompasses a wide scope, primarily targeting actions to enhance underdeveloped aspects of village economies. Key areas in rural India that require new development initiatives include- enhancing human resources, focusing on literacy (especially among women), education, skill enhancement, health, sanitation, public health improvements, and land reform, alongside the advancement of each locality's productive assets.

Development of infrastructure, such as electricity, irrigation, financial services, marketing, and transportation, including building roads within villages and connecting them to major highways, along with providing facilities for agricultural research, extension services, and the dissemination of information.

Specific actions to reduce poverty and markedly enhance the living standards of the less privileged population segments, focusing on access to productive job opportunities.

This implies providing individuals involved in agricultural and non-agricultural activities in rural areas with resources to boost their productivity. Additionally, they should be offered chances to expand into different non-farm sectors.

Core components of rural development: Regardless of geographical location, cultural background, or society's historical development phase, there are at least three fundamental elements that are believed to define the essence of rural development.

Figure 1: Overview of the Chapter Rural Development (Credit: Jarial,S)

1. **Basic needs**: Essential for survival, basic needs include access to food, clothing, housing, education, primary healthcare, and security for individuals and their property. A lack of or severe shortage in any of these areas signifies a state of profound underdevelopment. Thus, ensuring the provision of life's essentials to all is a fundamental duty of all economic systems, be they capitalist, socialist, or mixed. Economic growth, or the increased per capita availability of these essentials, is crucial for enhancing the quality of life in rural areas, constituting rural development.
2. **Dignity**: Every individual and nation aspire to achieve dignity, self-respect, or honor. The absence or deprivation of dignity points to an undeveloped state.

3. **Freedom**: Here, freedom encompasses political or ideological liberty, economic independence, and liberation from social oppression. A society bound by servitude to nature, ignorance, others, institutions, or rigid beliefs has not reached its developmental goals. Any form of servitude is indicative of underdevelopment.

Concepts and Connotations of Rural Development

Development is a subjective and value-laden idea, making universal agreement on its definition elusive. Its usage varies across different contexts, often implying the act of unfolding, revealing, or unveiling something hidden. It signifies unfolding or opening potential human powers. The development of rural areas in India is a multi-dimensional problem viewed by policymakers and academicians, mainly from the economic aspect. However, rural development in India is not only an economic problem but also a more social one. **Michael P. Todaro** views rural development as most suitable, in the Indian context, in the following manner:

i. Enhance living standards, including employment, education, health, nutrition, housing, and various social services.

ii. Decreasing equality in the allocation of rural incomes and the rural-urban imbalances in incomes and economic opportunities.

iii. To sustain the capacity of the rural sector.

In the Indian context, rural development appears to be more of a sociological issue than an economic one. As economic development progresses and awareness increases, the social fabric becomes more complex and less conducive to economic conditions. The caste system remains a significant social phenomenon in India, influencing marriage norms, community participation, social control, and political dynamics, all of which negatively impact the rural development process. Therefore, rural development policies should aim to address and reform the existing social structures in the country.

Growth vs Development

Development transcends mere economic processes and cannot be reduced to only economic growth. It should embrace the broader spectrum of human life, including both material and non-material aspects. Viewing development as a multifaceted process that reshapes both economic and social systems is essential. While typically framed within a national context, achieving development on a wider scale might require significant changes to the global economic, social, and political frameworks.

Why Rural Development?

India has always been, and is expected to continue being, a country of village communities for the foreseeable future. Since the Vedic age, the village has served as the fundamental administration unit, with mentions of the gramini (village leader) found in the Rig Veda. Mahatma Gandhi wrote in Harijan 4th of April 1936.

"If the villages perish, India would perish too".

Hence, rural development is an essential and immediate requirement for India's progress; it is indispensable for its development.

Rising Expectations and Development

The average Indian aspires to improve living standards for themselves, their family, their community, and their country. Expectations differ regionally, with desires for better food, clothing, housing, education, security, and freedom. This represents a revolution in expectations across the developing world.

Several factors contribute to this phenomenon. Initially, the consumption habits of the rural elite, urban affluent, and foreign tourists, known for their taste for exotic and luxury items, have influenced the consumption patterns and preferences of the poorer sections. Additionally, exposure to modern goods and lifestyles through movies, television, radio, and advertising has heightened public expectations. Political promises of modern amenities to rural populations by local and national leaders have further elevated these aspirations. Moreover, the prioritisation of poverty eradication by central governments underscores this shift. Lastly, widespread media coverage has introduced the average person to new products, technologies, and services, transforming curiosity into demand.

The economic systems of many developing nations, India included, are unlikely to meet these rising expectations in the near term, leading to an inevitable clash between heightened aspirations and economic realities. The consequences will differ across countries but will likely include disillusionment, demoralization, unrest, and political turmoil. This situation underscores the urgent need for swift agricultural and economic progress as a national priority.

Development and Change

Change both drives and results from development, creating a reciprocal relationship. This change can manifest in various forms, including physical, technological, economic, social, cultural, attitudinal, organizational, or political. While every indicator of development is associated with some form of change, the direction of this change can lead to progress (development) or decline (retrogression). Changes can occur spontaneously or can be deliberately induced.

"Human Beings as the Cause and Consequence of the Development"

Even though studying humans is essential to development, humans cannot be studied in isolation. Instead, humans must be studied about each other, in society, and their environment.

Human development comes after economic development, but only if economic development is based on equality and respect for each person. Human dignity cannot be bestowed upon an individual through the benevolence of others; indeed, well-intentioned acts of charity can sometimes undermine it. This is because human dignity is rooted in equality, freedom, and respectful interactions among individuals.

Challenges and Conflicts in Development

Urban vs. Rural Development

The increase in urbanisation, associated with economic advancement in Western nations, is evidenced by the rising urban population. Consequently, economists often regard urbanisation as an indicator of development. This urban growth results from clustering infrastructure and capital-intensive industries in urban areas, creating distinct economic subsystems within the economy.

Industrial vs Agricultural Development

The idea that only through industrialization can agriculture be modernised, agricultural productivity and wage rates be increased, and labour displaced by mechanisation be utilized mirrors the rural versus urban development debate. Numerous economists associate development with the process of industrialisation.

Labour vs Capital Dogma

Today's development economists inherited this from their developed country forebears, who regarded capital as the key to development. The Harrod-Domar model illustrates this idea. In this model, the growth rate is equal to the sum of the rate of saving and the ratio of output to capital. If capital and labour are non-substitutable and there is a surplus of labour, capital constraints become the primary barrier to economic growth. This viewpoint is further reinforced by techno-economists who argue that new technology is inherently tied to capital investments.

In developing countries, development economists and planners have uncritically embraced the concept of capital as the cornerstone of economic growth. This adherence has given rise to various policies focused on boosting savings, shifting income from labourers to capitalists, granting exclusive rights to national and multinational corporations, reallocating resources from the private to the public sector, increasing reliance on foreign aid and loans, and undervaluing capital, especially foreign exchange for capital goods. These practices have adversely affected their economies. Specifically, the undervaluation of foreign exchange for capital goods has discouraged the development of technologies conducive to local labour, leading to premature and excessive mechanisation in certain sectors. This, in turn, has caused unemployment and the underuse of other domestic resources.

Human capital development is integral to capital-centric ideologies. In numerous developing countries, significant resources are allocated to support higher education. Consequently, millions of graduates from colleges and universities enter the unemployed white-collar workforce annually. India, for instance, has made substantial investments in universities, particularly in fields like engineering, technology, agriculture, medicine, and management. Despite this investment, many graduates from these institutions are dissatisfied with the domestic work environment and compensation levels, prompting them to seek opportunities abroad. As a result, the country forfeits the returns on its investment in their education and training. It is hoped that our new educational policy will address these challenges effectively.

Induced vs Autonomous Development

Every nation undergoes a process of natural or autonomous development over time. However, the extent and speed of this progression may not be sufficient to ensure a decent standard of living. In such instances, intervention becomes imperative to accelerate this natural development.

In developing nations, development planning arises as a trend and a crucial pathway for nurturing growth. Even developed countries turn to economic planning or government intervention. Any planning method is preferable to having none, and decentralized planning offers advantages over centralized approaches.

Determinants of Rural Development

The factors affecting rural development favourably or adversely are so varied and have combined over time in so many ways., that is, very difficult to isolate a small number of crucial variables or determinants.

The factors are as follows:

1. Technology
2. Capital
3. Institutions and organisations'

4. Natural resources
5. Human resources

All these factors operate within limits imposed by finite, non-growing and closed planet earth. This suggests that economic growth and development have a natural ceiling. The most significant factor in rural development is technological advancement; it is essential to development. To develop a steady stream of technological breakthroughs, however, a big pool of technically trained, talented, and motivated labourers and a conducive domestic environment are required. Although it is impossible to produce anything without employing natural resources and environmental amenities, a lack of natural resources does not necessarily preclude a high level of rural development. As Japan and Israel have amply proved, human resources and technologies can be substituted to a limited extent for natural resources. In India, a substantial portion of natural resources is utilised daily. Such resources must be created and exploited prudently for ordinary people's benefit to achieve sustainable and equitable development.

To keep the development process going, it is crucial to have domestic surpluses (savings) that can be mobilised and used correctly through a network of well-developed financial institutions. In terms of human resources, developing countries like India would do well to give the most important to developing human resources to make rural development more stable. Returns to investment in human resources development are the highest. Human resources are the only way for developing countries like India to reach sustainable development, but they hurt the environment because they are renewable and never run out. Human resources are the only way for developing countries like India to reach sustainable development, but they hurt the environment.

Paradigms of Rural Development

So far, no theory of rural development works for everyone. However, the different paradigms and theories of development that we look at in this chapter can help us understand how and why rural development happens. Let us investigate the ideas of past economists and their thoughts about rural development.

The Modernisation Theory

Modernisation theory is a way to look at how societies change over time. It evaluates a country's internal elements, assuming that 'traditional' countries can develop like more developed' countries with some help.

Max Weber, a German sociologist, looked at the role of rationality and irrationality as societies change from traditional to modern. His ideas were used in modernisation theory. The thesis focuses on more prosperous and developed countries, stating that a rise in technology will make all nations wealthy, especially if developing nations may follow the path of these more affluent countries. Wealthier countries are one answer to poverty.

The Dependency Theory

A way of looking at economic underdevelopment that focuses on the supposed limits that the global political & economic order imposes. Argentine economist and statesman Ral Prebisch first proposed dependency theory in the late 1950s. Later, Talcott Parsons, a sociologist at Harvard, gave his view of modernisation. Then, in the 1950s and 1960s, the theory became more well-known.

According to dependence theory, underdevelopment is caused by countries' periphery economic position. Underdeveloped countries offer cheap labour and essential materials. Advanced economies buy these resources to turn them into finished items. Underdeveloped countries buy finished items at excessive prices, depleting capital they could use to improve their production. This creates a vicious loop that perpetuates the world's rich centre and poor periphery. Moderate dependency theorists, like the Brazilian sociologist Fernando Henrique Cardoso, believed development was possible within this system. More radical scholars, like the German American economic historian Andre Gunder Frank, argued that the only way out of dependency was to create a non-capitalist (socialist) national economy.

The Big Push Theory

Rosenstein Rodan introduced this theory. According to this viewpoint, a significant push or complete investment package can help generate economic progress. A minimum level of resources must be allocated if developmental programmes succeed, as takeoff requires some ground speed. Similarly, development efforts need essential resources. This idea holds that 'Bit by Bit' allocation cannot lead to economic development; instead, a particular quantity of investment is required. If several interdependent industries are formed, economies of scale will be realised. Investing in external economies will aid economic growth.

Leibenstein's Critical Minimum Effort Thesis

The main idea of the theory is that economic growth in underdeveloped and overpopulated countries is impossible unless a minimum level of investment is injected into the system as a consolidated dose that pulls the system out of the doldrums. This minimum level of investment is called 'minimum critical effort'. Leibenstein says shocks and stimulants influence every economy.

Shocks reduce output, income, employment, and investment. Shocks reduce development forces. Shocks depress development, reversing progress.

Stimulants boost income, output, employment, and investment. Stimulants boost growth. "Income Generating Forces" lubricate development. Stimulants enhance per capita income over equilibrium.

Lewis Model of Economic Development with Unlimited Supplies of Labour

Arthur Lewis' concept of "Economic Development with Unlimited Supplies of Labour" envisions capital accumulation in the modern industrial sector to draw labour from subsistence agriculture. Fei and Rains improved and extended Lewis' model, although the two are similar. Both models (Lewis's and Fei-modified Ranis's version) assume surplus labour in the economy, primarily disguised as unemployment in agriculture.

Further, they see a "dual economic structure" with factories, mines, and plantations constituting the modern sector, which uses replicable capital, produces for the market and profit and employs wage-paying labour.

Agriculture is a subsistence or traditional sector that uses non-reproducible land, self-employment, inadequate production techniques, and hidden unemployment. Thus, current sector productivity per head is higher than in agriculture. In agriculture, marginal productivity is assumed to be zero. Therefore, the average productivity is estimated to be above the subsistence level.

Gunnar Myrdal Thesis of "Spread and Backwash" Effects

Gunnar is a top development theorist. His books "The Asian Drama" and "Economic Theory and Undeveloped Regions" explain the caves of underdevelopment in impoverished countries and how the state promotes institutional reforms to raise development.

The two key terms Myrdal used in his development analysis are "Cumulative Causation" and "Backwash Effects". According to Myrdal, Cumulative Causation enables an economy to progressively move a society from the spectre of underdevelopment towards development. Myrdal believed that most underdeveloped nations suffer from the "dualism" of developed.

Due to dualism in undeveloped regions of underdeveloped countries, growth impetus is mostly enjoyed and goes to more prosperous regions. The advanced regions leap ahead, leaving the poorer ones behind. "Cumulative Causation" describes this. Another cumulative cause in impoverished countries is migrating people and capital to more developed regions. When younger, better-educated people relocate from less-developed regions to more developed regions for work, the less-developed regions are left with an unskilled, dependent populace. This worsens their suffering and underdevelopment. High fertility in undeveloped countries diminishes per capita income, increases poverty, and continues low progress.

The Human Capital Model of Development

Schultz proposed this idea in his book Investment in Human Capital; however, he experienced negative feedback from other economists. He says that knowledge and talent are a sort of capital, and investing in them increases economic output and workers' pay. Due to slavery, many economists refused to embrace his thesis of humans as capital, which was understandable then. Schultz's ideas did not reject humanity but encouraged self-investment. He encourages people to invest in their health, internal migration, and on-the-job training, but he concentrates on education to boost productivity. If people did these things, they would have greater economic chances.

Gandhian Model of Rural Development

Gandhi's approach to rural development is characterized by idealism, placing morality above materialism. Followers of Gandhi, known as Gandhians, believe that moral principles are derived from religion and Hindu scriptures such as the Upanishads and the Gita. Gandhi envisioned an ideal social order termed "Rama Rajya," wherein the sovereignty of moral individuals prevails. He conceptualized Rama Rajya not as a monarchy with a king and subjects, but as a state where "Rama" symbolises God or one's inner conscience. Gandhi advocated for a democratic and people-centric societal structure.

Gandhian Approach to Rural Development

The ideal village constitutes the fundamental unit of Gandhi's envisioned social order." If the village perishes, India will perish too". Gandhi's ideal village was a federation of self-governing republics. The central government will merely coordinate the activity of the village republics and supervise common interests such as education, primary industries, health, currency, banking, etc. The central authority will only have moral coercion or persuasion to implement decisions on village republics.

The Principal Component of the Model

Decentralisation: Gandhi believes village republics can only be formed via social and political decentralisation. The Village Panchayat will make decisions instead of the state and capital in this arrangement. Panchayat is legislative, executive, and judicial. It would oversee education, health, and sanitation. Panchayats must safeguard and uplift "untouchables" and poor people. Villages would raise resources for Gandhian village management. The village would resolve all problems and disputes. The Panchayat promotes moral and spiritual ideals among ruralites for rural rehabilitation. Volunteers would defend the village non-violently.

Self-sufficiency: Food, clothing, and other basics should be self-sufficient in the village. The village imports stuff it cannot make. We must generate more than we can to get what we cannot. The village economy should provide full employment for the villagers, so they do not have to migrate to towns. Gandhi said every man must work to eat. Moral discipline and mental development require physical labour. Body needs must be met. There would be enough food and leisure if everyone worked for their food.

Industrialisation: Gandhiji said industrialisation benefits few and concentrates economic power. Industrialisation exploits villages passively or actively. It is competitive. Market large-scale manufacture requires marketing. Marketing is predatory profit-seeking. Industrialisation replaces labour, increasing unemployment. Village and cottage businesses should be revitalised. Gandhians are not against machines if they boost self-sufficiency and employment. Only they should not be used as a means of exploiting others.

Trusteeship: Gandhiji supported private property. He aimed to limit private property's entitlement to a decent living. Gandhiji mandated trusteeship for the excess. Capitalists cared for themselves and others. Some of their excess wealth would benefit society. Gandhiji believed a trusteeship would improve worker welfare and reduce worker-employer conflict. Gandhiji felt God owned land. Individual land ownership should be discouraged. Community land must be used for community welfare. If landowners continue to exploit poor employees, they should organise nonviolent, non-cooperation, civil disobedience struggles.

Rural Development Strategies in India

After independence, India's rural development programmes and policies revealed four development strategies.

1. **Growth-Oriented Strategy**: This assumes rural people are logical decision-makers. Given the chance and circumstances, they will maximise their revenues. In this technique, the state builds infrastructure and maintains a favourable climate to promote rural enterprise growth. This method assumes that increasing production will benefit the poor. Market mechanisms regulate and coordinate private and public agency activity. This paradigm formed the foundation of the broader agricultural

development strategy during the 1960s by introducing programs like IADP, ICDP, and HYVP. However, it proved ineffective in tackling poverty, unemployment, and inequality, leading to its abandonment.

2. **Welfare-Oriented Strategy**: This approach aims to enhance the welfare of rural and impoverished populations through extensive social initiatives such as the Minimum Needs Programme, Applied Nutrition Programme, and Mid-day Meals programme, among others. It hinges on providing essential goods, services, and municipal facilities in rural areas. This approach operates under the assumption that individuals cannot identify and address their challenges, relying instead on government experts utilising financial and administrative resources. Villagers are relegated to a passive role as recipients of services within this framework, reflecting a paternalistic orientation. The effectiveness of rural-focused programs varies, with some regions experiencing benefits for the rural poor while others do not. However, this approach fosters dependency and demands resources beyond the capacity of governments to sustain.

3. **Responsive Strategy**: This approach empowers rural communities to take charge of their development by establishing organizations and support systems. It is responsive to the needs of rural people as identified by them. The government facilitates self-help initiatives among villagers by providing them with technologies and resources. This concept operates on the premise that rural communities can address their challenges when given limited support and autonomy. This strategy's primary indicator of success is community participation and control over projects.

   Operation Flood, initiated in India in 1970 across 18 milksheds in 10 states, is a notable example of this approach. Operation Flood aimed to modernise and bolster India's dairy industry by establishing a three-tier Anand pattern dairy cooperatives structure. Many voluntary organizations also adopt this development paradigm.

4. **Integrated or Holistic Strategy**: This approach amalgamates the advantageous elements of the preceding three strategies to foster growth, welfare, equity, and community involvement. This paradigm offers a comprehensive, unified perspective on poverty, unemployment, and inequality, addressing their physical, economic, technological, social, motivational, organizational, and political foundations. Its objective is to enhance the community's capability to engage in development initiatives led by the government. This strategy operates on the assumption that the government can reconfigure societal power dynamics and that centralized agencies can collaborate with community groups in

power-sharing. Achieving vertical and lateral integration necessitates both specialized and generalist skills, institutional leadership, social intervention proficiency, and adept systems management. Sustaining this approach requires a permanent decentralized matrix structure.

Measures of Rural Development

A variety of indicators have been used to measure rural development.

Gross National Product (GNP) refers to the total value of all the goods and services produced by the residents and businesses of a country, irrespective of the production location.

GNP considers corporate and resident investments inside and outside the country.GNP considers corporate and resident investments inside and outside the country. It also considers domestic product value.GNP does not include foreign nationals' incomes or foreign-made items in the country's industrial units.

Physical Quality of Life Index (PQLI)

Morris David Morris made the Physical Quality of Life Index (PQLI) for the Overseas Development Council in the middle of the 1970s. It was designed because GNP was not a good progress indicator. The Physical Quality of Life Index looks at three factors to determine a country's quality of life or well-being introductory literacy rate, infant mortality, and life expectancy at age one. All are equally weighted on a 0 to 100 scale.

PQLI could be seen as a step up, but it has the same problems as other quantitative attempts to measure the quality of life. It has also been challenged because infant mortality and life expectancy overlap substantially. As a result, the United Nations Human Development Index is a more prevalent method for gauging well-being.

Human Development Index (HDI)

The HDI was created to emphasise that people and their capabilities should be the ultimate criteria for assessing the development of a country, not economic growth alone.

In conclusion, it can be said that rural development, as a crucial element of the broader developmental agenda, aims to bolster the village economy across multiple fronts, including human resource development, infrastructure enhancement, poverty alleviation, and job creation. Core principles such as the provision of necessities, dignity, and autonomy are central to rural development efforts, transcending geographical and cultural diversity. In the Indian context, rural development extends beyond mere economic progress, encompassing socio-economic dimensions that grapple with the intricacies of the social framework and the enduring caste system. While economic growth remains essential, true development necessitates a restructuring of both economic and social systems. India's historical reliance on its villages underscores the pivotal role of rural development in the nation's advancement.

The escalating aspirations of the average Indian for an improved standard of living underscore the urgency for rapid agricultural and economic progress. Development is inherently linked with change, with each influencing the other in a reciprocal manner, whether it be physical, technological, economic, or social. Human beings serve a dual function as both instigators and products of development. Nevertheless, human dignity cannot be bestowed solely through external benevolence; it must be founded upon equality and dignified interpersonal relationships. India's development strategies have transitioned from growth-centric and welfare-focused approaches to more responsive and integrated methodologies, each possessing its own merits and demerits.

The integrated approach amalgamates the strengths of preceding strategies to comprehensively address issues such as poverty, unemployment, and inequality. Various metrics, including Gross National Product, Physical Quality of Life Index, and Human Development Index, have been employed to assess rural development, each offering unique perspectives and limitations. Notably, the Human Development Index emphasizes that human capabilities should serve as the ultimate yardstick for evaluating a nation's development, transcending mere economic indicators.

Answer the Following Questions

1. Why is rural development considered a multidimensional issue, and how does it extend beyond economic progress in the Indian context?
2. Compare and contrast the growth-oriented, welfare-oriented, responsive, and integrated strategies of rural development in India, highlighting their respective advantages and disadvantages.
3. Discuss the significance of human dignity in the context of rural development, considering its relationship with equality, freedom, and social structures. How can rural development initiatives uphold human dignity while addressing socio-economic challenges?

7

Rural Development Programs

Arnab Roy

Department of Agricultural Economics and Extension, Lovely Professional University Phagwara, Punjab

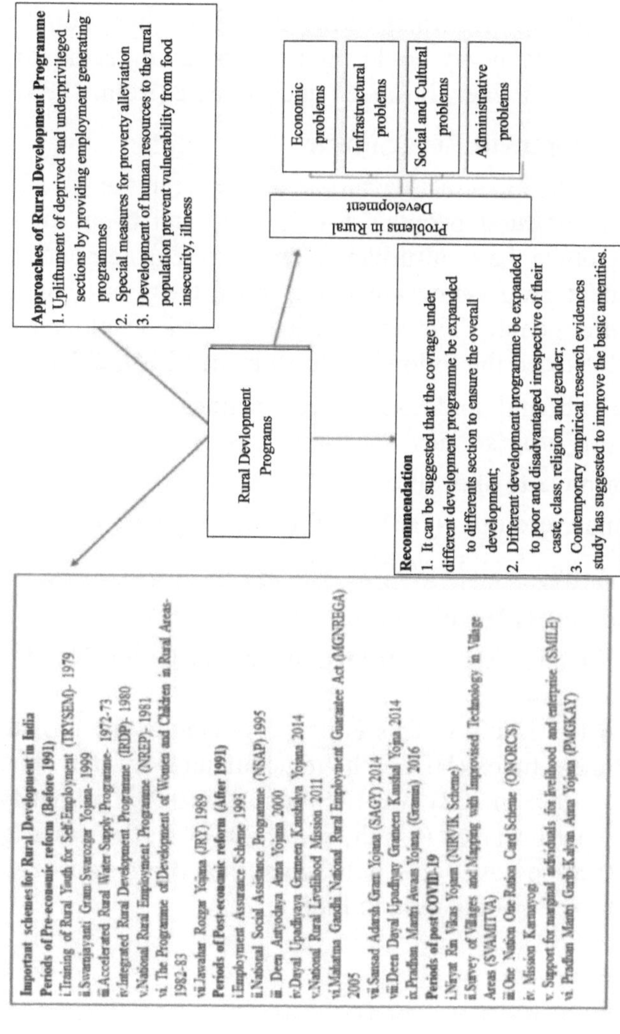

Figure 1: Overview of the chapter (Credit: Jarial, S)

"India lives in its villages. If the village perishes, India will perish too"

- Mahatma Gandhi

Introduction

Rural development programmes are designed as an integral part for socio-economic development, especially of developing country like India. These rural development programmes connotes greater social transformation which has recognized as a sine qua non. Since from independence, rural development programmes mainly focusing on poverty reduction (Dev, 1995). The number of public and private organizations focus on rural development as a way to poverty[1] reduction has grown up with the comprehension that most impoverished people lives in rural and tribal areas. But The focus of rural development programmes Although the trickle-down theory was based on the belief that an expanded macro economy could improve the living standards of impoverished people, its effectiveness has been questionable (Rath, 1985).

Approaches of Rural Development Programme

The prime objective of holistic rural development programme is the improvement of the quality of rural people's life in rural and tribal areas accompanied by narrowing down the rural-urban income gap. The approaches of holistic rural development programme are not to raise the profit but to maximise the welfare of the people. The approaches of rural development programme strategically restressed the following thrust areas (Basu, 2013):

1. Upliftment of deprived and underprivileged sections by providing employment generating programmes
2. Special measures for poverty alleviation
3. Development of human resources (HRD) to the rural population
4. Prevent vulnerability from food insecurity, illness

Need and Importance of Rural Development

The Human Development Report 2021–22, brought out by the United Nations Development Programme, shows that India's global rankings have gone down from 130 in 2020 to 132 in 2021. This is not surprising as the growth in India's Human Development Index (HDI). The regional numbers show that the highest decline in HDI values in 2021 was in South Asia (0.9%) primarily on account of India's poor performance (Singh, *et al.*, 2001). In this respect, there are always a need to come with some new schemes and programs that upthrusts the position of the rural population in India.

---

[1] Amartya Sen's definition, "poverty indicates a lack of basic human capabilities i.e., potential selective capability of individuals

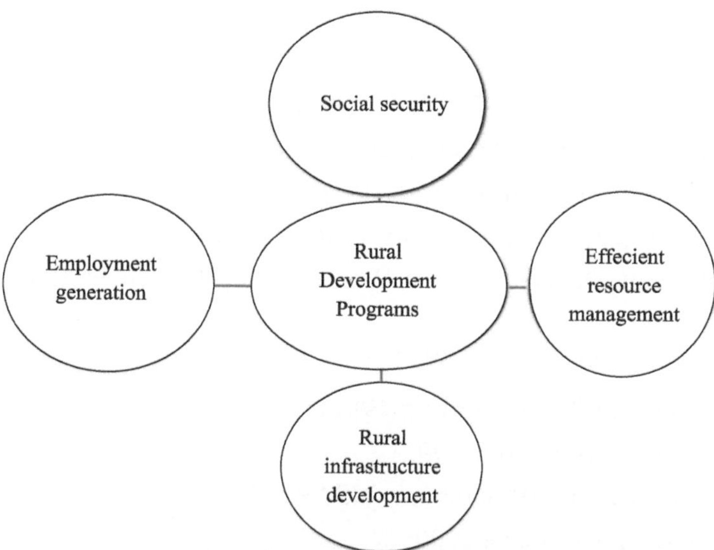

Figure 2. Dimension of Rural development programmes

Important Schemes for Rural Development in India

In this subsection, the several schemes of rural development has been discussed. The social security programmes which are very popular globally primarily focus on unemployment security (18.6%), children welfare (26.4%), vulnerable and very poor persons[2] (28.9%), pensions for rural labour (32.5%), benefits for the incapacitated force (33.5%), work injuries compensation and accident cases (35.4%), and maternal welfare (44.9%) (Anonymous, 2022). Here the major rural development schemes in India are classified as following subdivision (Fig. 2):

Indira Awas Yojana

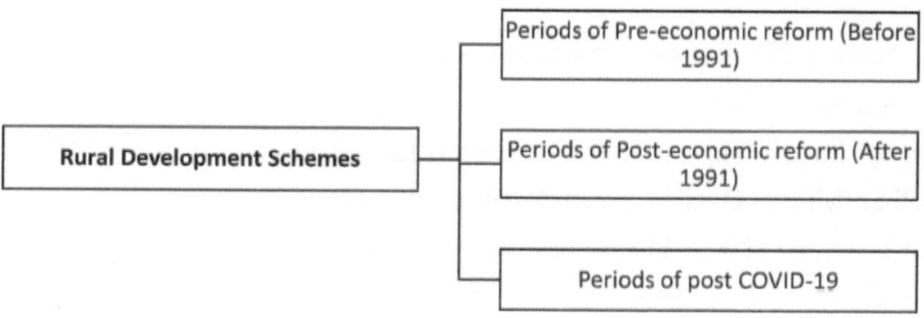

Figure 3. Subdivision of Rural development programmes in India

[2] *The Very Poor person is defined as people whose per capita monthly expenditure (PCME) lies below three fourth of the poverty line*

Periods of Pre-economic Reform (Before 1991)

i. Training of Rural Youth for Self-Employment (TRYSEM)- 1979
ii. Swarnjayanti Gram Swarozgar Yojana- 1999
iii. Accelerated Rural Water Supply Programme- 1972-73
iv. Integrated Rural Development Programme (IRDP)- 1980
v. National Rural Employment Programme (NREP)- 1981
vi. The Programme of Development of Women and Children in Rural Areas- 1982-83
vii. Jawahar Rozgar Yojana (JRY) 1989

Periods of Post-economic Reform (After 1991)

i. Employment Assurance Scheme 1993
ii. National Social Assistance Programme (NSAP) 1995
iii. Deen Antyodaya Anna Yojana 2000
iv. Dayal Upadhyaya Grameen Kaushalya Yojana 2014
v. National Rural Livelihood Mission 2011
vi. Mahatma Gandhi National Rural Employment Guarantee Act (MGNREGA) 2005
vii. Sansad Adarsh Gram Yojana (SAGY) 2014
viii. Deen Dayal Upadhyay Grameen Kaushal Yojna 2014
ix. Pradhan Mantri Awaas Yojana (Gramin) 2016

Periods of Post COVID-19

i. Niryat Rin Vikas Yojana (NIRVIK Scheme)
ii. Survey of Villages and Mapping with Improvised Technology in Village Areas (SVAMITVA)
iii. One Nation One Ration Card Scheme (ONORCS)
iv. Mission Karmayogi
v. Support for marginal individuals for livelihood and enterprise (SMILE)
vi. Pradhan Mantri Garib Kalyan Anna Yojana (PMGKAY)

The aim of Ministry of Rural Development, under Govt. of India is responsible for the progress and welfare of rural people through allocation of fund through different schemes. The intentions of this ministry is to increase livelihood opportunities and providing social security as well as improving rural infrastructure for overall development. The Ministry allocate budget to difference schemes depends upon the urgent need of the rural people and priority of the particular area (Agrawal, 2016). The followings table presents the budgetary allocations to the Ministry of Rural Development for 2022-23.

Table 1: Budgetary allocation to the Ministry of Rural Development (Rs. in crore)

Department	20-21 Actuals	21-22 RE	22-23 BE	% Change (22-23 BE/21-22 RE)
Rural Development	1,96,417	1,53,558	1,35,944	-11%
Land Resources	1,176	1,485	2,259	52%
Total	1,97,593	1,55,043	1,38,204	-11%

Note: BE is budget estimate and RE is revised estimate.

Sources: Demands for Grants 2022-23, Ministry of Rural Development

The Standing Committee on Rural Development in India (2021) had noted that the allocation to the rural department is very much lower than the amount demanded by the Ministry of Rural Development. Such lack of funds generally affects the appropriate progress of the schemes to right direction. However, during 2021-22, the Standing Committee noted that unexpended balance of more than forty thousand crore had accrued over all the schemes of the Department, which may raise queries on utilisation of the capitals.

It can be explained from the figure 3 that departmental expenditure during the period of 2012 to 2021 increased but during 2021 to 2022 has been decreased. It also has been observed that the per cent change of expenditure was found negative during 2021-22 to 2022-23.

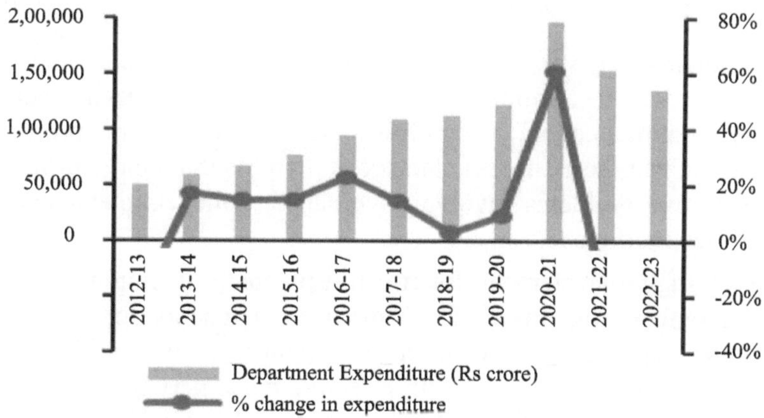

Figure 4. Expenditure by the Min. of Rural Development over the years (Rs crore)

Sources: Union Budgets 2012-13 to 2022-23

Problems Faced for Rural Development Programme in India

Efficient execution and monitoring of rural development programmes can be confirmed only if the personnel associated with the programmes appropriately trained and motivated. It is often observed that the objective of one flagship programme skirmish with others. There is lack of coordination of institutional mechanism for reconciliation. Therefore, many rural development programmes utterly fail to achieve their objectives. Insufficient amount of capital resources, decisions related with different economic impacts of the development programmes and spending huge amounts of money on unproductive purposes are some of the factors which hinder the road of the rural development programmes in India.

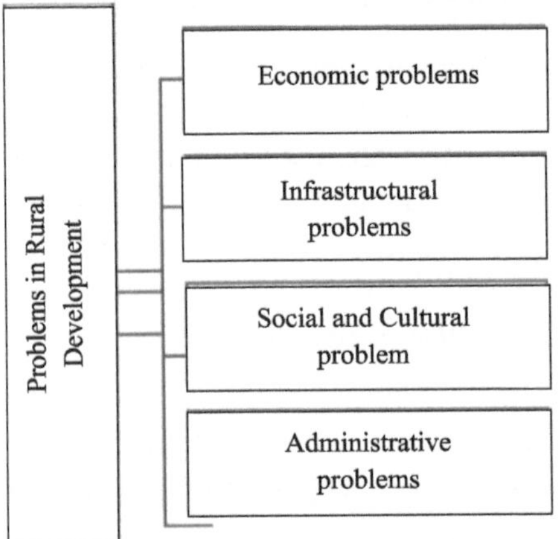

Figure 5: Problems in rural development

Economic problems refer to issues such as poverty, unemployment, or lack of financial services. Infrastructural problems encompass inadequate transportation, communication, and utilities. Social and Cultural problems include education, healthcare access, and societal norms that hinder progress, while administrative problems involve governance, policy implementation, and public service inefficiencies.

The World Bank suggested elements for effective planning and implementation of Rural Development Programs are The National plan of action for supporting regional policies and adequate local level monitoring for achieving the objectives, Greater decentralization with effective machinery at the regional and local level to coordinate the sectoral activities of national departments operating in the regional and local departments, Participation of the rural poor in the planning and implementation process through local government and other group organization / voluntary organizations (Sinha, 2022).

Suggestions and Recommendations

1. It can be suggested that the coverage under different development programme be expanded to different section to ensure the overall development;
2. Different development programme be expanded to poor and disadvantaged irrespective of their caste, class, religion, and gender;
3. Contemporary empirical research evidences study has suggested to improve the basic amenities.

Conclusions

The impoverished people actively involving in the different development schemes then only poverty can be truly eradicated. Finally, all policies related with poverty alleviation from launched by the government are very supportive to figure out robust financial stand for the people who belong from Below Poverty Level group (BPL). As per World Bank's Policy Research, extreme poverty is 12.3 percentage points lower in 2019 as compared to 2011 specially in rural areas, since various poverty mitigation programmes initiated by the Government of India in both rural and urban areas through rural housing, skill development for self-employment, training for rural youth. There has been a lot of discussion around the effectiveness and intensity of antipoverty in the pre-reform and post-reform period in India. But the effectiveness of Pradhan Mantri Garib Kalyan Anna Yojana packages and insurance *scheme* for health care workers to alleviate the pain and sufferings launched during Covid-19 pandemic is irrefutable.

Answer the Following Questions

1. Explain the fundamental objectives of rural development programs in the context of socio-economic development. What are the key challenges faced by rural communities in countries like India that necessitate the implementation of such programs?
2. Summarize the historical context and evolution of rural development programs in India. How have these programs evolved over time to address the changing socio-economic needs of rural populations? Provide examples of specific initiatives or policies introduced at different periods to illustrate this evolution.
3. Evaluate the effectiveness of rural development programs in India by analyzing their impact on various socio-economic indicators. How do these programs contribute to poverty reduction, employment generation, infrastructure development, and social empowerment in rural areas? Support your analysis with relevant data and case studies showcasing successful outcomes of specific interventions.

8

Community Development: Meaning and Concept

Priyanka Lal

Department of Agricultural Economics and Extension, Lovely Professional University Phagwara, Punjab

Introduction

What is community development?

Community development refers to the process of bringing community people together after identifying issues related to them and taking a collective action. Community development empowers residents and builds stronger, more integrated communities. Community development is an all-encompassing approach based on the ideas of empowerment, human rights, inclusiveness, social justice, self-determination, and collective action (Kenny, 2007).

Figure 1: Overview of chapter

Community development views individuals of the community as experts in their own lives and communities, and it emphasizes community knowledge and wisdom. Community people lead community development projects at every stage, from problem identification to action planning and implementation. Community development places a strong emphasis on power redistribution in order to address the root causes of inequality and poverty.

Approaches of Community Development Model

McMillan and Chavis in 1986 discussed about the prerequisites of community which will help in interdependence and value creation. The elements are as follows:

1. Membership
2. Influence
3. Integration and needs satisfaction
4. Shared emotional connection

Participation in community development refers to community members' full involvement and leadership in planning, developing, delivering, and assessing community actions or initiatives. Participation must not be tokenistic; rather, community members must participate in ways that are important to them as well as to the community development initiative itself. Building full and meaningful engagement takes time.

Figure 2: The wheel of participation
Source: Dooris & Heritage, (2013), adapted from Davidson (1998)

Principles of Community Development

- Encourage active and representational citizen engagement so that individuals of the community can have a real impact on decisions that affect their position.
- Engage community members in problem identification so that individuals impacted can comprehend the root causes of their condition.
- Assist community members in comprehending the economic, social, political, environmental, and psychological consequences of possible solutions to the problem.
- By emphasizing shared leadership and active citizen participation, assist community members in developing and implementing a strategy to overcome agreed-upon challenges.
- Seek alternatives to any effort that has the potential to harm the most vulnerable members of a community.
- In the community development process, actively endeavour to improve leadership capacity, skills, confidence, and aspirations.

Philosophy of Community Development

Basic philosophy of community development programme was

1. Individual development
2. Development of family.
3. Awareness of the responsibilities and self-motivation among the people
4. Community development
5. Development of Cooperativeness among the people
6. To create confidence towards science and technology
7. Development of rural leadership
8. Development of rural institutions
9. Development of other resources for community development

Steps for Community Development

Figure 2 depicts the steps needed for undertaking community and economic development. They are as follows:

Step 1: Identify the Issue

To identify community challenges, capacities, and needs, both formal and informal methods can be used. Identifying the issue helps in bonding the common interest of the people that leads to overall development of the community.

Step 2: Determine Stakeholders

Involve community and organizational stakeholders for a specific common cause. Include citizens who are affected by the problem/issue.

Step 3: Develop Strategies

Engage the community in a discussion about the issues, and discover potential solutions to concerns. Always consult experts for solutions.

Step 4: Locate Resources

The solutions for a common problem should always be sustainable in nature. Choose a suitable strategy. Identify local in-kind and monetary resources that can be linked with other resources to help the community implement a certain programme approach.

Step 5: Execute

Implement the strategy in collaboration with the community, with an emphasis on shared leadership and collaboration.

Step 6: Evaluate

Formative and summative evaluations are used to examine whether the program's impacts on the target audience and others are met.

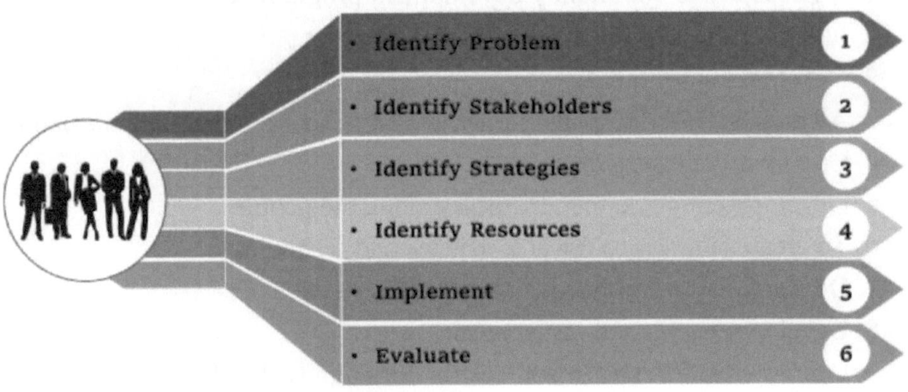

Figure 3: Steps for community development

The specific objectives of the plan may be categorized under the following heads:

i. Agriculture and improvement of agricultural production
ii. Setting up of cooperative societies in each village
iii. Animal husbandry
iv. Public health

v. Rural education
vi. Improving the means of communication and transport in rural areas
vii. Setting up village level small-scale cottage industries
vii. Organizing and strengthening the village panchayats

When should Community Development Approach be Used?

Community development approach is not always the best route to take. Community development may be very beneficial:

a) To address social and community issues: Community development is an effective strategy for bringing about change at the community or neighbourhood level. For example, if you want to improve community safety, cohesion, social isolation, or develop communities that are better for children.

b) Community development approach is useful technique to utilize resources to empower self-determination and strengthen the ability of local Indigenous organizations and grassroots community groups (Higgins, 2010).

c) Community development efforts are likely to perform successfully in impoverished neighbourhoods, where they can mitigate some of the effects of adversity on children and families by increasing social capital and social inclusion (Ife, 2016; McDonald, 2011; Price-Robertson, 2011; Wallerstein, 2006).

History of Community Development in India

To foster community development, the Indian government established the CDP, or Community Development Programme, in 1952. In India, the planning commission has defined the community development programme. It is an endeavour, according to them, to bring about and initiate economic and social transformation in the lives of peasants through their efforts. Historically, rural communities have been the primary focus of community development programmes in India. Nonetheless, many social workers focused on urban rather than rural areas, and they were professionally trained. According to the United Nations, community development is a process in which members of a community collaborate to solve common problems. Despite the fact that the primary focus of community groups in India was rural, social workers worked hard to balance the programme by focusing on urban regions as well.

This programme has also been suggested by A.R. Desia as a way for the Five Year Plans to begin the economic and social transformation of rural areas. In other words, it is a community-controlled community development project. In this scheme, the villages are referred to as the community. The Indian government outlined the goals of this initiative in 1973. The effort for community development began in 1952 and was officially launched on October 2, 1952. The primary purpose of this programme was to achieve integrated development in rural society, which included all aspects of people's lives.

The current CDP schemes are entirely based on the previous paradigm. As a result, the history of community development programmes in India has been documented and is being preserved. Panchayat Samities receive in-aid under the headings of Social Education and General Education. This category contains activities that contribute to educational growth. Funding is provided for the completion of residential buildings for personnel or construction blocks, as well as Gram Sewak Huts. These funds are also utilised to finish the continuing development of office buildings.

The three phases

The CDP has been divided into three different phases, which are:

1. National Extension Phase
2. Intensive Community Development Project Phase
3. Post-Intensive Development Phase

The selected areas are subjected to the approach utilised for providing services based on the pattern of ordinary rural development in the first phase, the National Extension phase, with less government investment. The selected blocks are exposed to greater composite in the second phase, and the development programmes are more intensive and entail a considerably higher government spending. The third phase, a post-intensive phase, assumes that the foundation of the process launched for self-perpetuation was formed during the previous phases, together with a reduction in the special government's required expenses.

National Extension Phase: From 2nd October, 1953, NES was implemented. This was implemented in places not covered by the CDP so that the entire country may benefit from development. In terms of character, the NES was less intense than the CDP. Because CDP and NES shared fundamental concepts, they were merged at both the centre and the periphery state. All By October 1963, NES blocks had evolved into CD blocks. NES encompassed nearly all of the communities in the country; aside from this national programme. A new administrative organisation was created using the existing system. The Planning Commission at the highest level, led by the Prime Minister, was in charge of development planning and coordination. It was an advisory board comprised of secretaries from many Central Ministries is assisting. A CDP administrator was chosen to serve under the supervision of the Central Committee for the general administration of the programme. A state development committee chaired by the chief minister was formed at the state level. Its members include various ministers. It received development assistance from the state level advisory board.

Organization for Community Development Programme-1958

An organisation known as Community Project Administration was formed to carry out community development projects. The Planning Commission was in charge of this organisation when it was established. However, it is now run by the Ministry of Community Development. This organization's structure is divided into four categories:

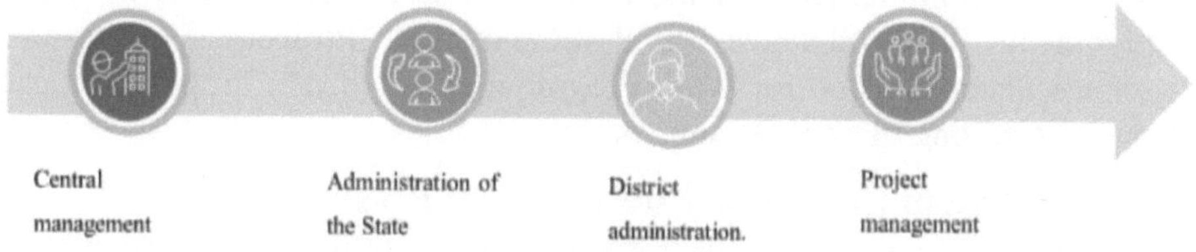

Figure 4: Organisation Structure of community development

Control and power flow begin with Central Administration and end with project administration. It is a hierarchical organisation.

Panchayati Raj's Emergence

When the Balwanth Rai Mehta Committee proposed the formation of Panchayati Raj to execute the CDP, things changed dramatically. The main premise for establishing Panchayati Raj was that people should be given authority over their villages. The programmes would be implemented by Panchas elected by the village residents. This will ensure that people are involved in the development of villages. Thus, under this system, progress was envisioned from the bottom up, from the masses of people. The Third Five Year Plan was also amended with the role of Panchayati Raj in mind. In the Third Plan, the Planning Commission proposed numerous new tactics for village development. Increased agricultural production was also emphasised. The Third Plan also proposed a new approach to some of the existing initiatives.

Among the new types of development programmes were:

1. Increased agricultural output,
2. Area development initiative, as well as
3. Special target group programme.

The Intensive Agricultural Area Programe (IAAP), Projects for Intensive and Integrated Agricultural Development (PIAID), and the High Yielding Variety Programme (HYVP) were the three key programmes developed to increase agricultural production. Some of the programmes, such as the Drought Prone Area Programme (DPAP), Hill Area Development Programme (HADP), Command Area Development Programme (CADP), and Tribal Area Development Programme, were created to assist specific areas (TADP). The most recent programmes in this area are the Integrated Rural Development Programme (IRDP) and the Regional Development Programme (RDP). However, the third type of programmes in the Third Plan and succeeding plans were intended for specific target groups. Small and marginal farmers and agricultural labourers Development Programme, Tribal Sub-Plan, Rural Industries Programme, Rural Artisans Programmes, Crash Scheme for Rural Employment, Pilot Intensive Rural Employment Projects, Employment Guarantee Scheme, Food for Work Programme, Antyodaya Programme, and others were among these programmes.

Important Indian Community Development Programs

Shriniketan, a rural rehabilitation effort established by Rabindranath Tagore in 1921, received assistance from Mr. Elmtirst. The project's key goals were agriculture, village welfare cooperation, Scout organisation, industries, education, and so on.

Mr. F.L. Brayne conceptualized and implemented the **Gurgaon rural welfare project** in 1920. The project's goals included enhancing agricultural production, reducing waste in social services, and improving health.

Marthandam Project: This project is a collaboration between the YMCA and Christian churches. The project's goals were to improve education, health, and economic aspects of life, as well as moral and spiritual development and social development.

Gandhian Constructive Program at Sevagram: The initiative began in 1920 at Sevagram and then moved to Wardha in 1938. The goals were to be realised by self-help, labour dignity, self-respect, simple and honourable life, and so on.

Rural Development Program: This was a government programme launched in 1935-36 with a grant of Rs. 1 crore from the Government of India. The program's goals include encouraging village industries, improving village communication, rural sanitation and recreation, medical help, agriculture, and so forth.

Etawah Pilot Project: In September 1948, a project for rural development and welfare was launched in Etawah (U.P.) with the active help of Mr. Albert Myer and Mr. Horace Holmes. The project's aims were to assess the extent of agricultural progress in terms of production and social improvement, as well as to assess people's efforts, confidence, and cooperation.

Firka Development Scheme: The Government of Madras initiated the intense Rural Reconstruction Scheme, also known as the Firka Development Scheme, near the end of 1946. It aimed to enhance the area's living conditions and instil in my residents an active interest in their problems in order to make them self-sufficient and self-reliant.

Sarvodaya Scheme: The Sarvodaya Scheme is built on Gandhian ideas as well. Since 1948-49, the state of Bombay has taken an active interest in the plan. The system focuses on cooperative concepts and tactics, attempting to instil in people the habits of self-help, mutual aid, and saving.

Conclusion

The history of community development programmes in India is extensive and informative. Even today, the community development programme adheres to all of the objectives and goals established before its inception. In recent years, the CDP has helped many rural communities to grow. There are outcomes at both the individual and communal levels. Directly involved children and families in community development programmes may benefit from increased skills, knowledge, empowerment, and self-efficacy, as well as increased social inclusion and community connectedness (Kenny, 2007). Community members can become more empowered through community development activities, allowing them to recognise and confront conditions and institutions that are leading to their disempowerment or negatively influencing their wellbeing (Ife, 2016). Community development and empowerment projects at the community level can result in long-term results such as stronger and more cohesive communities, as indicated by changes in social capital, civic participation, social cohesion, and improved health (Campbell, Pyett, & McCarthy, 2007; Ife, 2016; Kenny, 2007; Wallerstein, 2006).

Answer the Following Questions

1. Define community development and explain its fundamental principles. How does community development empower individuals and strengthen communities? Provide examples to illustrate your explanation.
2. Summarize the approaches and models of community development, citing McMillan and Chavis's elements of community as a reference. How do these elements contribute to building strong and interconnected

communities? Provide real-world examples to demonstrate your understanding.

3. Analyze the steps involved in community development and their significance in achieving sustainable outcomes. Using the provided steps for community development, discuss how each step contributes to the overall process of community empowerment and improvement. Provide a hypothetical scenario or case study to apply these steps in a practical context

9

Rural Leadership: Concept and Definition Types of Leaders in Rural Context

Termaric Oinam

Department of Agricultural Economics and Extension, Lovely Professional University Phagwara, Punjab

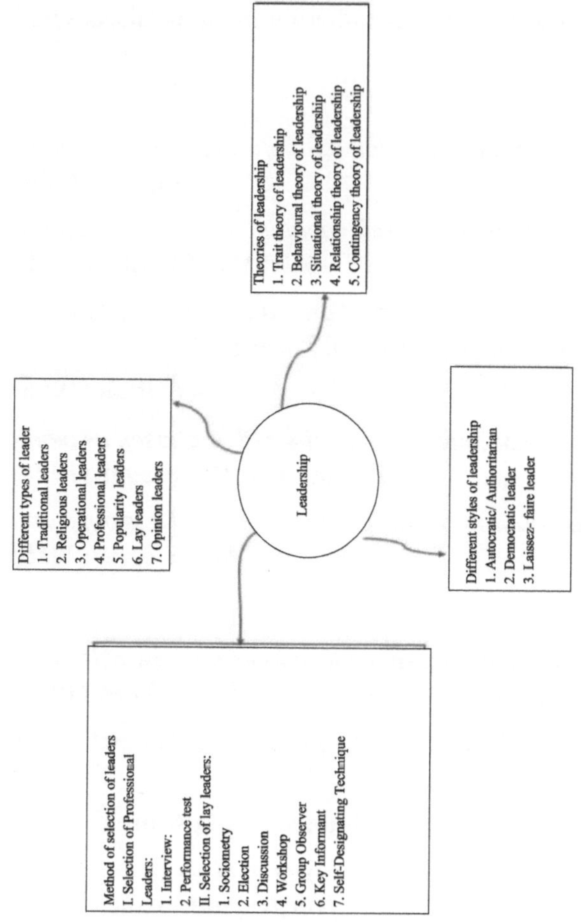

Figure 1: Overview of the chapter (Credit: Jarial, S.)

Introduction

Leadership as such has a broad connotation per se. It is an interesting social phenomenon. It could be stated that leadership is a part of the power structure and any form of group life can be traced back to some form of leadership. Stogdill (1950) said that the word "leader" originated back in the 1300s and the word "leadership" in the 1800s (Muhammad and Sameen, 2019). Different authors have given different definitions and outlooks at different times. "There are almost as many different definitions of leadership as there are persons who have attempted to define the concept" (Bass, 1990). As far as rural leadership is concern, some of the definitions propounded by various authors for thorough understanding of rural leadership are being discussed in this chapter as one single definition would not suffice to truly determine what leadership is as different leaders have different strengths and weaknesses, different styles and approaches and different means and ends. Before an in-depth discussion on the verb – leadership, it is rather pertinent to discuss and define who is a leader?

Leader

A leader is one who, in a social situation, can elicit (stimulate) positive reaction from other members of the group. **– Stogdill (1950)**

Leader is a person who instructs and controls people in order to secure predefined goals or targets. **– Hicks and Gullet (1975)**

Leaders are people who shape the goals, motivations, and actions of others. Frequently they initiate change to reach existing and new goals.

– Cuban (1988)

Leader is a person who has been spontaneously considered or chosen as being influential. **– Dhama and Bhatnagar (1991)**

Leader is one who is flexible to adapt to the differences among the groups and the changing situations. **– Khan *et al.* (2015)**

Leadership

Leadership is the activity of influencing people to cooperate towards some goal which they come to find desirable. **– Tead (1936)**

Leadership is defined as the art of influencing people so that they will strive willingly towards the achievement of group goals.

– Koontz and O'Donnel (1988)

Leadership is a form of art in mobilizing others to want to struggle for shared aspirations. **– Kouzes and Posner (1995)**

Leadership is creative problem solving. **– Reiter-Palmon and Illies (2004)**

Leadership is the process of influencing others to understand and agree about what needs. to be done and how to do it, and the process of facilitating individual and collective efforts to accomplish shared objectives.

– Yukl (2006)

Leadership is a process whereby an individual influences a group of individuals to achieve a common goal. **– Northouse (2010)**

With the inception of 21st century, it has become more widely acknowledged that a leader's moral character is not only essential for society but also essential for long-term organisational success. (Freeman et al., 2004; Gulati et al., 2010; Padilla *et al.*, 2007), thus marking a substantial shift in leadership qualities and ideologies. At this crossroads, ***servant leadership*** seems to be the most promising and most investigated over the last few years, particularly due to the holistic approach and vast focus adopted in comparison to other philosophies, as well as to its significant influence on personal and team level outcomes, such as, organizational citizenship behaviour, organizational commitment, job performance and job satisfaction. The phrase "servant leadership" was first used by Greenleaf in his 1970 essay "The Servant as Leader" to refer to a newly emerging leadership style in which leaders prioritised their followers' personal development by treating them ethically. The author stressed that the servant leader is "*primus inter pares*" or "*first among equals*", meaning that his/her highest priority is service to others in order to fulfil their needs, rather than fulfilling his or her personal needs. Servant leadership is a kind of moral leadership in which leaders put the needs of their followers—their employees, clients, and other stakeholders—ahead of meeting their own needs (Alice and Eliana, 2021). Despite the fact that the idea is not new among academics or practitioners, it has gained more attention in the last decade.

Theories of Leadership

There are a number of leadership theories propounded by different authors from different school of thought. Nevertheless, a modest number of theories has been analyse in this chapter which the author considers significant.

1. Trait theory of leadership

It is known as the "Great Man Theory," according to Thomas Carlyle. This viewpoint contends that some innate or inborn characteristics and behaviours exist in leaders. Among these qualities are personality traits, persuasiveness, intelligence, physical characteristics, bravery, dependability, and a host of other qualities. Between the 1930s and the 1950s, this theory had a surge in popularity, but it also suffered a severe setback. Whilst it kick-started the study of leadership and leadership traits, some limitations came across with the coming of *Behavioural theory of leadership*.

2. Behavioural theory of leadership

In contrast to the trait theory, this approach views leadership in terms of "what leaders do rather than what they are." The premise of this notion is that exceptional leaders are created, not born. This leadership paradigm, which has its roots in behaviourism, places an emphasis on the behaviours of leaders rather than their internal or mental states. This idea holds that individuals can learn to lead through instruction and observation (Amanchukwu *et al.*, 2015).

3. Situational theory of leadership

According to this theory, leaders decide on the optimal course of action based on contextual factors. Different leadership philosophies might be better suited for particular sorts of decision-making. An authoritarian style could be most effective, for instance, when the group's leader is the most informed and experienced person in the room. In other circumstances, a democratic system would be more efficient where the group's members are knowledgeable experts. (Cote, 2017).

4. Relationship theory of leadership

The connections made between leaders and followers are the focus of relationship theories, also referred to as transformational theories. By assisting group members in seeing the significance and greater good of the job, transformational leaders inspire and encourage their followers. These leaders are concerned with the output of the group, but they also want each individual to reach their full potential. This type of leader frequently upholds strong moral and ethical standards. (Groves and LaRocca, 2011).

5. Contingency theory of leadership

Contingency theories of leadership concentrate on specific environmental factors that could influence which specific style of leadership is most appropriate for the circumstance. This viewpoint contends that no one leadership style is best in every circumstance. (Khan *et al.,* 2016). According to leadership academics White and Hodgson, genuinely effective leadership is about achieving the proper balance between behaviours, needs, and context rather than merely the traits of the leader (Hodgson and White, 2003). Good leaders are able to evaluate the demands of their followers, evaluate the circumstances, and then modify their behaviour as necessary. Success is influenced by a variety of factors, including as the followers' traits, the environment, and the leader's leadership style (Khan *et al.*, 2016).

Different Styles of Leadership

1. Autocratic leader (Authoritarian leader)

In this type of leadership, the decision-making is completely up to the leaders. He believes that his subordinates never carry out their duties properly. With power in his hands, subordinates approach him with all of their issues, regardless of the issue's nature or severity. He is the lone decision-maker, sets all organisational policies, activities, and goals, and stifles his subordinates' capacity for originality and innovation.

Limitations

- Conflict, low morale, and frustration are common.
- Subordinates often try to avoid taking on responsibility.
- The pace of work slows, and employees experience job insecurity

Advantages

- Effective when the employees follow the assumptions of Theory X by McGreggor
- Effective when the leader is highly competent for making a right decision and subordinates are incompetent and inexperienced.

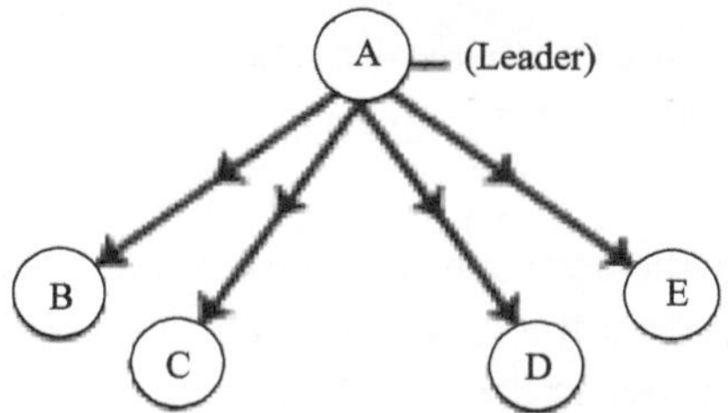

Boss-Centred-Leadership
(A is the leader who bosses around and give orders)

Figure 2: Autocratic Leadership Style *(Source: https://ask.learncbse.in/t/discuss-in-brief-the-different-styles-of-leadership/9337)*

2. Democratic leader

This leadership style is just opposite to autocratic style of leadership. The leader takes decision in consultation with the subordinates whereby participation of subordinates in decision making satisfies their social and ego needs making them more committed to their organization.

Limitations

- Decision making is cumbersome
- It require good communication skills on the part of the leader

Advantages

- Subordinates typically take on more responsibility and develop their potential.
- It increases employee satisfaction and boosts employee morale, which boosts productivity.
- Individual as well as group morale are high and employees fell secure

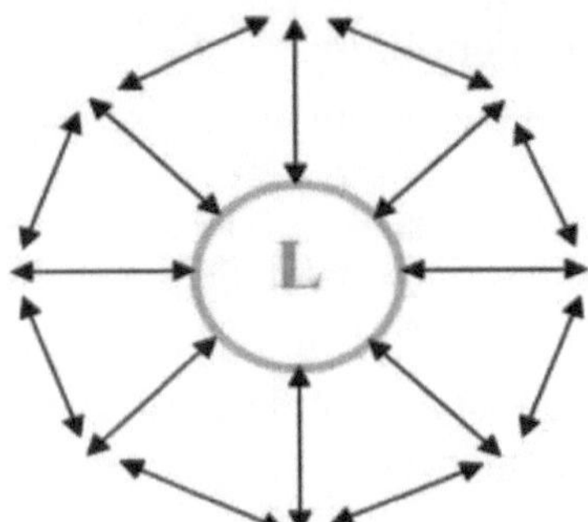

Figure 3: Democratic Leadership style *(Source: https://keydifferences.com/difference-between-autocratic-and-democratic-leadership.html)*

3. Laissez-faire leader

In this type of leadership, the boss defers to the workers when making decisions. They have complete freedom to choose how and what they want. The boss is of the opinion that if employees are left alone, the job will be done. The leader appears to have less self-assurance.

Limitations

- The biggest limitation of this style of leadership is that due to full freedom to the subordinates, it could create chaos and mismanagement in decision making
- Employees may experience agitation and poor teamwork coordination
- Often and informal leader arises

Advantages

- There could be possibility of developing innovative and creativity problem solving ideas among the workers.

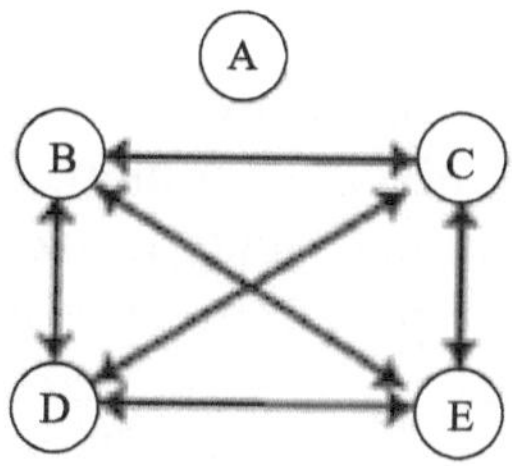

Subordinate- Centred- Leadership
(A is the leader, who avoids use of power and gives freedom to subordinates)

Figure 4: Laissez-faire Leadership Style *(Source: https://ask.learncbse.in/t/discuss-in-brief-the-different-styles-of-leadership/9337)*

Different Types of Leader

Whilst there are different types of leaders, this chapter particularly focuses on the different leaders which are generally found in Indian context.

1. Traditional leaders

These types of leaders emerge out of tradition and always stick to their tradition. They uphold established norms and institutions and meet a variety of social norms (i.e. performing traditional rites and ceremonies). They resist change, have entrenched interests, and worry that it will force them out of their positions of authority.

E.g. Tribal chiefs

2. Religious leaders

These leaders are created by the practise of religious rituals or the proclamation of religious concepts. Such leaders' primary duty is to counsel followers on topics of religion.

3. Operational leaders

Whether or not they are in an elected position, these leaders actually start the action within the group. An operational leader is someone who understands how the various components of an organisation interact and contribute to the overall result. When they consider problems, they concentrate on what systems and procedures are required or will be affected. They guarantee the organization's stability.

E.g. Volunteer Leader

4. Popularity leaders

Popularity is a measure of how much other people enjoy or value a particular person, idea, location, thing, or other notion. Reciprocal liking, interpersonal attraction, and other related elements can all contribute to liking. A person is elected to a leadership role by a group of people because they like him. Sometimes, this person may or may not be the group's true leader.

E.g. Ornamental Leaders/Nominal Leaders

5. Professional leaders

One who is a professional leader has gotten precise, specialised training in a certain field. He is paid for his full-time employment as a profession.

E.g. Extension Officer, Gram Sevak, Agricultural Officer

6. Lay leaders

A lay leader is someone who has been chosen by their peers to lead them. They might or might not have had specialised training. Such leaders typically don't get paid and just work part time. These individuals can be formal or unofficial leaders.

E.g. Youth club president

7. Opinion leaders

These leaders are the most effective in the rural areas of India and are also beneficial to extension efforts. These are the leaders that other people go to for guidance on specific matters. They also legitimise actions and have an impact on judgement. They are global citizens who accelerate the spread of ideas.

Roles of Leader in a Group

It is believed that man is a sociable animal. He lives in groups. He is always interacting socially with other group members, and each person has different needs. A person's life is a never-ending battle to meet his requirements and decompress. In our culture, interactions with other people or groups of people are the primary means of meeting needs. The group's members seek to one another for help in meeting their needs. It is true that there must be a group of people for leadership situations to arise. He is a key participant in the group's activities.

1. Group initiator and Group spokesman

He is the one who takes the initiative for any task, programme, plan of action, project, etc. by uniting the members of the organisation around a single idea and goal. He converses in the locals' tongue, making it easy for them to understand him. He is also responsible for elevating the voices of a group to the public and higher authorities. As new methods are more likely to be accepted as a result of their standing and personal support, innovations spread faster throughout society as a whole.

2. Group harmonizer

There are frequently conflicts of interest among the group members. He serves as a mediator in this case to help the members reach an agreement. Additionally, he is in charge of upholding equity and proper homogeneity within the group.

3. Group planner and educator

A group leader serves as a mentor and a guide for the other group members. He may analyse neighbourhood issues that eventually serve as a foundation for the creation of programmes. He is in charge of organising and assuring the local community's participation in extension programmes, which furthers the group's and the community's development. He is constantly prepared to give all members the proper guidance.

The definition of a group leader varies from place to place, but in general, he is a well-wisher who continually pursues and aspires for the improvement and development of the group as well as for society as a whole.

Method of Selection of Group Leaders

There are numerous ways and methods of selecting both professional and lay leaders. Some of these are discussed as:

Selection of Professional Leaders

1. Interview
2. Performance test

1. Interview

It is on of the most common strategy for choosing a professional leader. This approach is mostly based on an interview and a review of the person's prior academic and professional records. Through this procedure, a great deal of data about a person can be gathered. There have been attempts in business and management to complement interviews by giving candidates a battery of exams. These exams evaluate a person's skills, aptitudes, attitudes, and interests as well as their academic background and professional experiencc. Instead than relying solely on the interview for selection, consider administering a battery of tests in addition to it.

2. Performance test

This technique has occasionally served as the foundation for choosing professional leaders. For instance, the method known as "Leaderless group tests" involves giving a group of seven or eight people a task to do and letting them decide who will be the leader. A different kind of test involves designating a person as the group's leader and then watching how successfully that person manages the group's members' activities.

Selection of lay leaders

1. Sociometry
2. Election
3. Discussion
4. Workshop
5. Group Observer
6. Key Informant
7. Self-Designating Technique

1. Sociometry

It is a technique for describing the social relationships among individuals in a group. (Kothari, 1996). Jacob L. Moreno (1953) defined sociometry as 'the inquiry into the evolution and organization of groups and the position of individuals within them'. It tries to use numbers to quantitatively characterise social phenomena. Tools for measuring, examining, and fostering relationships are available in sociometry. Group members take part in group development by reflecting on and analysing their own interpersonal and group behaviour using information from these tools. Sociometry helps us to quantify, map, and construct linkages in order to make invisible organisational dynamics apparent and explorable. Sociometry is a crucial tool for people to develop healthy interpersonal relationships and mature group networks. In other words, it largely deals with making decisions about interpersonal relationships, such as choosing people with whom to work, play, etc., or deciding who to consult for guidance or to solve other issues. It can be applied to choosing lay and professional leaders.

An illustrative diagram has been depicted in figure 4.

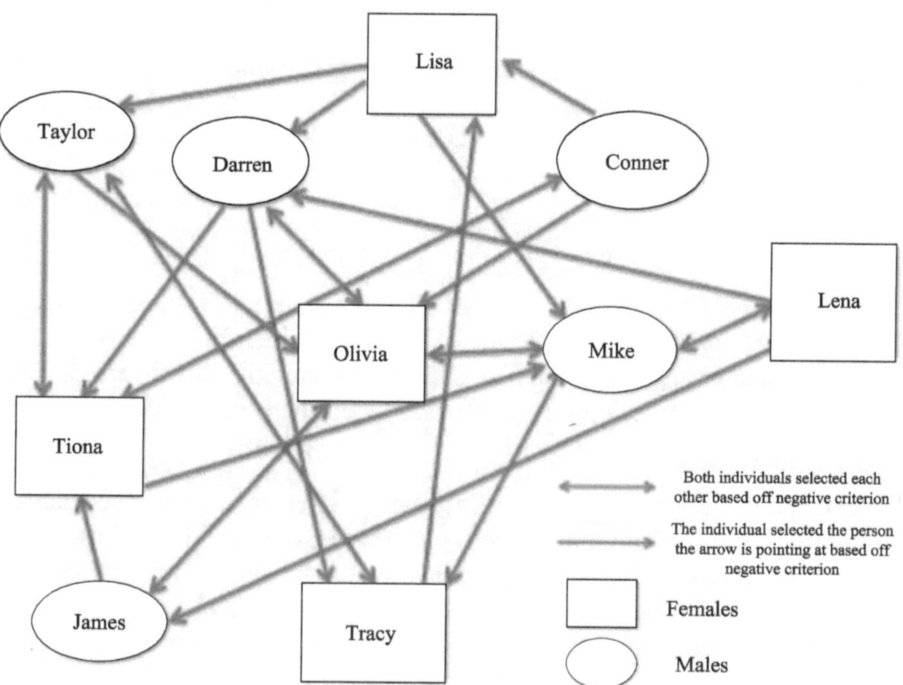

Figure 5: Sociometry *(Source: https://study.com/academy/lesson/sociogram-definition-examples-quiz.html)*

2. Election

Another popular approach for choosing leaders simply entails having the group members choose a leader by vote or another means. By describing to the group the roles of leaders in relation to specific problems and highlighting the qualities of a good leader for the given purpose, the extension worker may help the locals choose the appropriate person for the right job. The election of such leaders through Panchayati Raj institutions is one of the best examples.

E.g. Ward members, Sarpanch

3. Discussion

The person with sound knowledge and aptitude is quickly identified through discussions (on any subject), while a simple talker is easily identified. The potential leader is encouraged and given the certainty to express himself during discussion. Over time, this may give him greater confidence to accept a position of leadership and help him establish himself as a valuable leader.

4. Workshop

In this approach, a large group is divided into smaller units, and the smaller units are in charge of the programme and decision-making. Each little group develops a leader. The extension worker can identify specific leaders who step up to assume responsibility over time. The extension worker's responsibilities in the workshop include consulting, observing, leading discussion groups, etc.

5. Group observer

The extension worker will be able to identify potential leaders by seeing (observing) a community or group in action. He is free to observe the neighbourhood in any circumstance. The group shouldn't be aware that the extension worker is watching them in order to get the best results.

6. Key informants

The extension worker may ask key informants or people who have relevant information about a community, such as teachers or VLWs (village level workers), to identify opinion leaders in that region. Based on their suggestions, he will choose the leader. When compared to the sociometric approach and other methodologies, the key informant method is less expensive and takes less time.

7. Self-designating technique

A series of questions are posed to the responder in order to ascertain how much he believes himself to be an opinion leader, and the results are then analysed.

Conclusion

Any type of workgroup, programme, extension activity, or developmental effort depends on the leadership's effectiveness. A capable leader may turn a failing team or organisation into a productive one. On the other hand, a weak leader might undermine the group's productivity and spirit of cooperation. The main responsibility of a leader is to direct and instruct the group. In all actions, a leader always provides guidance, advise, and leadership. A good leader works hard to ensure the general well-being of his group and acts as a friend and philosopher to his followers. A good leader may inspire a sense of unity and belonging among the people in his organisation. As team captain, he strives to settle interpersonal conflicts that could otherwise prevent the team from functioning well.

Discipline is a vital component of success for every objective that needs to be attained. A leader ensures that there is order, complies with laws and regulations, and refrains from disruptive behaviour while also treating each member of his group equally. A leader emphasises self control. The group is motivated by the leader. He strengthens the group's resolve, loyalty, and confidence. The group's leader serves as a genuine link to the outside world. A leader represents his followers and speaks on behalf of the group before different authorities. Each of his members has him as a guardian by nature. In a nutshell, it can be argued that effective leadership keeps the group cohesive, orderly, enthusiastic, full of optimism, and—most importantly—functioning as a team that looks out for the interests of the whole group.

Answer the Following Questions

1. What distinguishes the Trait theory of leadership from the Behavioural theory of leadership, and how did the emergence of the Behavioural theory challenge the assumptions of the Trait theory?
2. Compare and contrast the roles and responsibilities of an Autocratic leader with those of a Democratic leader within a group setting. How do these leadership styles impact group dynamics and member satisfaction?
3. Critically assess the effectiveness of different methods for selecting both professional and lay leaders within a community or organization. What are the strengths and weaknesses of each method, and under what circumstances might one method be more suitable than another?

10

Extension Administration Meaning and Concept, Principles and Functions

Termaric Oinam

Department of Agricultural Economics and Extention, Lovely Professional University Phagwara, Punjab

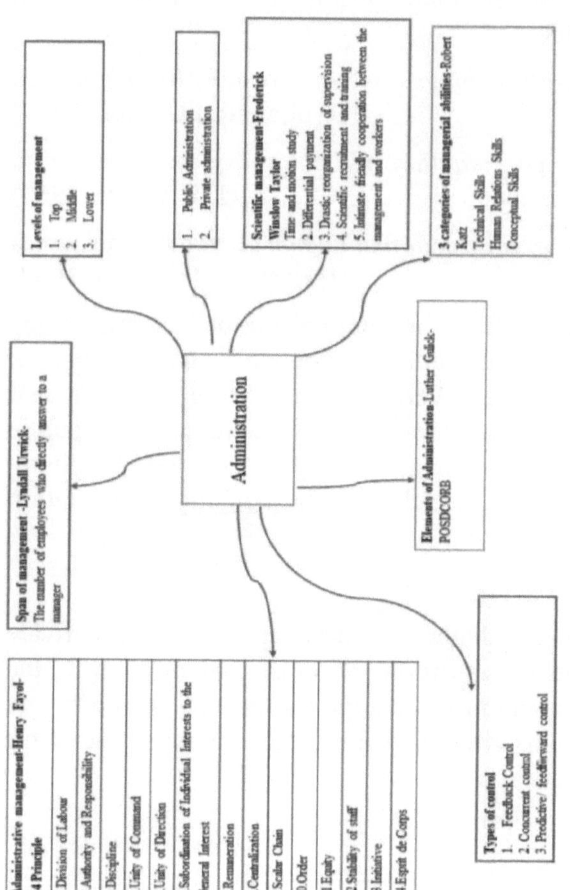

Figure 1: Overview of the chapter (Credit: Jarial, S)

Introduction

To accomplish the objectives of the organisation, the administration often performs a standard set of tasks. Administration is the direction, leadership, and supervision of a group's actions toward certain common objectives (Newman, 1950). It suggests sincere efforts made to plan and manage human activities in order to accomplish set or desired goals. Organising, leading, and controlling people and resources to achieve predetermined goals.

A detailed manual outlining the best ways to perform duties as an extension administrator is impossible. Most of management concepts are common sense guidelines that develop from experience. The concepts are, at best, rudimentary tools, but they have great potential if applied properly and judiciously. They serve as an action manual.

The Latin word ***ad*** and ***ministiare,*** which meaning to take care of or manage matters, is the root of the English word administration. Several well-known administration definitions include

Administration has to do with getting things done; and accomplishing defined objectives. **(Gulick and Urwick, 1937)**

Administration is the direction, coordination and control of many people to achieve some purposes and objectives. **(L.D.White, 1955)**

Administration is the organization & direction of human & material resources to achieve desired ends. **(Pfiffner & Presthus, 1967)**

According to the aforementioned definitions, "administration" can be defined more broadly as a group activity that requires cooperation and coordination to achieve specific goals or objectives. Woodrow Wilson, the 28th President of the United States (1913–1921), is revered as the founder of public administration (Jayanta, K.D. & Ratnaprava, B). In an article titled "The Study of Administration," published in 1887, he acknowledged public administration for the first time.

Private and Public Administration

The motivations are the primary distinction between public and private governance. While most private organizations prioritise making a profit, the primary goal of public administration is to serve the general public.In any case, the benefit of private administration is that it is quick to make decisions, businesslike, and devoid of political pressures.

Table 1: Difference between Public and Private Administration

S.No.	Public administration	Private administration
1	Bureaucratic	Business
2.	Political direction	No political influence
3.	Diversified nature of the function	Limited
4.	More public accountability	Less
5.	Less efficiency	More efficiency

Management or Administration

Administration includes management. A method of administration used in the conduct of public affairs is management. An administration is a term used to describe the conventional structure in which a civil service performs its duties.

History of Management

Management as an idea has existed for thousands of years. According to Pindur, Rogers, and Kim (1995), the earliest forms of management existed at least 3000 years before the birth of Christ, when Middle Eastern clerics began keeping records of economic transactions. Around 400 BC, Socrates claimed that management was a skill distinct from having technical knowledge and skills (Higgins, 1991).The hierarchy of power was used by the Romans, known for their legions of warriors led by Centurions, to establish accountability. The structure of the Roman Catholic Church was based on defined areas, a chain of command, and job descriptions. A group of artisans and merchants known as guilds produced things made by hand during the Middle Ages, which spanned around 1,000 years from 476 AD to 1450 AD.These goods ranged from bread to armour and swords during the Crusades. Similar to the Catholic Church, there was a structure of authority where masters held the apex of the power and journeymen and apprentices were subordinate to them. These artisans were essentially small firms that produced goods of diverse quality, with low productivity rates, and no need for administrative oversight beyond that of the proprietor or master craftsperson.The late 1700s to the early 1800s saw the Industrial Revolution, a time of enormous upheaval and profound change in how people lived and worked. Prior to this, the majority of people lived in rural areas and earned their livelihood through farming or other manual labour. The steam engine's development led several innovations, such as the automated transportation of coal from underground mines, the powering of factories that could mass-produce made-by-hand goods previously, and railroad locomotives that could swiftly and effectively transport goods across international borders. Workers were necessary for factories, and those workers needed order and leadership. The demand for management and coordination increased as these facilities grew larger and more productive.

Table 2: Historical Development of Management

Era	Description
Pre-3000 BC	Earliest forms of management with Middle Eastern clerics keeping records of economic transactions.
400 BC	Socrates distinguished management as a skill separate from technical knowledge and skills.
Roman Era	Romans used a hierarchy of power for accountability, exemplified in their military structure.
Middle Ages	Guilds of artisans and merchants produced handmade goods, with a structured hierarchy of authority.
Industrial Revolution	Massive change with the development of steam engines, leading to the need for management in factories.
Modern Times	Prominent management theories developed, including administrative management and scientific management.

Although there are many management theories, the two most prominent and extensively researched theories — **administrative management** and **scientific management** — have been covered in this chapter.

Scientific Management

The scientific management father is Frederick Winslow Taylor (1856–1915). Throughout his 26-year career, he had a significant impact on the advancement of management philosophy through his experiments and writings. He carried out a several trials at three businesses: Bethlehem Steel, Simon's Rolling Machine, and Midvale Steel. Taylor produced several significant contributions that fall under the category of scientific management while working as the chief engineer for Midvale Steel Company.

1. Time and motion study

Taylor, who worked as a machinist, was aware of how pieceworkers used to limit productivity to a third of its previous level out of concern that their employers would reduce their piece rates as soon as production increased. Taylor began time and motion study because he believed that no one knew how much labour a man could reasonably be expected to accomplish. In this method, the ideal way to complete a task was identified by timing each motion using a stopwatch and developing shorter, simpler variations. This has taken the place of the worker's old general knowledge.

2. Differential payment

In his differential piece work payment plan, which he introduced, Taylor connected incentives with output.

3. Drastic reorganization of supervision

Taylor suggested 2 new concepts 1) Separation of planning and doing 2) Functional foremanship

Back then, it was common for each worker to organise his job, choose his tools, and determine the sequence in which the tasks should be completed. This foreman merely instructs the worker on what tasks to complete rather than how to do them. Taylor argued that a foreman, not the worker, should plan the task.

4. Scientific recruitment and training

It stressed the necessity for scientific worker selection and development to bring out their finest faculties and enable them to perform higher-class, more fascinating, and more lucrative work than they previously could.

5. Intimate friendly cooperation between the management and workers

According to Taylor, management and labour must undergo a total mental revolution for the proposals above to be successful.

Contributions and Limitations of Scientific Management

Time and motion are first. Second, the emphasis that scientific management placed on the scientific selection of workers has made us recognise that a person cannot be expected to perform his job properly without ability and training. Third, studies have made us aware that the tools and physical movements involved in a task can be made more efficient and rational. Finally, managers are now pushed to seek out the best way to do a task. Both blue-collar manufacturing occupations and white-collar office and service positions have become specialised and standardised, which increases worker productivity and facilitates management control. Taylor's scientific management emphasised the floor-level administration of solely physical tasks while ignoring problem-solving and decision-making. No man is a purely economic man. Therefore, Taylor's assertion that economic incentives are powerful enough to urge people to increase is false. Man's actions are not always determined by his needs for money. At least after he has advanced past the point of starving, he has a variety of other needs, such as security, social, or egoistic needs, which drive him much more powerfully than his desire for money.

Administrative Management

With an emphasis on the establishing of broad and administrative concepts applicable to general and higher managerial levels, **Henry Fayol** (1841–1925) is regarded as the founder of administrative management theory. He was a French mining engineer who become an important industrialist and effective manager. Before his book *General and Industrial Administration* was translated into English in 1929, the western world knew very little about him. He wrote a monograph in French in 1916. As broad guidelines for the management procedure and management practice, he offered 14 management principles. Below is a discussion of them:

Table 3: Principles of administrative management

S.No.	Principle	Description
1	Division of Labour	Division of work into manageable, discrete components, leading to increased efficiency.
2	Authority and Responsibility	Managers should have the authority to give orders and expect obedience, with a balance of responsibility.
3	Discipline	Discipline is crucial for smooth operations, requiring good leadership, fair agreements, and appropriate sanctions.
4	Unity of Command	Each employee should only receive instructions from one superior for a specific task to avoid confusion.
5	Unity of Direction	Departmental goals should align with organizational goals without conflicting.
6	Subordination of Individual Interests to the General Interest	The general interest should be prioritized over individual interests to maximize productivity.
7	Remuneration	Fair remuneration determined by several factors, improving employee productivity and morale.
8	Centralization	The balance of centralized and decentralized authority based on various factors for efficient utilization of staff.
9	Scalar Chain	The hierarchical structure of authority for communication, with flexibility for immediate actions ('gang planking').
10	Order	Organizational orderliness through scientific selection and organization of personnel and materials.
11	Equity	Fair and impartial treatment of employees to foster positive labor-management relations.
12	Stability of staff	Job security is essential for employee motivation, loyalty, and productivity.
13	Initiative	Encouraging employees to think creatively and execute plans boosts zeal and innovation.
14	Esprit de Corps	Fostering team spirit and unity among workers, using verbal dialogue to resolve misunderstandings.

Elements of Administration

The abbreviation **POSDCORB**, which reflects the traditional understanding of organisational theory, is frequently used in the fields of management and public administration. It was highlighted the most in a 1937 paper by Luther Gulick. POSDCORB was initially intended to foster the development of public service professionals. The components are: Planning, Organizing, Staffing, Directing, Co-Ordinating, Reporting, and Budgeting, in Gulick's own words.

Luther Gulick denoted the functional elements by the letters: "POSDCORB"

1. Planning

Thinking about the steps necessary to accomplish a goal is the process of planning. It is the first and most important thing to do to get the desired outcomes. It is developing a general description of the tasks to be completed and the approaches to be used to get them done. It involves planning a future course of action and choosing the most suitable path of action in advance.

2. Organizing

For the group to collaborate effectively, effective authority connections must be established among the chosen tasks, people, and work locations. Identifying activities, classifying grouping of tasks, and assigning of responsibilities are all parts of the organising process.

3. Staffing

Planning with manpower: (estimating manpower in terms of searching, choosing the person and giving the right place), Training and development, as well as recruitment, selection, and placement. Compensation Performance Evaluation.

4. Directing

According to this definition, directing is a process in which managers give instructions, provide guidance, and monitor employee performance to meet predetermined objectives. The management process is stated to be at its core while directing.

Direction has the following elements:

a) **Supervision** To check that work is being done as necessary, directed, and allocated based on the work plan, supervision entails watching over subordinates, workers, or other members while at work. When people are given motives based on their unmet wants, motivation can be characterized as a planned managerial process that encourages them to work to the best of their ability.

b) **Leadership** Leadership is the process through which a person persuades others to achieve a goal and guides the group in a way that makes it more rational and organized.

c) **Communications** Communication is the process of communicating information between two or more people. Information is sent from a sender to a receiver in this process.

d) **Co-ordinating** Linking the many components of the task together and preventing conflict from overlapping. Integration and synchronization of group members' actions create unity of action in the pursuit of shared objectives.

e) **Reporting** Keeping both superiors and subordinates informed of events and making arrangements for gathering information through record-keeping, research, and inspection.

f) **Budgeting** Budgeting is the process of creating a spending plan. The budget alludes to this financial strategy. Be creating a spending plan, one can analyze one's financial status and determine whether one will have enough money to achieve one's goals. Budgeting is simply about striking a balance between one's income and expenses.

Levels of Management

Depending on their rank, managers require different skills. An individual can perform a physical or mental job with a desired result. Not all skills are innate; some can be learned via practice and application of previously acquired knowledge and experience. A manager must have these three key talents to carry out his responsibilities successfully. Top managers require great conceptual abilities, whilst middle managers require strong interpersonal skills, and lower level managers require technical abilities. Strong communication, decision-making, and time management abilities are essential for all managers. The three main competencies are:

i. Lower -level (first line): foremen & white collar supervisor

ii. Middle management: sales manager, personnel managers, other departmental heads

iii. Top management: company's presidents, executives, vice presidents

The three fundamental categories of managerial abilities, according to American social and organizational psychologist Robert Katz (1955), comprise:

Technical Skills

Lower- level managers need to possess these abilities. When a manager refers to a person's knowledge and skill in any production department method or technique, he refers to that person's knowledge and competency in that process or technique. This would entail having a technical understanding of the industrial process. A manager 's technical skills consist of specialised knowledge and competence and the capacity to use that knowledge. Technical abilities include creating financial statements, programming computers, constructing office buildings, and conducting market research. Since supervisory managers frequently work with employees creating the company's products and or services, these talents are crucial for them. As the manager advances to higher ranks, its value as a component of the manager role decreases. The technical component becomes less significant in higher functional positions like a marketing manager or production manager as the conceptual component relating to these functional areas becomes more significant.

Human Relations Skills

Managers employ interpersonal abilities known as human relations skills to use people resources to achieve goals. This set of abilities includes the capacity to comprehend human behaviour, effectively interact with others, and inspire people to achieve their goals. Giving employees constructive criticism, being aware of their particular needs, and being willing to provide authority to subordinates are all instances of strong human relations practices. Companies should prioritis finding and elevating managers with strong interpersonal communication abilities. An authoritarian leadership style and employee enmity can result from a manager with poor or nonexistent people skills. In a nutshell, it is the capacity to communicate clearly with people of all ranks.

Conceptual Skills

It refers to a manager's capacity to see the organization and its future from a broad and long-term perspective, and his capacity to think abstractly, evaluate the forces at play, and appraise the environment and the changes it is undergoing. It entails observing the organization as a whole, comprehending the interdependence of the many components, and evaluating how the organization interacts with its external environment. Managers can analyze issues using these talents and come up with several solutions. Strong conceptual abilities are extremely important for managers at the top of the management pyramid, where strategic planning occurs.

Developing Organizational Skills

Organisation might mean two different things. The first interpretation focuses on the organizational procedure. The second interpretation refers to the institution or group that forms due to organizing. Formal and informal organizations are the two main categories of organization. Making provisions for the provision of relevant information and other instruments for performance in that capacity is necessary to ensure that a role functions effectively. An organization structure should be created to clarify who is responsible for what tasks and outcomes, to remove performance barriers brought on by ambiguity and assignment uncertainty, and to provide decision-making and community networks that reflect and support business objectives. The creation of Departments is one component of the organization. The term "department" refers to a separate geographic division for a section of an organization over which a manager has control to carry out particular tasks. Departmentalization is the process of combining similar or logically connected work activities so that they take place at the same time.

Organizational Levels and the Span of Management

The goal of an organization is to improve human cooperation, and stages of the organization are necessary due to the span of management's constraints. The number of employees who directly answer to a manager is the span of management. Few organizational levels are connected with a large span of management, while numerous levels are associated with a restricted span of management. **Lyndall Urwick**, a well-known British consultant, determined that eight to twelve subordinates are the appropriate amount at the lowest level of a business. For all superior authorities, four is the ideal number of subordinates.

Problem with Organizational Levels

There are several levels, and departmental levels make communication difficult. An enterprise with many levels has greater difficulty communicating objectives, plans, policies etc., downward through organizational structure than does a firm in which top manager communicates directly. Planning and control are hampered by the presence of numerous departments and levels. As a plan is broken down at lower levels, it loses coordination and clarity since it is clear and comprehensive at the top level. With the addition of levels and managers, control becomes challenging.

Operational Management Position- a Situational Approach

The Span of Management (SOM) approach from the classical school focuses on identifying the precise number of subordinates needed for an efficient SOM. The span of management principle states that there is a limit to the number of subordinates a manager can effectively supervise. Upper level (SOM) is from three to eight subordinates. However, more recent operational management theorists have taken the position that there are too many underlying variables in management situations for us to specify any specific number of subordinates that a manager can effectively supervise. However, the precise amount will depend on how underlying factors such as:

Factors Determining an Effective Span

1. Subordinate training
2. Clarity of delegation of authority
3. Clarity of plans
4. Use of objective standards
5. Rate of change
6. Communication techniques
7. Amount of personal contact needed
8. Variation by organizational levels
9. Other factors

Decentralization, or the propensity to distribute decision-making authority, is another crucial idea. On the other side, centralization is the concentration of power. It can be a geographical departmental concentration or a propensity to limit decision-making delegation.

Assigning tasks, delegating authority, and holding people accountable for results are all parts of the delegation of authority or decentralization process. Individual mindsets impact the art of delegation. The secret to effective decentralization is balance. Giving people authority to do something inspires them to work hard for the company.

Controlling

One of the main mission-driven responsibilities of management in a company is control. To make sure that operations are carried out by the plans, it is a process of comparing the actual performance with the company's established criteria and, if necessary, taking corrective action.

The basic control process involves (1) Comparing performance with standard (2) Determining where negative deviations occur, and (3) Developing remedial measures to correct deviations.

Features of Controlling

An effective control system has the following characteristics:

a) It aids in the achievement of organizational goals;
b) It facilitates the best use of resources;
c) It assesses the standard's accuracy;

d) It also establishes discipline and order;
e) It inspires employees and raises employee morale;
f) It ensures future planning by revising standards;
g) It enhances an organization's overall performance;
h) It also minimizes errors.

Process of Controlling

The following steps in the control process are depicted in the figure.

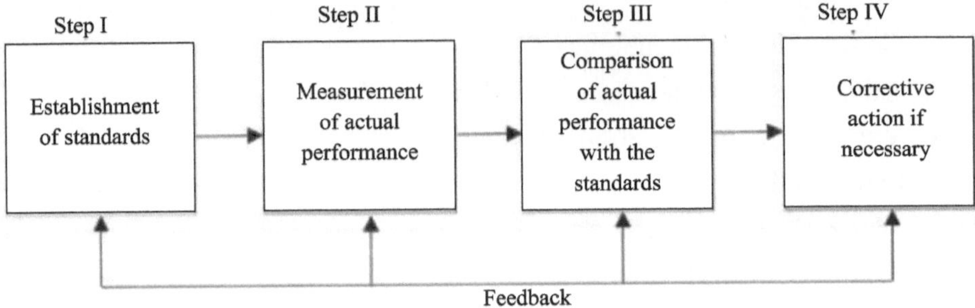

Figure 1: Process of Controlling *(Source: https://businessjargons.com/controlling.html)*

1. **Establishing standards**: This means setting up the target, which needs to be achieved to meet organizational goals eventually. Standards provide performance standards.
2. **Measurement of actual performance**: The employee's actual performance is compared to the goal. The measurement of performance becomes challenging as management levels rise.
3. **Comparison of actual performance with the standard**: This assesses how far the actual performance deviates from the standard.
4. **Taking corrective actions**: The manager starts it and fixes any flaws in actual performance.

Thus, controlling processes control business operations to ensure that actual performance adheres to the standard plan. Managers can avoid situations that could result in losses for the organisation using an efficient management system.

Types of Control

There are three types of control, viz.

1. **Feedback Control**: This procedure entails gathering data about completed tasks, analysing that data, and improving similar jobs in the future.

2. **Concurrent control**: This procedure entails gathering data about completed tasks, analysing that data, and improving similar jobs in the future.
3. **Predictive/ feedforward control**: This kind of control enables problem detection before it occurs. Consequently, action could be taken in advance of such a situation.

Advantages of Controlling

- Saves time and energy
- Allows managers to concentrate on important tasks. This allows better utilization of the managerial resource
- Helps in timely corrective action to be taken by the manager
- Managers can delegate tasks so that routinely chores can be completed by subordinates.

Supervision

Instructing, directing, monitoring, and observing the workers while they accomplish their duties for the company is what is meant by supervision. Supervision is made out of the words super and vision, where super stands for above and beyond and vision for seeing. Therefore, it entails observing employee activity above and beyond. The supervisor is a link between the superior and the subordinates, acting as a mediator.

Typical Roles in Supervision

The nature of the organization's culture, the complexity of the department's goals, the department's staff's level of knowledge, and most importantly, the supervisor's capacity for effective delegation to their direct reports all affect how dynamic the job of a supervisor is. For example, a manager could take on multiple responsibilities on the same day.

Advocate- The supervisor frequently has to speak on behalf of the employee to management and to argue the employee's case for meriting a reward. For instance, if a worker warrants a promotion, the supervisor frequently needs to defend the decision to the supervisor's boss.

Boss - Organizational leaders go by various labels, and people have diverse opinions. Boss, on the other hand, is the phrase that is most commonly used and understood. When employees in the department are ultimately seeking direction and advice on their tasks, the supervisor is regarded as the boss.

Coach - With the recent expansion of the personal and professional coaching industries, the term "coach" has acquired a new connotation. In that area, coaches are skilled at assisting clients in bringing out and using their wisdom.

They frequently ask probing inquiries to facilitate that.

Facilitator - A facilitator's role is to assist a group of individuals in defining their intended outcomes and collaborating to reach those outcomes. When a group is just starting, a facilitator may give somewhat directive counsel or offer insightful questions, paraphrasing, and summarizing. Consequently, a facilitator functions much like a coach working with an established team.

Mentor - A mentor is a person who supports another's (a mentee's) professional and personal growth. The mentor may have formally agreed to play that function, for instance, as a component of a larger mentoring programme, or may have explicitly agreed to play the position based on a mutual connection. As a result, the mentee believes they can depend on the mentor for support.

Trainer - When a new employee has to learn the job, or when an employee is having trouble increasing performance on the job, the supervisor is frequently the first person who is taken into account. Workers frequently consult the supervisor with questions on personnel policies. For example, progressive workers could inquire about the culture of the company. The supervisor must ensure that training takes place; they may conduct the training personally or arrange for it to be done by a subject-matter expert.

Conclusion

Various activities are included in agricultural extension that aims to raise people's quality of living and food production. Therefore, extension needs to be controlled and directed to reach the intended outcomes. Extension administration illustrates the administrator's efforts to organize, direct, and coordinate the staff members' actions to fulfil the extension service's mission and support farmers in achieving their goals. As a result, extension administration is the skill of managing the human and material resources inside an extension system.

The extension administration is aware that there are individuals with various interests, abilities, attitudes, and social backgrounds. Extension is therefore created to assist farmers with different orientations. To save the entire agricultural system and improve the overall state of the economy, extension must restrain competing interests and discourage farmers from being uninteresting. Administrators of extensions should concentrate their efforts on the desired improvement. Through strong ties between extension agents and other development organizations, change can be effected. Extension administration aims to achieve results primarily through the activities and efforts of other individuals tasked with carrying out certain tasks.

Answer the Following Questions

1. What are the key differences between public administration and private administration according to the text? How do these differences impact decision-making and operational processes in each sector?
2. Discuss the contributions and limitations of both scientific management and administrative management as outlined in the text. How have these management theories shaped modern organizational practices?
3. Explain the significance of the POSDCORB framework in the field of management and public administration, as highlighted in the text. How does this framework aid in the effective functioning of organizations, particularly in terms of planning, organizing, staffing, directing, coordinating, reporting, and budgeting?

11

Transfer of Technology: Concept and Models

Mukesh Chaudhary

Department of Agricultural Economics and Extension, Lovely Professional University Phagwara, Punjab

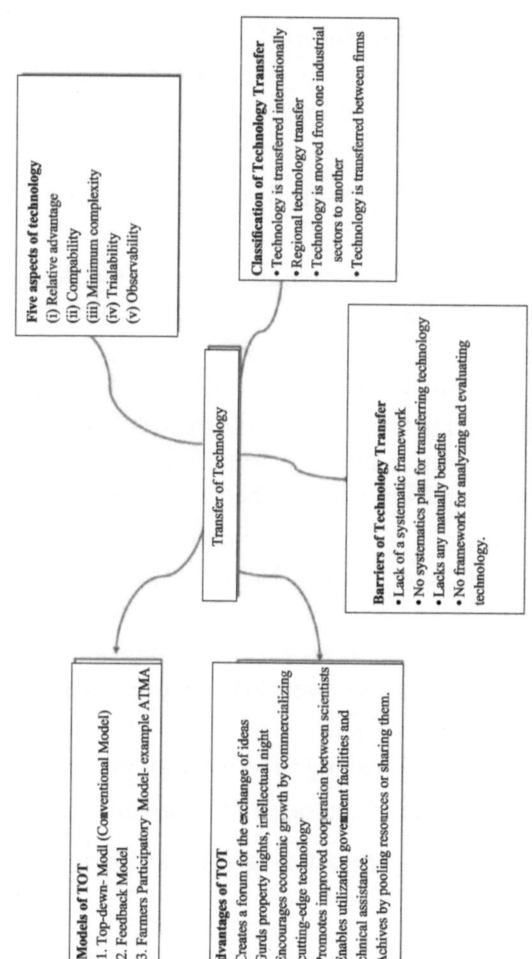

Figure 1: Overview of the chapter (Credit: Jarial, S)

Introduction

The interest in technology transfer traces back to the colonial era, which began by disseminating knowledge about the core industries of mining, plantations, and agriculture, which was seven decades ago. Technology has had a significant impact on human development and life growth throughout history. People's life are constantly changing due of technology, whether or not they are ready for it. There has been so much change brought about by technology, and it has occurred at such a rapid pace that many times people lose their capacity to handle it successfully and pleasantly. In this scenario, more ideas are being created in the smaller globe, and technology's residence time is getting much shorter.

Keywords

Transfer: It is the process of transferring data, knowledge, and objects from one location or person to another.

Technology: It refers to application of knowledge for practical purposes.

OR

Technology is scientific knowledge that is applied to address a variety of human problems in the real world.

Agricultural technology: It is a collection of information that is methodically arranged and relevant to local production issues, with the goal of enhancing current productivity and/or broadening the scope of production.

Transfer of technology (ToT): Technology transfer, often known as the transfer of technology, is the process of transferring technology from its owner or holder to another person or organisation in an effort to turn inventions and scientific discoveries into novel goods and services that benefit society.

Transfer of technology in agriculture: ToT means translating the research findings or technologies into actual practice in the farms by recipients or farmers themselves.

Technological development: It is the process of **research** and **development** of **technology.** Many **emerging technologies** are expected to become generally applied soon.

Need: it is difference between what is and what ought to be desirable situations.

Objectives: it is expression of ends towards which our efforts are directed.

The degree of acceptance of a technology depends on five criteria

i. Relative advantage

ii. Compatibility

iii. Minimum complexity
iv. Trialability
v. Observability

Extension vs ToT

One of the objectives of extension is to transfer technology, and as part of this process, the extension agent is also tasked with educating farmers and deciding for technical inputs and services. As a result, many individuals confuse the terms extension and technology transfer.

Though extension is a crucial and significant component of technology transfer, Swanson and Claar (1984) claimed that the two concepts are not interchangeable. Additional "function of technical input services" are included in the transfer of technology. On the other hand, extension focuses mostly on teaching farmers how to manage their resources and make decisions, which may help with the transmission of technology. It is crucial to realize that extension focuses on educating farmers rather than providing them with technical input and services. Many institutions place a strong emphasis on the supply of inputs and technical services, which are listed as extension activities, due to the misconceptions regarding the function of extension.

However, extension organizations frequently take on tasks that are not directly related to extension education, such as providing inputs, monitoring credit repayment, enforcing government rules, collecting statistical data, setting up cooperatives, etc. (Arnon, 1989). The question of whether providing technical inputs and services counts as "extension" is still up for debate.

Examples of Technology Transfer in Agriculture

New crop varieties

High yielding or disease resistant strains often genetically engineered.

Manufactured inputs

Fertilizers, pesticides, and other agricultural chemicals.

Machinery

Tractors and cultivators. Grain drying equipment and other postharvest technology.

Management techniques

Computers, financial statements, and tillage practices.

University research and training

Biotechnologies and new crop varieties. Training for scientists and farmers.

Models of TOT

1. Top-down-Model (Conventional Model)

Salient features

- Farmers were passive users of technology.
- Farmers and scientists had little to no interaction with one another.
- One of extension's responsibilities was to convince people to use new technologies.

A similar strategy was used during the Green Revolution. Clients' concerns and opinions were not given enough consideration in this model or strategy to address them. One illustration of the top-down ToT model is the T & V system.

2. Feedback Model

With the development of FSR and the inclusion of on-farm experimentation into agricultural research techniques, this approach has gained popularity.

Key characteristics

- The researcher appreciates understanding the challenges and responses of the target population.
- Close collaboration between the extension system and research.
- Both a research farm and farmer fields are used for research.
- To gain a comprehensive grasp of farmers' issues, the research team comprised social scientists and extension workers.

3. Farmers Participatory Model

To promote sustainable development in rural regions, there has been a growing trend toward the need to increase farmers' capacities for research and extension. The new model is based on several observations on research and extension projects in several global regions. Farmers have an innate curiosity in experimenting with novel farming techniques due to their deep interests, strong ties to their profession, and experience. Their native knowledge of agro-ecological conditions and wisdom are excellent resources for developing appropriate technology. As a result, the new model had adopted the stance that agricultural research must start and conclude with farmers.

The characteristics of such approach are as given below:

1. Farmers are viewed as active collaborators in extension and research.
2. Farmers' knowledge of indigenous cultures is appreciated & considered.
3. Farmers and academics are considered to work together in research to address issues that farmers are facing.

4. A crucial component of the participatory paradigm is the establishment of physical infrastructure and educational facilities to support local experimentation.
5. It focuses on the requirement that scientists have greater sensitivity in order to comprehend, interact with, and work with farmers.

An illustration of this kind of ToT model is ATMA.

4. Farmer-back-to-Farmer Model

The "Farmer back-to-Farmer" paradigm is an alternate to the two types mentioned above (Rhodes and Booth, 1982). The model's fundamental presumption is that research must start and end with the farmer. By starting with farmers, it completely flips the top-down paradigm. This calls for including farmers as full participants in the problem-solving team.

Classification of Technology Transfer

The practice of transferring technology generated by one organization to other potentially valuable objectives is known as technology transfer (NASA). The following categories can be used to categorize technology transfer:-

i) **Technology is transferred internationally**, spanning international borders. For instance, technology moves from developed to poor nations.

ii) **Regional technology transfer** is the movement of technology from one area of the nation to another, such as from one state to another within the nation.

iii) **Technology is moved from one industrial sector to another** in a process known as cross industry or cross sector technology transfer. For instance, innovations from the space programme are used in commercial applications.

iv) **Technology is transferred between firms**; one company gives it to another. As an illustration, consider the transfer of CAD expertise and CAM equipment from a machine tool manufacturing company to a furniture manufacturing company.

Technology that is moved from one place within a company to another is known as intra-firm technology transfer. For instance, technology can be transferred from a company's Mumbai division to its Chennai division, or from one department to another inside the same building.

Advantages of ToT

- Creates a forum for the exchange of ideas.
- Guards property rights, intellectual rights.

- Encourages economic growth by commercializing cutting-edge technology.
- Promotes improved cooperation between federal and non-federal scientists.
- Enables non-federal organizations to utilize government facilities and technical assistance.
- Achieves objectives that neither party could complete on their own by pooling resources or sharing them.

Barriers for Technology Transfer

The following are the ultimate international technological difficulties with obstacles and the difficulty with technology transfer:

- A lack of a systematic framework for studying technology and a weak comprehension of the subject in general.
- The poor nations acquiring the technology do not have a systematic plan for transferring it.
- The method of technology transfer lacks any mutually beneficial scientific or technological advantages.
- The absence of an appropriate framework for analyzing and evaluating technology.
- Failing to take ergonomics into account when transferring technology.
- Failure to appraise the influence of technology and consider environmental factors.
- Failing to identify the local market's potential for technology adoption.
- Failing to identify potential uses for the transferred technology.
- Limiting the technology transfer feasibility research to financial analysis.
- A misunderstanding of the idea of a technology's appropriateness, which has so far been limited to modest, low-investment technologies.

Conclusion

Technology transfer, a critical process that has evolved since the colonial era, plays a significant role in human development and growth. Initially focused on core industries like mining and agriculture, ToT has broadened in scope and complexity, reflecting the rapid pace of technological advancements. The concept encompasses various forms, including the transfer of data, knowledge, and application of scientific methods to practical problems, especially in agriculture. Tot in agriculture, specifically, involves translating research findings into practical farming applications. This process has seen several models, including the Top-Down Model, Feedback Model, Farmers Participatory Model, and Farmer-Back-to-Farmer Model. Each model reflects a different approach to integrating farmers into the technology transfer process, ranging from viewing them as passive recipients to active collaborators. The classification of ToT highlights its diverse applications - international, regional, cross-industry, inter-firm, and intra-firm - showcasing its expansive reach and potential impact. The advantages of effective ToT are manifold, including the promotion of economic growth, protection of intellectual property rights, and fostering collaboration. However, ToT faces several barriers, including a lack of systematic framework for technology study, inadequate plans for technology adoption in developing countries, and a limited understanding of technology's appropriateness. Addressing these challenges requires a comprehensive approach that considers local markets, environmental factors, and the potential for technology adoption.

Answer the Following Questions

1. How does the process of technology transfer in agriculture differ from other sectors, and what are the key factors that influence the successful adoption of technology by farmers?
2. Considering the models of technology transfer discussed, such as the Top-Down Model, Feedback Model, Farmers Participatory Model, and Farmer-Back-to-Farmer Model, how might agricultural extension services tailor their approach to better engage with farmers and facilitate the effective transfer of technology?
3. What are the primary advantages and disadvantages of international, regional, cross-industry, inter-firm, and intra-firm technology transfer in agriculture, and how do these different forms of transfer impact the development and adoption of agricultural technologies globally

12

Capacity Building of Extension Personnel

Mukesh Chaudhary

Department of Agricultural Economics and Extension, Lovely Professional University Phagwara, Punjab

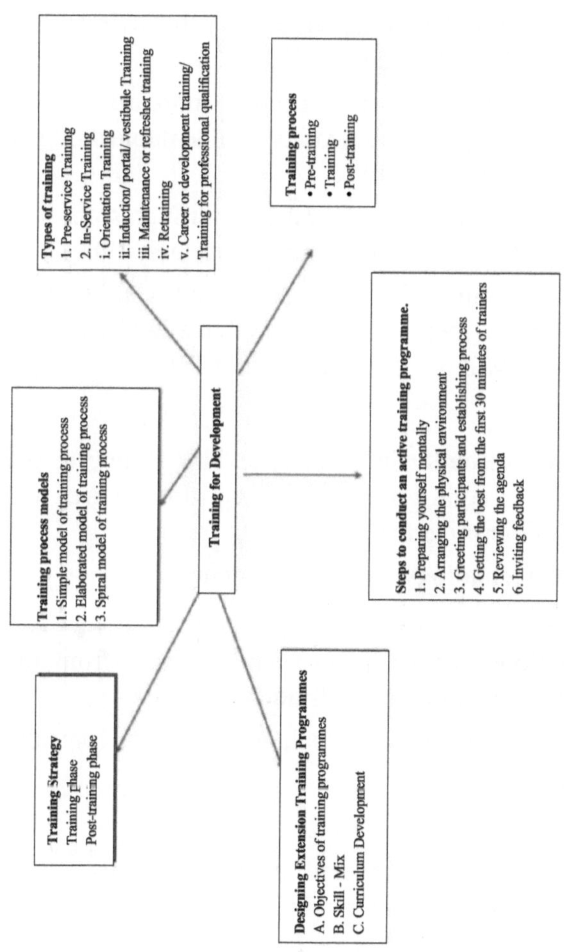

Figure 1: Overview of the chapter (Credit: Jarial, S)

"Activities which develop individual knowledge, talents, skills, and behaviour and improve institutional structures and processes so that the organization may efficiently accomplish its mission and goals in a sustainable manner" it refers as a capacity building. One of the crucial elements of capacity building is training.

Training for Development

Training is becoming an integral component of HRD. It has developed into one of the elements that allows any institution to produce its personnel who are the most productive and qualified.

Training – Definitions

- Training is the art of improving a worker's knowledge and ability to do a specific profession.
- Training is a learning process that aims to modify behaviour into something more permanent after experience.
- Training is the process of assisting workers to become more effective in their current or future work through the development of suitable thought, action, skill, knowledge, and attitude habits.
- Changing employee behaviour, attitudes, or opinions through some sort of supervised experience is the process of training (Krietner, 1989).
- Training is a methodical procedure for altering the attitudes, skills, and/ or motivation of current employees in order to better align employee traits with job requirements (Milkovich and Boudreau, 1998).

Need for Training

Training has largely caught up, especially in industries. This is due to the abrupt and competitive shift that is taking place in the world. However, the following factors can be used to determine the requirement for training:

- The quick changes in both technology and employment.
- Acute and chronic skill deficit

Changes in workforce expectations and demographics. Pressure from the market and competition to raise the calibre of goods and services.

Training programmes offered to extension staff include There are basically two forms of this:

1. Pre-service Training

It is a procedure through which people are prepared to enter a certain type of professional career, such as one in engineering, medicine, or agriculture.

Prior to any appointment, an individual must complete professional training designed to prepare them for starting a new line of work. According to Swanson (1984), it is a course of instruction that gets someone ready for a career in extension and typically results in a diploma, certificate, degree, or other credential in one or more of the following fields: agriculture, fisheries, forestry, animal and/or veterinary science, or home science.

The Veterinary Department likes to accept only Veterinary graduates released from the Universities, just as the State Departments of Agriculture currently favour University graduates for admittance into their extension services.

2. In-Service Training

It is intended for employed candidates who are currently in service. In-service training is a procedure for staff development that aims to enhance an incumbent's performance in a position with specific work responsibilities.

It encourages people to advance their careers. The chance to establish a feeling of purpose is offered by in-service training, which is a problem-centered, learner-oriented, and time-bound set of activities. boost the participants' capacity to learn new information and develop technical proficiency.

In-Service training is of different types, some of them are as follows:

i. **Orientation Training** Typically, newly assigned extension staff receive this training. It offers an introduction to working for the government and addresses queries that a new hire is likely to have. This phrase is also used to describe in-service training In order for staff to be suitably oriented toward meeting the requirements of a new circumstance, extension personnel in a new responsibility enjoys a new operational programme.

ii. **Induction / portal / vestibule Training** New extension staff receives induction training as soon as they are hired and before they are placed in a specific location to serve, typically as an Assistant Agriculture Officer, Agriculture Officer, or Extension Officer.

iii. **Maintenance or refresher training** To refresh their knowledge and abilities before passing them on to trainees, trainers from training centres and universities were the original target audience for this course. The phrase refers to any new training intended to improve the professional competence of extension staff, particularly in their area of expertise.

    This instruction is typically given to extension staff later in their careers. As it comes to upgrading technical knowledge and skill of extension staff, this training is quite important to them. This covers the review of older materials as well as fresh information and new methodologies.

Employees receive this kind of training in order to maintain their highest level of performance and avoid becoming stagnant.

iv. **Retraining** It refers to the efforts designed to prepare an individual for a new assignment or a broadened aspect of the old specialty.

v. **Career or development training / Training for professional qualification**

The purpose of this kind of training is to improve an employee's knowledge, abilities, and skills so they may take on more responsibility as they advance in their careers.

To encourage personnel to advance to higher levels of the administrative hierarchy, this training may result in the employees earning a higher degree (undergraduate or postgraduate) or diploma (promotions).

The Directorate of Extension runs such a programme on an annual basis under which it provides extension employees with fixed monthly stipends to cover their costs of housing, lodging, and tuition fees in addition to the salaries and benefits they receive from their own employing companies. Only exceptional extension staff who are younger than 45 years old are eligible for these courses.

Training to Farmers

All agricultural universities offer a regular farmer training programme. For aspiring farmers, there are training facilities. They also set up quick courses for farmers in some places. Crop management, livestock feeding and management, and plant protection are all covered in the course. The following points should be taken into account for such training.

1. Time of holding the training, i.e., when they are comparatively unburdened by such agricultural activities. The variations here will depend on the weather and season. If T.N., March through May for the Kharif crop and August through September for the Rabi crop are the best times to hold agricultural training courses.
2. Duration of course: For farmers who are actively farming, a one-week course is adequate. For special topics like using irrigation facilities and water management, operating tools, and plant protection, it may be of two or three days in length.
3. Course location: In addition to physical facilities, the location where the farmers may observe the actual crop, method demonstrations, operations with certain tools and implements, or specific treatments like the application of fertiliser, must be given significant consideration.

4. Production cum demonstration camps and discussion groups of the farmers: based demonstration camps should be set up in the villages because the farmers cannot afford to be away from their crops and homes.

Each primary crop should have these planned beforehand. To allow the farmers to return home the same evening, the training should only last one or two days and the participants should all be from the same village or a group of surrounding villages. The farmers will receive technical training right in their communities, and the subjects may be relevant to their particular needs.

Training Process

The individual who is currently working for the organisation will be the focus of any training. The focus will be different depending on where it is in the training process, both at the beginning and the finish. The effectiveness of training is defined as the implementation of what a person has learnt during the training process.

The training process has three phases as follows

- Pre-training
- Training
- Post-training

Pre-training phase

- The pre-training process begins with comprehension of the circumstance, which necessitates more effective behaviour.
- Analysis of the circumstance and job on which improved performance is to be attained is a key component of the process.
- The pre-training process begins with an explanation of the task that will be altered.
- For the training programme to be created to satisfy those needs, knowledge of the operational requirements of the work must also be known in addition to the technical requirements of the position.

Training process – models

There are several models for training processes, of which there are three important models.

1. Simple model of training process
2. Elaborated model of training process
3. Spiral model of training process

Simple Model of the Training Process

The main goal of the training process as a whole is for employees to behave more effectively while they are working for the firm. Improvement is the dependent variable in the straightforward training process, whereas individuals and organisations are the independent factors. Fig. 1 displays a training model in its most basic form.

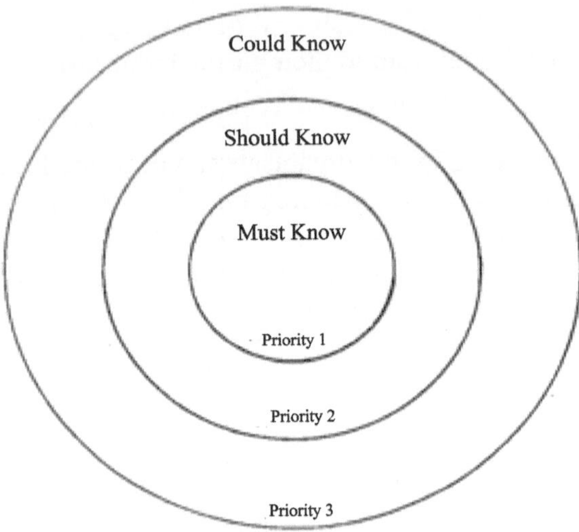

Figure 2. Simple Model of the Training Process

Elaborated Model

But contrary to what figure 1 might imply, training is a more intricate process. First and foremost, the training system must be integrated. It could be a transient system, like a one-time programme, or a long-term organisation, like a training department. In either scenario, the system's trainers gain knowledge from the many possibilities for evaluating their efficacy, or via feedback. As a result, the intervening and independent variables change into dependent variables.

In figure 2, this elaboration is displayed.

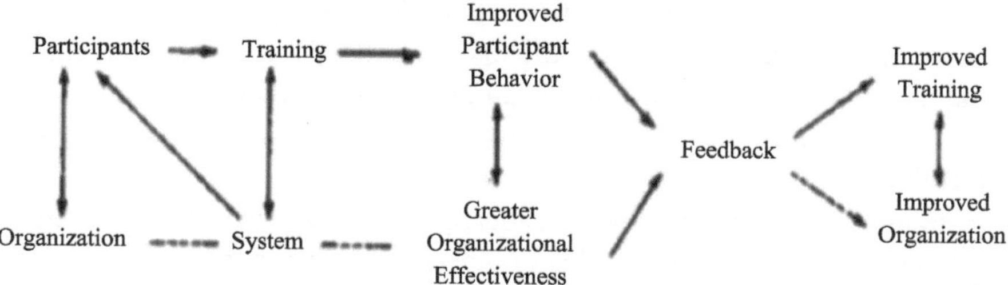

Figure 3. Elaborated Model of the Training Process

Figure 3 shows the process as a whole, with its three partners and three stages. It is a spiral model that overlaps the employees currently working for the firm. A training programme, as well as each event and sequence of events that make up the programme, can be visualised using this spiral model. For instance, the stage where new knowledge and abilities are really developed and acquired.

Spiral Model

The spiral diagram in figure 3 depicts the stages that participants go through as they learn, then they return to their occupations (hopefully with improved skills). The other two partners provide "inputs" to help the participants at different points throughout the process. These inputs are represented by arrows, with arrows coming from inside the spiral representing the work organization's inputs and arrows coming from outside the spiral representing the training institutions' inputs. The arrows serve only as visual aids. The spiral feedback system is built into the huge helix itself. This spiral model will be used to explain the training process, with a further turn toward participants and work organisations.

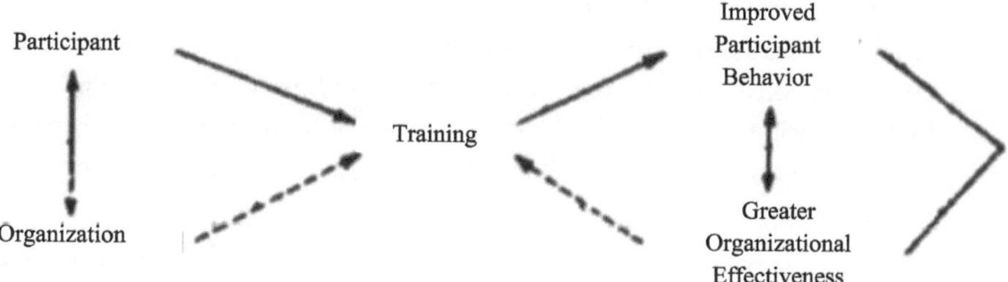

Figure 4. Spiral Model of the Training Process

Training Strategy

First and foremost, clear objectives and methods are necessary for effective training. In that sense, it is similar to a production process in that both methods and ends must be appropriate for the task at hand. Clear guidelines must be provided for each component of the training task, including the time, talent, and facilities needed for it, to relate them. The first responsibility is to make sure of this.

Four strategic questions must be considered, each of which will be looked at in turn. First and second are examples of outside techniques,

- Establishing training goals
- Defining training specifications
- The next two are outcomes of internal strategy.
- Organizing the training inputs and
- Improving the training institution
- The actions of the instructed individuals. It should also be taken into account how the organisation will react to the trainee's newfound knowledge and abilities after he returns from training.
- Who feels that this new behaviour is necessary? For a training programme to be effective, consideration must be given to the student's immediate supervisor, the organisation, or the trainee himself.

Training phase

- The majority of training programmes would be one-time events like sessions, evening classes, or residential courses.
- In the training programme, the trainee is exposed to new material, new people, and a new environment, which initially makes the participant uneasy. Later, when the subject that would be useful and stimulating is taught, the participant will concentrate on the subject of his interest and will be in step with the other participants.
- He would be asking himself a few questions, such as whether he has the necessary skills for the position, whether he has been given the chance to work honestly for the organisation, or whether the organisation is trying to keep him away so that it may implement the programme he had fiercely opposed.
- There is no assurance that the student will learn what he has chosen to learn with all of these questions running through his head. His thoughts would wander, and he would pick up information from the offered training programme that was of interest to him. This selection

error would be brought about by the trainee not possessing the requisite skills, by the training institution using inappropriate training design and technique, etc.

- Finally, after conquering all of the challenges in the initial phase of the training programme, the participant would investigate what interests him the most in a training environment. If he finds it useful after exploring, he gives it another try and evaluates its success and satisfaction. There would be numerous trials that were repeated.
- If he is happy with the outcomes, he decides to implement it in his company; but, if he finds it to be ineffective, he discards it and tries a different approach, and in some situations, he may opt to stop learning altogether.

Post-training phase

- At this point, the circumstance changes, and the participant returns to his workplace where he meets his coworkers, family members, etc. Since he had been away from them for some time and had returned having learned some new concepts, he goes prepared and with some eagerness.
- Newly acquired skills are modified to match the demands of the workplace. The participant would put his training to use for the advancement of his organisation if the organisation was supportive and encouraging. Some organisations would provide assistance to the trainees so they could stay in touch with the training facility even after the training programme. On the other hand, he would feel more burdened and work harder to make up for missed time if the company disliked his absence and if his desk was full of work. He would lose interest in using his training, and his relationship with the training facility would likewise end.

Designing Extension Training Programmes

A training plan gives training a structure, while a training program's design determines its substance. A training plan outlines the general criteria that must be followed for training to occur in accordance with the extension personnel's evaluated training needs within the framework of the extension training policy.

The training strategy is operationalized and actual instruction is provided through the design of the training programme. The success of a training intervention will be greatly increased by a well-designed training programme. Therefore, a poorly constructed training programme is considered to be unsuccessful. The steps in creating a training programme are as follows:

A. Objectives of training programmes

A precise explanation of the training program's objectives is the first step in the design process. These goals must be founded on the extension staff's Training Needs Assessment (TNA) and listed in priority order from general to specific goals. These goals must be expressed in terms of the information, abilities, attitudes, and characteristics that the trainee will have attained by the completion of the training course.

The learners will be able to clearly understand what to expect from training if the program's objectives are clearly stated.

The goals of a training programme can be divided into two groups, general behavioural goals and specific behavioural goals, at the most basic level of treatment. The objectives of a training programme must include both kinds of objectives.

At a more advanced level of therapy, the training objectives can be divided into three classes of Cognitive Objectives, Psycho-Motor Objectives, and Affective Objectives, and their sub-classes, in accordance with Bloom's taxonomy of educational objectives.

If the objectives, learning experience, and evaluation components of the design of a training programme are conceptualised as (a), (b), and (c), respectively, then the objectives serve as the foundation upon which the learning experience and evaluation components of the design of a training programme could be built. This emphasises the significance of the objectives in the design of a training programme.

B. Skill - Mix The second step in the design of training programme is determination of appropriate skill-mix for different levels of extension personnel.

Katz postulate three types of skills for a manager, namely (i) Technical Skills, (ii) Human Skills, and (iii) Conceptual Skills as proposed by Misra (1990).

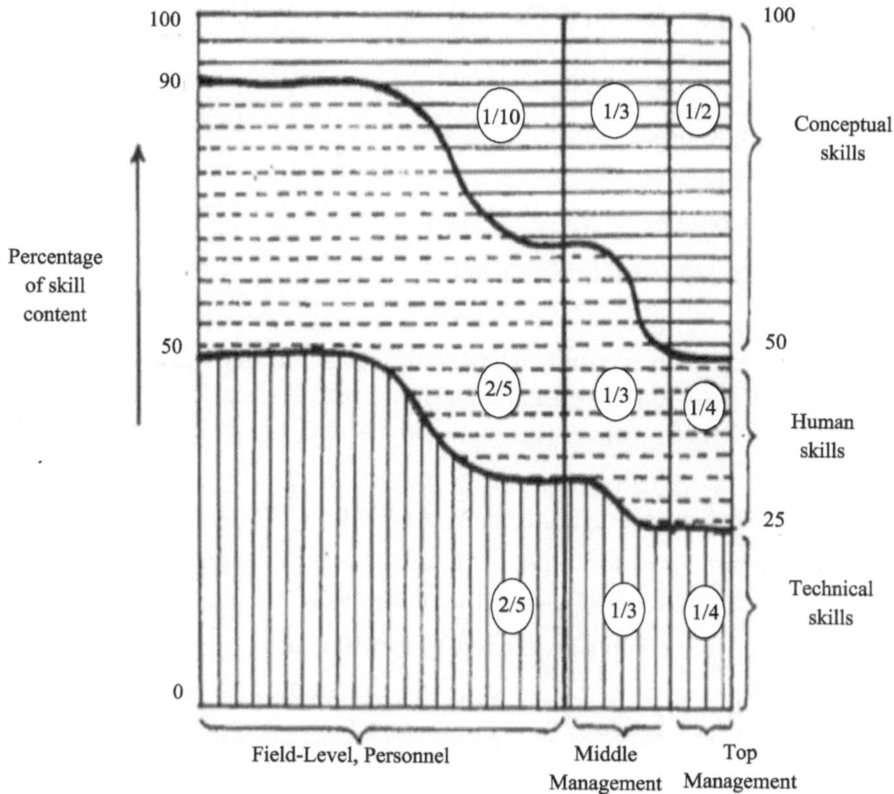

Figure 5. Skill mixes for the different levels of Extension Personnel (Source: Misra, D.C. 1990, New Dimension in Extension Training)

For example, field-level personnel like Village Level Extension workers and Agricultural Extension Officers require technical skills in ample measure, human skills in fairly good measure and conceptual skills in moderate measure.

C. Curriculum Development

The creation of a suitable training curriculum is the next stage in the design of a training programme. There are two reasons why curriculum development is necessary. It is necessary to establish a specific curriculum for a training course that is organised in response to the assessed training needs of extension employees that result from the shifting needs of farmers. Since there is no pre-existing curriculum for the purpose, a unique curriculum must be created for a unique training course with a unique target audience. Its transdisciplinary nature presents a challenge. The creation of curricula is necessary to prepare for upcoming demands.

Components of a Standard Curriculum

- Course objectives
- Achievement Targets
- Course Structure
- Assessment
- Course Contents

Developing Standard Curriculum

Objective

Prior to creating the curriculum, we must decide on the general and specialised training goals based on the estimated training requirements of extension staff. In the end, the precise objectives should be divided into distinct informational components.

a) Subject Matter - Decision Structure Matrix

The target group's position on a decision structure - subject matter matrix is crucial for selecting the training curriculum's content.

b) The concentric circles approach to curriculum

Thirdly, we must choose the subjects and the amount of them that must be taught in order to create the training objectives. Subject prioritization is necessary.

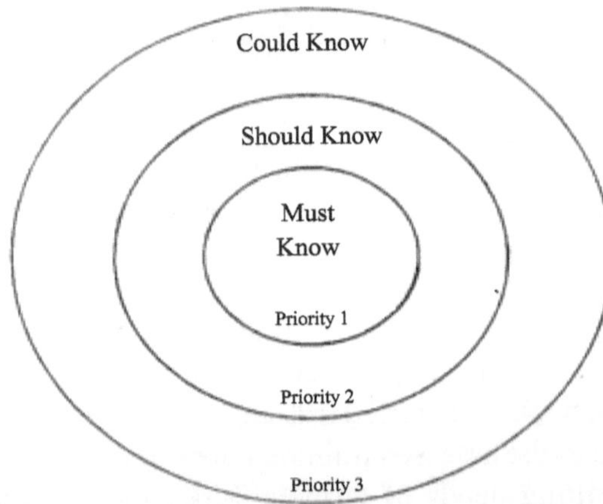

Figure 6. The Concentric Circles Approach to Curriculum

The three types of knowledge that make up the "Concentric Circles Approach to Curriculum" are what must be known, what should be known, and what could be known.

In order to avoid drifting to the middle or outer circles at the expense of the inner circle, which has frequently been seen in practise, it is crucial to focus your efforts on the inner circle of "must know" concepts.

c) The Information Unit

A definition or description of a single concept constitutes an information unit. Every feature of the topic is expressed in terms of a distinct technical unit that can be enhanced, analysed, and connected to other elements in a logical or psychological order. It is simple to alter and combine objectives to get fresh training answers because all the material for each activity has been broken down into information units.

d) Training Methodology

If curriculum serves as the "heart" of a training programme, training techniques could be thought of as the "arteries" and "veins" that carry training messages to trainees and allow trainers and learners to simultaneously get feedback on the training programme. The level and educational background of the trainees, the training curriculum, and the amount of training time must all be taken into consideration when choosing the best training methodology. A training program's efficacy will undoubtedly increase if the training methods are chosen properly, but it will also almost surely decrease or be ruined if the wrong training methods are chosen.

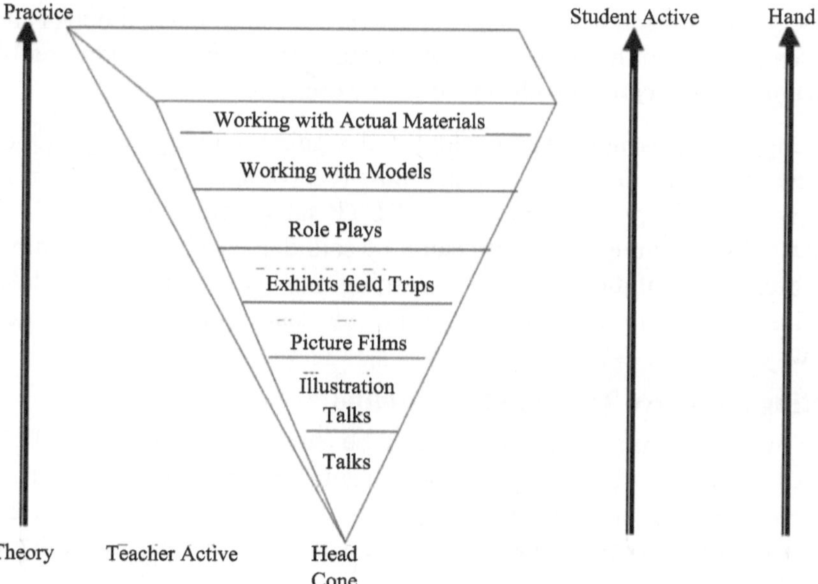

Figure 7. Extension training methodology cone (Source: Misra, D.C. 1990. New Direction in Extension Training)

Never forget a training technique. It is merely a tool to help you achieve your training goals. Never should it be considered a goal unto itself. Such a propensity is frequently observed in training practise and must be controlled since it interferes with the training objectives and decreases the efficacy of a training programme. The training process in detail is shown in Fig. 6.

e. Training Media

- Books, handouts, graphics, flipcharts, photographic prints, other printed materials, real targets, specimens, models, and simulation tools, as well as chalkboards, magnets, and flannel boards, are examples of non-projected media.
- Projected media, such as closed-circuit television video tape, slides and filmstrips, microfilm, projection, and opaque projectors (epidiascope).
- Audiovisual media, including public address systems, reel-to-reel and cassette tapes, records, and broadcast radio.

The proper training media selections will be influenced by the training methods as well as the audience and training objectives. Chalkboard and overhead projector may be sufficient for group discussions, although handouts may also be used as support. Training materials should only be used when necessary and not just because they are available.

f. Training Manuals and Handbooks

The training manuals and handbooks fall between the thorough text books and sporadic leaflets and bulletins in terms of coverage and content. Additionally, they concentrate on a carefully chosen area of expertise.

The training institutes are responsible for designing training programmes (DTP). The numerous DTP sub-systems must receive special attention from the training institutions. Only once several DTP subsystems have been handled expertly by a training institution can it be said that a training programme has been created. Institutions of higher learning must acknowledge this duty. Training institutions are no exception to the rule that reputations are earned the hard way.

Conducting an Active Training Programme

The only way a training programme can be completely successful is if effective exercises have been practised beforehand. It is important to focus on the program's physical arrangement, rapport-building, and content. Even the most beautiful programmes on paper are useless if the trainer has the delivery abilities to carry out the design specifications.

Steps to Conduct an Active Training Programme

1. Preparing yourself mentally

Feeling at ease with the course material thorough planning with plenty of notice preparation of training program's material activities Get connected with the participants and access course materials, manuals, spaces, audiovisual equipment, etc. If a question is posed and you do not know the solution, you might provide it as a group exercise or write it down and pledge to research it.Repeating a lesson may bore the instructor, but it won't bore a new student. Make sure to keep the participants' needs in mind rather than your own and create opportunities for you to learn from their experiences through dialogues.

2. Arranging the physical environment

The initial physical setup that participants experience will leave a lasting impression of the programme. The number of attendees, the speaker's style, and other aspects should all be taken into consideration while choosing the seating arrangements. If there isn't much writing involved in the programme, the participants might remove the tables and arrange the seats however they find most comfortable. Alternatively, if small subgroups are to be established, care should be made to ensure ample room between groups to prevent disruptions. Horseshoe arrangements are a common design. This can be transformed into a circle or a square. These all encourage group conversations with direct touch between each member. The participants themselves can assist in creating these arrangements for their personal comfort.

3. Greeting participants and establishing program

A strong welcome address makes for the best and most desired start. The trainer should be able to get inside each person's head, make them feel comfortable in their new surroundings, and let them express their emotions unreservedly. Consequently, a trainer should make sure that his programme has a positive greeting in order to establish connection with the participants. Prior to the session, participants can mingle more easily by taking a quick break. By getting to know each participant's name and making them feel at ease, the trainer can develop relationships. He or she should present each of them to the participants during the opening session, and then introduce himself with a hint of humble better knowledge.

Many other wordings are possible and can be addressed. The phrase "I have something for you" is just one example. "I've been through this too" creates a sense of "we" among the participants and the trainer, giving the impression that they are working with someone who has much more expertise and experience. The fact that the participants believe the trainer can relate to their issues and heavy workloads allows them to share their own experiences in this area. This salutation elevates the participants by saying, "I admire you." This is the best approach to show how much you admire the participant's traits and actions. Even if it may be for relatively simple deeds, the people are nonetheless greatly encouraged by such admiration.

4. Getting the best from the first 30 minutes of trainers

The most important 30 minutes of any class time are those, and a teacher should not squander them. According to Napien and Gershenfeld (1999), this time period, known as the "grave period," is when any excess hostility or antagonism will be masked by an air of politeness, caution, and reserve. During this period, the participants begin to understand what part they intend to play in the training programme and what they hope to accomplish.

Once participants are aware of their competency, start the class when scheduled without inciting impatience among them. One should establish trust by becoming a good fit for the group. The participant should have a clear understanding of the activities available to them as well as how and when they can connect with their hometown.

5. Reviewing the agenda

One should be made aware of what is going to be done, including what is anticipated of the programme and of the participants, from the very beginning of the programme. Writing down and clearly outlining the training objectives is a requirement. It is also necessary to offer the list of tasks that must be completed. They should be notified of the program's operation, including details about the accommodations, meal plans, and phone messages, among other things. It should also include a content outline and an explanation of the activities planned.

6. Inviting feedback

One must not neglect to ask for input on the agenda after examining it. The participants are given the chance to express their opinions or describe what they would like to see the programmes focus on more. Asking explicitly, "Does this fit what you intend to earn from this programme?" is the easiest strategy. Are there any additions you would like to make?The participant's input assists the trainer in adapting his programme, if possible, to meet their needs and continue to be compatible with them. Otherwise, the programme will be a waste of time with uninteresting content. After completing all of these procedures, one can confidently and easily begin the training programme itself.

Conclusion

Capacity building is a vital process in organizational development, focusing on enhancing individual and institutional capabilities to achieve mission objectives sustainably. At its core, training plays a pivotal role in capacity building, emerging as an indispensable component of HRD. This training encompasses various forms, including pre-service and in-service training, each tailored to meet the distinct needs of professionals at different career stages. The essence of training lies in its ability to enrich knowledge, skills, behavior, and attitudes, thereby fostering a more competent and productive workforce. With the rapid evolution of technology and shifts in workforce demographics and expectations, the need for continuous training has become more pronounced than ever. Training strategies, therefore, need to be carefully crafted, considering the dynamic nature of organizational and individual requirements. This includes setting clear objectives, developing appropriate curriculum, and employing effective training methodologies. Through a well-structured training process that includes pre-training, training, and post-training phases, organizations can significantly enhance their capacity, ensuring long-term success and adaptability in an increasingly competitive and changing world.

Answer the Following Questions

1. How does the design of a training curriculum contribute to the overall effectiveness of a capacity-building program, considering factors such as training objectives, skill-mix determination, and curriculum development stages?
2. Assess the significance of post-training phases in the capacity-building process, highlighting the impact of organizational support, work environment, and employee motivation on the successful application of newly acquired skills and knowledge in the workplace.
3. Develop a comprehensive training strategy for a hypothetical organization aiming to enhance its capacity in response to emerging technological advancements and shifting workforce expectations, outlining specific objectives, training methodologies, and post-training support mechanisms to ensure sustainable organizational growth and competitivene.

13

Information and Communication Technologies Applications in Transfer of Technology

Yanglem Lakshimai Devi

Department of Agricultural Economics and Extension, Lovely Professional University Phagwara, Punjab

Information and Communication Technology: Concept

ICT refers to an extensive array of systems and technologies dedicated to managing and delivering information and facilitating communication. This includes digital platforms such as the internet and the World Wide Web, as well as traditional media like radio, television—through cable and wireless methods—mobile phones, and printed materials. Accompanying these technologies are services and applications such as videoconferencing and online learning that utilize these mediums. Essentially, ICT is concerned with the utilization of technology to enable the flow of information via telecommunications, encapsulating all modalities used for capturing and broadcasting information on a global scale.

Key terms

Application: The action of putting something into operation

Technology: Application of scientific knowledge for practical purpose

ICT: Information and Communication Technology

ICT: Definition

Information and Communication Technology (ICT) can be defined as the collection of technologies that aid in the storing, processing, or transmission of data or information, or both.

Information and Communication Technology

The history of ICT for Development

ICT 4D 0.0: 1950s to late 1990s

ICT 4D 1.0: Late 1990s to Late 2000s

ICT 4D 2.0: Late 2000s Onwards

Role of ICT for Agricultural Development

Enhancing Agricultural Practicals Economically

E-commerce Integration

Advanced Warning Systems

Streamlined Access to Government Resources and Services

ICT Application	Disciption
Aqua (Almost All Questions Answered)	Farmer Knowledge Exchange form on the Internet, answering agricultural queries with context-specific information
Agrisnet (Agricultural Informatics and Commication Network)	Goverment scheme to provide ICT-enhanced servies to farmers, informing on inputs, schemes, soil health, and technology
Agmarknet (Agricultural Marketing Information System Network)	Portal for access to daily prices and arrivals data for commodities, including market trends and future prices
Aaqua (Almost All Questions Answered)	Online plateform responding to agricultural questions in four languages, providing expert advice with contextual information.

Agricultural Knowledge and Information System (AKIS)	World Bank and FAO system linking farmers with agricultural educators, researchs, and extension workers.
AGRIS	Global agricultural information network by the FAO, covering all aspects of agriculture.
AgNIC	Network of public and private agricultural libraries and information centers, providing global access to agricultural data.
CGIAR Learning Resource Centre (CGLRC)	Resource center providing electronic versions of CGIAR learning resources for agriculture and natural resource management.
VASAT	E-learning platform by ICRISAT, offering resources for rural communities, including an e-library and weather data.

According to Wikipedia, "ICT is a larger word for Information Technology (IT) that includes specifically the field of electronic communication in addition to IT". The definition of information technology is "the study, design, development, implementation, support, or management of computer-based information systems, including software applications and computer hardware." Information Technology (IT) is the "application of electronic computers and computer software to transform, store, protect, process, transfer, and retrieve data".

Overseas Development Institute (ODI) research defines ICT as "those technologies that can be utilized to interconnect information technology devices like personal computers (PCs) with communication technologies like telephones and their telecommunication networks." The PC and laptop with Internet and e-mail are the best examples.

The History of ICT for Development

The evolution of ICT may be loosely separated into three distinct phases. This is provided afterwards to De and Jirli (2011).

ICT 4D 0.0: Mid-1950s to Late 1990s

In this period, before the term 'ICT 4D' was coined, the primary use of technology revolved around computing and data processing within significant government operations and large-scale corporate sectors.

ICT 4D 1.0: Late 1990s to Late 2000s

Coinciding with the introduction of the Millennium Development Goals and the expansion of the Internet in affluent countries, there was a surge in the deployment of ICT infrastructure, along with numerous ICT initiatives in the developing world. Telecentres became prevalent, serving as hubs for disseminating knowledge on development topics such as health, education, and agricultural outreach to underserved populations. These centers began to increasingly offer government services online or in a hybrid format.

ICT 4 D 2.0: Late 2000s Onwards

While there's no clear boundary separating 1.0 from 2.0, this era is marked by a shift from reliance on telecentres to the adoption of mobile phones as the primary tool for ICT applications.

Role of ICT for Agricultural Development

The following factors have a crucial role in the development of agriculture through ICT:

Several key factors underscore the significant impact of ICT on agricultural advancement:

1. **Enhancing Agricultural Practices Economically:**
   a) ICT provides farmers with immediate access to essential information, such as best practice methods, availability of inputs and credit, weather predictions, market trends, and optimal pricing for their products.
2. **E-commerce Integration:**
   a) Farmers gain direct contact with local manufacturers, retailers, and wholesalers, enabling them to market their goods and manage transactions like orders online, with payments potentially processed offline. This digital marketplace offers entrepreneurs global market insights.
   b) Creation of Employment Opportunities
   c) ICT opens up job possibilities in rural areas for telecentre operators, expert consultants, and IT professionals by establishing rural information hubs.
3. **Advanced Warning Systems:**
   a) ICT can provide prompt alerts about potential threats of pests or diseases, as well as impending natural calamities such as droughts or floods, helping to minimize material losses.
4. **Streamlined Access to Government Resources and Services:**
   a) Utilizing ICT can streamline and lower the costs of obtaining information from government agencies, including services like accessing land records, online registration, and obtaining government forms.

Table 1: Popular ICT applications for Transfer of Technology

ICT Application	Description
AQUA (Almost All Questions Answered)	Farmer Knowledge Exchange Forum on the Internet, answering agricultural queries with context-specific information.
AGRISNET (Agricultural Informatics and Communication Network)	Government scheme to provide ICT-enhanced services to farmers, informing on inputs, schemes, soil health, and technology.
AGMARKNET (Agricultural Marketing Information System Network)	Portal for access to daily prices and arrivals data for commodities, including market trends and future prices.

Aaqua (Almost All Questions Answered)	Online platform responding to agricultural questions in four languages, providing expert advice with contextual information.
E-Krishi	Market-driven agriculture program in Kerala supported by IT-enabled agribusiness centers.
E-Sagu	IT-based system providing personalized agricultural advice to each farm, aiming to reduce costs and increase productivity.
DISK (Dairy Information and Services Kiosk)	ICT application to enhance milk production quality and manage dairy services, developed by the Indian Institute of Management.
M-Krishi (Mobile phone based ICT)	Mobile-based system offering farmers weather, soil, and market information tailored to their specific plots.
IRRI Rice Web	Comprehensive educational resource on rice by IRRI, including its history, cultivation, processing, and research.
Agricultural Knowledge and Information System (AKIS)	World Bank and FAO system linking farmers with agricultural educators, researchers, and extension workers.
AGRIS	Global agricultural information network by the FAO, covering all aspects of agriculture.
AgNIC	Network of public and private agricultural libraries and information centers, providing global access to agricultural data.
CGIAR Learning Resource Centre (CGLRC)	Resource center providing electronic versions of CGIAR learning resources for agriculture and natural resource management.
VASAT	E-learning platform by ICRISAT, offering resources for rural communities, including an e-library and weather data.
VERCON	FAO network using the Internet to strengthen research and extension connections within national agricultural systems.
Krishi Vigyan Kendra	ICT tool for monitoring activities of Krishi Vigyan Kendras and disseminating agricultural innovations.
Expert system	Software using knowledge and inference to solve complex problems, drawing on AI for knowledge-based information generation.

Conclusion

The integration of Information and Communication Technology (ICT) into the agricultural sector marks a transformative step in modernizing agriculture across various regions, particularly in developing countries. ICT applications like AQUA, AGRISNET, AGMARKNET, and others have revolutionized how farmers access critical information, enabling them to make informed decisions that enhance productivity and sustainability. These tools provide up-to-date information on weather patterns, market trends, and best agricultural practices, and they facilitate direct access to markets, contributing to the economic empowerment of farming communities. The employment opportunities created by these initiatives, such as telecentre managers and IT technicians, demonstrate the positive socio-economic impact of ICT beyond mere agricultural practices. Additionally, early warning systems for natural disasters and pest infestations contribute to risk mitigation and the preservation of agricultural investments. Access to government services and information has been streamlined, making it easier for farmers to navigate bureaucratic processes and benefit from governmental schemes. This not only saves time and reduces costs but also promotes transparency and efficiency in government-farmer interactions.

Answer the Following Questions

1. What is the distinction between Information Technology (IT) and Information and Communication Technology (ICT)?
2. Explain the evolution of ICT for development outlined in the text, distinguishing between the three phases identified and highlighting key developments within each phase.
3. Considering the role of ICT in agricultural development, propose a plan outlining how a rural community can effectively utilize ICT applications like AQUA, AGRISNET, and M-Krishi to improve agricultural productivity and market access.

14

Monitoring and Evaluation in the Extension Programme

Chethan Patil N.D.

Department of Agricultural Economics and Extension, Lovely Professional University Phagwara, Punjab

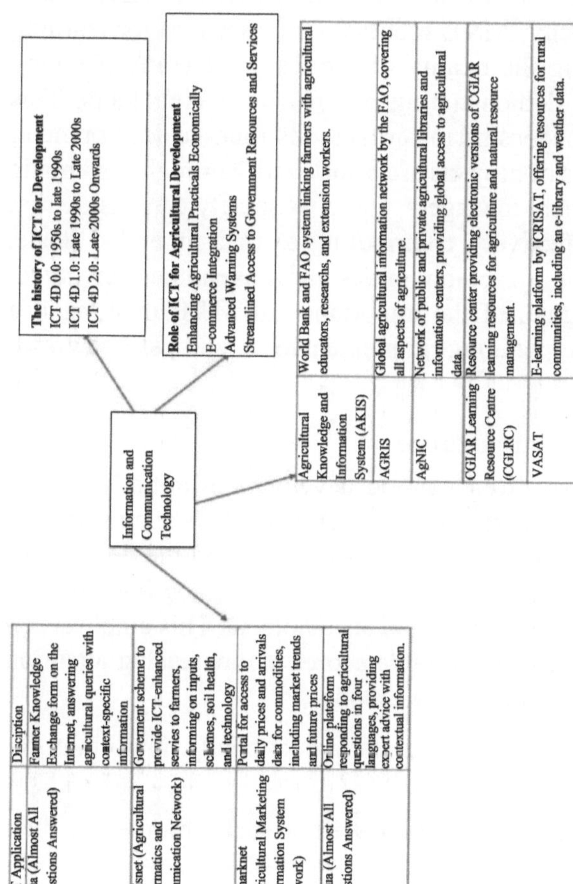

Figure 1: Overview of the presentation (Credit: Jarial, S)

Introduction

The 'cutting edge' of any development is the projects. No matter how well planned, a poorly executed project will waste valuable resources. India has pioneered many poverty-reduction programmes in agriculture, rural development, health and family welfare, education, women's and children's development, drinking water, and other fields. According to an analysis of these initiatives, monitoring and suitable mid-course corrective measures are crucial to accomplishing project objectives.

Monitoring and Evaluation (M&E) is becoming increasingly important for project and portfolio management. Development projects must perform better, and this is widely recognised. Monitoring and evaluation are crucial to the project cycle because they hold development investments accountable. Project success depends on proper monitoring and evaluation. The statement from the World Bank (2004) underscores the crucial role of Monitoring and Evaluation (M&E) in the development sector. M&E processes are essential for learning from past initiatives, enhancing the quality of services, efficiently planning and allocating resources, and demonstrating progress to stakeholders. This emphasis on M&E reflects a broader shift towards results-focused development, where the impact and outcomes of projects are prioritized. Through systematic M&E, governments, development managers, and civil society can ensure that development activities are effectively contributing to their intended goals, thereby maximizing the benefits for communities and stakeholders involved. The focus on results has heightened the importance of M&E, making it a fundamental component in the planning, implementation, and assessment of development projects.

Monitoring and Evaluation: Importance

The tracking and assessment of extension and development initiatives offer government representatives, development leaders, and members of civil society enhanced tools for learning from past experiences, enhancing the delivery of services, organizing and distributing resources, and showcasing outcomes as a component of being accountable to principal stakeholders. This emphasis on outcomes within the development sector underscores the increasing attention on monitoring and evaluation. (World Bank, 2004).

Monitoring and evaluation (M&E) processes are critically important for several reasons:

- They provide ongoing insights into how well projects are meeting their objectives.

- They enable the early detection of issues, allowing for timely interventions and solutions.
- They ensure that projects are accessible to all segments of the target population.
- They assess the efficiency of project components, recommending enhancements when necessary.
- They contribute to the formative assessment of a project's potential to meet its overarching goals.
- They lay the groundwork for developing effective planning guidelines for future initiatives, according to Bamberger *et al.* (1986).
- They inform sector assistance strategies by analyzing the outcomes of past policy and project evaluations, highlighting strengths and areas for improvement in implementation.
- They enhance project design through the application of tools like the logical framework, which facilitates the careful selection of performance indicators, thereby testing and improving project objectives.
- They involve stakeholders in the design and implementation phases, fostering a sense of ownership over project outcomes, which enhances sustainability and accountability. The collaborative setting of objectives and indicators ensures that goals are mutually embraced.
- They signal the necessity for adjustments during the project's lifecycle, as continuous information flow allows managers to monitor progress and make necessary operational changes.

Concept of Monitoring

"Monitor" comes from Latin root and means 'warn'. Management information systems need monitoring. Managers need information to manage extension and development projects.

Four main elements make up a conceptual framework for extension monitoring:

i. An organisation;
ii. A monitoring and evaluation (M & E) unit;
iii. A matrix of information needs; and
iv. A monitoring and evaluation cycle.

Top management gets information from the monitoring unit and other sources. This affects programme delivery, planning, and sustainability. This leads to institutional development, "the process of improving institutions' capacity to make effective use of available human and financial resources."

Monitoring as a concept involves comparing actual activity and outcome progress to previously established objectives. To learn from experiences (the learning function), account for resources used and results obtained (the monitoring function), and make decisions that will effectively move projects and programmes towards their goals (the steering function), monitoring is the systematic collection, analysis, and use of information from projects and programmes (War Child, 2006).

Bamberger *et al.* (1986) define monitoring as: "an internal project activity designed to provide constant feedback on the progress of a project, the problems it is facing and the efficiency with which it is being implemented." Monitoring is undertaken or performed while a project or programme or scheme is being implemented. It is done to improve its design and function while in action.

The term "monitoring" is typically used to refer to a process of periodically observing the progress of the programme or project to identify any weaknesses or shortcomings and take corrective action to maximise the effectiveness of the programme or project. This context typically refers to non-formal education or extension education and development. However, if any of the participants misreport facts, the monitoring system will lose its trust and be unable to fulfil any useful functions.

Approaches for Monitoring

Three monitoring methods exist: result-oriented, constructivist, and reflexive. Each approach includes principles, methods, and tools for (system) innovation projects. They differ greatly in their views of reality, processes, outcomes, and ways to facilitate, manage, or modify them. The best method depends on the project, setting, and monitoring and evaluation goals. In practical terms, it may be advantageous to integrate methods from various approaches to leverage their strengths.

Table: 1 Approach for monitoring

	Result-oriented approach	**Constructivist approach**	**Reflexive approach**
Methods	Log Frames, Logic Charts, Theory of Chang	Learning Histories, Evaluation, Most Significant Change	Reflexive Monitoring in Action/ Reflexive Process Monitoring / Interactive Learning Approach

Objective	Accountability and managing	Learning from each other and modifying processes Agenda setting	Learning, change of practices and their institutional setting
Paradigm	Reality exists and can be measured/defined objectively	Reality is constructed through interaction and negotiation.	Reality has to be reconstructed/ a new reality has to be developed
Focus	Results/predefined objectives or procedures	Meanings and values, based on negotiations	Calling existing practices and institutional settings into question

Source: Mierlo B. V. 2018. Approaches and Methods for Monitoring and Evaluation. http:/ edepot.wur.nl/185027

Principles of Monitoring

The acronym for monitoring is **STRDPFACTS.**

1. **"Monitoring must be simple"**: A complex monitoring system fails; simplification and prioritization of issues are key.
2. **"Monitoring must be timely"**: Timely monitoring is crucial for prompt management action, linking monitoring's credibility to its promptness.
3. **"Monitoring must be relevant"**: It should focus only on relevant parameters to program objectives, preventing the generation of unused or unusable information for management.
4. **"Information provided through monitoring should be dependable"**: Management will trust monitoring data if it is accurate.
5. **"Monitoring efforts should be participatory"**: Efforts should ensure participation from all extension stakeholders, including field staff, specialists, and clients (farmers).
6. **"Monitoring must be flexible"**: Its iterative and routine nature should not result in rigidity.
7. **"Monitoring should be action-oriented"**: Monitoring should be practical and focused on the needs of its clients, avoiding the generation of unnecessary information.
8. **"Monitoring must be cost-effective"**: Monitoring efforts should be cost-effective, emphasizing simplicity, relevance, and accuracy. Computerization can further enhance cost-effectiveness by saving staff hours in data processing.
9. **"Monitoring efforts should be top management oriented"**: Monitoring systems should align with top management's needs but also ensure benefits for information providers to maintain data quality.

10. "**Monitoring units represent specialised undertakings**": Monitoring involves diagnosing problems and proposing practical solutions as well as data collection and analysis.

Concept of Evaluation

Evaluation' is a derivative of Latin word 'Valere' means strength. From 'Valere' comes the word 'Value' meaning worth or quality of something. Evaluation may be defined as the process or method of determining the worth or quality of something.

Evaluation is a more thorough process than monitoring. Evaluation means deciding what an object or phenomenon is worth. To inform the design of future projects, evaluation is a study of a project's results (changes in income, housing quality, benefit distribution, cost-effectiveness, etc.). Evaluation is a procedure that is "primarily used to assist in the selection and design of future projects," according to Bamberger *et al.* Evaluation studies can determine how well a project achieved its goals (such as an increase in income, higher-quality housing, benefit distribution across various groups, etc.) and how cost-effective it was in comparison to other options.

The general goals of monitoring and evaluation can now be succinctly summarised as follows in light of the aforementioned discussion:

- To list the benefits and drawbacks.
- To offer the implementing agency feedback.
- To be aware of the actual arrangements being made
- To identify the issues that need to be fixed.
- To understand the degree of target-setting success.
- To assess if the funds were used in a suitable manner.
- To determine whether the project or programme is on track.

Monitoring and Evaluation Compared

Monitoring is the routine gathering of data about active projects, programmes, and programmes. Monitoring and assessment are essential for a programme, scheme, or project. The major goal of the review is to improve the programme by highlighting its strengths and weaknesses, not to demoralise the staff or the initiative. It is a procedure associated with reviewing the programming one last time and improving it. The programmes' pre-planning, planning, and implementation phases are all covered by the evaluation. In other words, evaluation addresses issues that arise before programme implementation, throughout programme operation, and following programme completion.

Evaluation is essential in science to determine what has been accomplished, what goals have been met, what flaws or failures have occurred, and how to weight them. The concerns of any other social process evaluation are similar to those of technologically based educational evaluation.

Types and Process of Evaluation

Even when planning and constructing a programme or project, the context in which it is being considered is assessed. After the project or programme is started, several inputs—physical, human, financial, and technical—are used in its execution. These inputs go through several processes aimed at producing the desired results, which are then manifested as various outcomes, products, or consequences. An evaluation may consider all of these factors collectively or concentrate on one or more specific aspects of a certain course.

However, to increase the validity, objectivity, and fairness of the assessment process, both internal individuals (those involved in the implementation of a policy, scheme, project, or programme) and external individuals or agencies can conduct the evaluation. Thus, we will concentrate on the various types and evaluation methods in this section.

Types of Evaluation

Different types of evaluation exist based on the many factors or criteria taken into account, which are covered in more detail below.

Types Based on the Aspects Covered

A program's actual context comes before it is planned and developed. After a programme or project is launched, various activities occur. Various inputs and processes result in the consequences, influence, output, or outcome. Thus, the program's aspects include the context, inputs, procedures, and effects/impact. Evaluations might be comprehensive and all-encompassing or can focus on a single area of the programme. Evaluation can be divided into the following forms according to the aspect(s) of the programme or project covered:

Context evaluation: It assesses the environment in which a project or plan is being developed and its viability. Before creating a programme based on a perceived need, this is done. In terms of the demands, requirements of the people, and the physical elements of the place in the context, it considers various factors of the current situation and the ground realities.

Input evaluation: It considers the various types of inputs used since the start of the implementation of a programme or project, including human, financial, and technological inputs. It aids in determining the kind, scope, calibre, sufficiency, and timeliness of various programming inputs.

Process evaluation: It entails assessing the nature and effectiveness of the project's activities or tactics. It assesses what has been accomplished, who has accomplished what and how much, the variety and calibre of the activities, *etc*. It looks for solutions to issues like the ones below.

Do all project activities follow the timetable and/or plan? If not, were the proposed actions modified in any way? And if so, why?

Are the materials, the content, and how it was presented high quality?

Are the right actions being used to ensure the project reaches its target audience?

Are the primary actors and the involved parties satisfied?

Impact/outcome evaluation: Evaluation of the project's impact and results entails determining whether the results met or exceeded expectations. In other words, the degree to which the pertinent endeavour has succeeded in achieving its aims. Impact evaluation assesses how well and far the goals were accomplished, whereas outcome evaluation assesses how effectively the aim was accomplished. It looks for answers to issues like: To what extent has the project achieved its goals?

How successful has the initiative been at achieving its goals?

Are there any outside-the-project variables that have aided or obstructed the desired change?

What steps have been taken to accomplish the goal?

Has the project had any unanticipated effects or changes?

Types based on the stage at which evaluation is done

A programme, project, or scheme may be evaluated while it is still in progress, after, or after it has ended. The evaluation is, therefore, one of the following sorts.

Formative evaluation: Pre-testing is a form of formative evaluation used to determine the campaign evaluation tactics or chosen process's strengths and shortcomings before and during execution. The programme is customised to the target audience thanks to formative research. Before they are deployed on a broad scale, messages, procedures, or products are tested on a small group of people. This kind of review enables essential changes before the entire effort is carried out. Before the activity is implemented on a broad scale or to improve the activity's quality, its primary goal is to maximise the change or effect of that activity for the programme's success.

Improvement of operations is the main goal of evaluation; critical decisions

1. An educational programme, in general, is an imperfect venture, achieving somewhat less competently than what its operators intend, and

2. The most important purpose of the evaluation is the improvement of operations; the important judgments to be made relate to factors that can be altered.

As a result, formative assessment aims to offer specific information and judgements that will help improve a subpar operation. Formative evaluation's logic must be entirely consistent with the requirement for social action in the actual world and the contextual uncertainties surrounding it. It refers to systems in process and attempts to provide ways and means of improving rather than just pronouncing judgment that will demoralise and defeat the motivated efforts of those involved in the process.

Summative evaluation examines the project, scheme, or Extension and programme monitoring and assessment from beginning to end. It is performed after the project, scheme, or programme. It is intended to serve as a summary and guide decisions regarding whether to continue the project (or its specific components) and whether using it in other contexts would be beneficial. It entails looking for answers to issues like:

1. What were the primary advantages and disappointments?
2. What were the main benefits and disappointments?
3. What factors helped and hindered the project?
4. What could be the advice to others willing to embark on something similar?
5. What aspects can and will be sustained, and how?
6. Is it worth continuing in its current form? Why/why not?
7. What recommendations have emerged about where to go from here

Summative evaluation: which is comprehensive and gathers data and renders judgements about all relevant elements, including strategies, processes, activities, and outcomes, gives an understanding of the eventual impact or outcome. The evaluation is a judgment on the value or merit of the specified plan, project, or programme. Usually, decision-making calls for this kind of examination. The following are some possible decision alternatives: spreading the intervention to additional organisations or sites, continuing funding, increasing funding; continuing on probationary status; modifying and trying again, or ending it if it is not justified to continue.

Types by Evaluating Agency

Evaluations are easily divided into two types by agency.

i) **Internal evaluation**: It is the evaluation conducted by the implementing agency itself to know the progress of the programme and its outcomes.

ii) **External evaluation**: It is the evaluation conducted by an external agency by following the same procedures and guidelines of evaluation in measuring the programme and its outcomes.

Suchman (1976) identified five different types of measurements as part of the evaluation: i) Measurement of effort; ii) Measurement of performance; iii) Measurement of the adequacy of effort; iv) Measurement of project efficiency; and v) Process evaluation - assess overall functioning of the project in all its dimensions of co-ordination, structure, planning, leadership roles and other aspects as its collective measures.

Steps Involved in the Evaluation Process

We must understand the procedures involved in the evaluation process to conduct the evaluation. The four crucial processes that makeup the most competent evaluations are best defined as steps or stages.

1. Description: The first stage describes the phenomena that need to be examined. These descriptions are typically verbal, graphic, and graphical and are frequently more profound.
2. Measurement: This stage is essential if a precise assessment is to come next. Most researchers in the physical and social sciences maintain that descriptions lacking quantitative data are insufficient as a foundation for comparative analysis. Sometimes, it is possible to "by inspection" identify any differences that may exist. Still, without measurements (expressions of the descriptions in numerical terms), the importance of the contrasts can only be inferred.
3. Assessment: Assessment is the comparison of two or more measurements. For instance, comparing two results from two learners can indicate which one has progressed more. It is also possible to determine whether a learning change occurred by comparing two measurements made of the same students at two distinct points. Assessment activities can even be used to identify the statistical significance of these changes (gains, losses, relative competence, *etc.*). However, making statements like "the gain is significant and the learners have achieved well" or "the competency is adequate" goes beyond assessment and instead represents the evaluation's findings.
4. Evaluation: This step involves assigning a value judgment to an assessment's findings. In other words, evaluation is assessing the value or significance of an empirical discovery.

Conclusion

Monitoring and evaluation are crucial components of any project or program. Through systematic monitoring, organisations can track progress, identify challenges, and make necessary adjustments to meet project objectives. Evaluation allows for an in-depth analysis of the project's effectiveness, efficiency, and impact. By gathering and analysing data, organisations can make informed decisions, learn from past experiences, and improve future interventions. Overall, monitoring and evaluation provide valuable insights for evidence-based decision-making, accountability, and continuous improvement in developing and implementing projects and programs.

Knowledge: Describe the main differences between monitoring and evaluation within the context of extension programmes as outlined by Dr. Chethan Patil N. D. How do these functions contribute to the effectiveness of development projects?

Answer the Following Questions

1. Explain the importance of the three approaches to monitoring (result-oriented, constructivist, and reflexive) and how each approach contributes to the overall success of extension projects. Provide examples of methods associated with each approach as mentioned in the chapter.
2. Considering the principles of monitoring summarized by the acronym STRDPFACTS, propose how an extension worker might apply these principles to enhance the monitoring of a rural development project. Include examples of simple, timely, and relevant monitoring activities.
3. Analyze the types of evaluation (context, input, process, and impact/outcome) and discuss how each type can inform different stages of a project lifecycle. Provide an example of how input evaluation might be used to improve a specific aspect of an extension project.
4. Critically evaluate the significance of incorporating both internal and external evaluations in the success of extension programmes. Discuss the potential strengths and weaknesses of relying predominantly on one type over the other, using insights from the chapter.

15

New Trends in Agriculture Extension and Communication

***Neela Madhav Patnaik*[1] *and Usha Das*[2]**

[1]*ICAR- Mahatma Gandhi Integrated Farming Research Institue, Motihari Bihar-845429*

[2]*Department of Social Science, College of Horticulture and Forestry, Pasighat Arunachal Pradesh-791102*

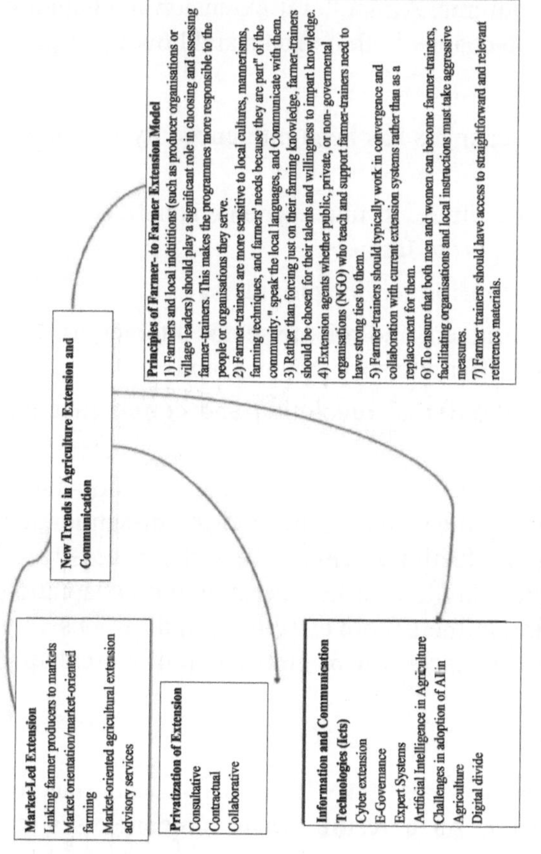

Figure 1: Overview of the chapter. (Credit: Jarial, S)

The 1980s and 1990s saw a few shifts in how we view development. There has been a significant ideological change in favour of privatisation. Since the 1990s, there has been an increase in the participation of the private sector (which deals with agro-inputs, agribusiness, and financial services), non-governmental organisations (both local and international), producer groups, cooperatives, and associations, as well as independent and connected to or employed by agri-business/producer associations consultants and ICT (Information and Communication technologies) based services.

Along with this, there is a growing understanding that those who provide agricultural extension services must assume new roles and possess new skills in order to effectively address the new challenges in agricultural development, including declining water availability, worsening soil degradation, changing and uncertain climate and markets, and the quick adoption of new ICTs. This chapter gives a broad overview of the general trends in agriculture extension and the forces that compelled it to widen its scope, accept pluralism, test out various finance and delivery methods, and re-evaluate some of its core presumptions and operational paradigms. Agricultural extension is changing everywhere, and there is pressure to change both its goals and how it is run.

Drivers of Change

The call for agricultural extension changes has been influenced by four main issues. Here are some of them:

1. The evolving character of agriculture, its unprecedented challenges, and the requirement to extend support to farmers;
2. Increasing the diversity of extension service providers;
3. A fresh look at how the government and private sector interact, as well as novel ways to finance and offer advisory services; and
4. Renewed perceptions from the digital revolution and communication and innovation research.

Due to the aforementioned emerging needs, extension services must now focus on a wider range of goals, including those that go beyond the dissemination of new technology and raising productivity. This covers the necessity of assisting farmers in better understanding the market, assisting with adaptation to market demands, and connecting farmers more effectively and responsively to domestic and international marketplaces where globalisation is escalating competitiveness.

Privatization of Extension

All around the world, extension services have historically been planned and provided by the public sector. As a result, when someone uses the term "extension," they usually mean public extension services. The goal of privatising extension services is not to replace public extension services with commercial ones. Private business companies, lending institutions, farmer's associations, non-governmental organisations, and media organisations are just a few of the diverse stakeholders that have taken part in privatisation in various ways.

The quality of planning at four levels- policies, programmes, projects, and strategy determines the success of an extension service. While projects and strategy can be developed by private extension organisations; policy and programmes must be set by the public extension system. There will probably be competition between the various extension providers when private extension organisations start supporting farmers in this way, leading to more effective and customer-driven service. The private extension agencies take good care of both technical and allocative efficiency, which are primarily economic in nature, leading to cost minimization, profit maximisation, and optimal use of resources, which are warranted in a competitive context.

Concept of Private Extension

As an alternative to public extension, private extension entails extension professionals working for the private sector who provide agricultural advisory services. In private extension, Van den Ban and Hawkins states, farmers are expected to contribute to the expense of this service and shoulder a portion of the burden.

The agricultural extension system should not be viewed as being privatised as a substitute for the public extension system. When it comes to spreading location-specific, system-based, and sustainable technology, the public sector has a comparative edge. In the areas of technological and commercial sectors, input supply, and other technical services, the private sector will succeed more.

Government agencies and agricultural organisations have put forward at least three scenarios for the privatisation of extension:

1. Only public services that directly affect the general public are funded by taxpayers.
2. Direct charging with the possibility of differentiating prices for particular scenarios or target groups for some individual services that directly result in a return in the form of increased income.
3. Mixed funding, including contributions from public and private professional associations for services with a delayed payback or collective services like applied research, farmer and agent training, and enhancements to Extension tools and processes.

There are Mainly Two Types of Private Extension Service

1. The first type is the wholly private kind, which engages in farming activities directly through consultants, agribusiness, agricultural input businesses, etc.
2. Farmer's organisations, NGOs, and other similar groups fall under the second category and are still heavily reliant on government subsidies.

The goal of privatising extension services is not to replace public extension services with commercial ones. In essence, it tries to lessen the role of the public sector in agricultural extension services to make room for a greater role for private ventures.

The following sorts of links between technology that could be extended or transferred are discussed:

1. Consultative

In recent years, there has been an increase in interest in the approach of commercialising public extension services, or switching from delivering a free public service funded by the government to a commercial operation funded by user fees. Consultative extension links are just temporary, yet they are very powerful. When developing an internal demonstration or performing an on-farm trial, the person or business that provides the technology is consulted to provide the extension or transfer of technology package.

2. Contractual

In the era of expanding intellectual property, these technological transfer linkages are anticipated to be stronger. To obtain a technological solution, private farms or franchisees may enter into a contract with public research services. In this case, a private farm provides the cash, and they also own the research's results. On the farmer's field, a demonstration and farm trial are conducted to make any necessary adjustments. The contract is for technological development, workforce training, and identifying a suitable technological answer. Another possibility is the widespread distribution of technologies by private organisations receiving state financing. With few exceptions, consumers typically purchase extension services at a set national price; although, in some situations, highly individualised projects are charged more, while projects for low-income users are provided at a lower cost.

3. Collaborative

This technology transfer is carried out in accordance with predetermined funding, benefit-sharing, and extension-related obligations. The operation of the programme, timely research, and the development of mutual trust all contribute to its success. These programmes enable the public sector to commercialise technology created through cooperative programmes while reducing transaction costs for private businesses.

Market-Led Extension

Concept of Market-Led Extension

Market-led extension is a method for effectively delivering adequate and high-quality information to farmers so that they can make prudent decisions about production and marketing that will maximise their return on investment without endangering the needs of future generations.

The extension functionaries' attention needs to go beyond output. The importance of quality, consumer preferences, market intelligence, processing, value addition, and other marketing data should be emphasised to farmers. This will lower production costs, increase product value, and enhance marketability for the farming community, all of which will result in excellent returns for the produce.

The main aspects of the paradigm shift in agricultural extension are the following:

a) Productivity to profitability
b) Subsistence to commercial agriculture
c) Commodity to farming systems orientation
d) Local to international markets
e) Monoculture to diverse crops
f) Exploitative to sustainable agricultural practises

Linking Farmer Producers to Markets

From very small and regional to very large and international enterprises, connecting farmers to markets can encompass a wide range of endeavours.

There are numerous ways to classify different linkage types. The connections could be between a farmer and a domestic merchant, a farmer and a store, a farmer and an agro-processor/ exporter, a farmer and a cooperative, or a farmer and a contract farmer. Relationships can be formalised through contracts or can be informal and based on trust. The idea does, however, presuppose the growth of long-term commercial partnerships as opposed to support for sporadic sales.

Market Orientation/Market-oriented Farming

Market orientation refers to the development of the value chain as a whole as well as a company philosophy or approach that focuses on finding and satisfying consumers' expressed or unstated demands or wants. Farming that is market-oriented uses more advanced production techniques, commercial inputs, and consistently high yields and quality agricultural products for sale.

SWOT analysis of the market: It is necessary to analyse the markets' strengths (demand, high marketability, good price, etc.), weaknesses (the opposite of the aforementioned), opportunities (export to other locations, right time of selling, etc.), and threats (imports and perishability of the products, etc.). The farmers must therefore be informed of this analysis in order to plan production and marketing.

Market-oriented Agricultural Extension Advisory Services

Market-oriented Agricultural Extension Advisory Services cover "a very broad range of services from technical know-how, understanding of markets, their needs, and business management, through organisational development, and facilitation of change in value chains. These services may also be referred to as value-chain development consultancy services or agricultural/rural company development services.

In market-oriented agricultural extension advisory services, agricultural extension specialists may play the following roles:

1. Technical know-how to increase production quality, quantity, and timeliness, etc. (such as choosing goods, breeds, and varieties that are suited for the market, and using sound agricultural practises including managing soil fertility, protecting plants, and managing water)
2. Knowledge of economics, business management, and markets (including guidance on legal, regulatory, and certification issues in addition to enterprise analysis, marketing, market analysis, business planning, and record keeping)
3. Knowledge to help value chain actors meet market or quality requirements (such as post-harvest handling and storage, processing and packing technology, adhering to standards for food safety and agricultural practises, or consumer rights)
4. Capacity building to support producers and other value chain actor groups (such as financial management, leadership, situation analysis and action planning, negotiation skills, participatory innovation development
5. Facilitating and supporting changes in value chain management (such as convening multi-stakeholder forums to understand market trends and drivers, to foster better mutual understanding and trust)
6. To identify bottlenecks along value chains and devise solutions, and to assist traders and processors to link up with reliable producers.

The agricultural extension system must change from the transfer of production technologies to enable farmers to get the most out of their businesses, as well as in part from ensuring adoption of a set of practises that will ensure high returns to farming communities by promoting agriculture as an agribusiness enterprise.

Farmer Led Extension/ Farmer to Farmer Extension

The provision of training by farmers to farmers, frequently through the establishment of a system of farmer promoters and farmer trainers, is described here as "farmer-to-farmer extension."

While we acknowledge that other terms (such as "model farmer," "volunteer farmer," "farmer trainer," "community knowledge worker," etc.) are also used and frequently have implications for the precise roles and tasks performed by the farmers involved, we use the term "lead farmer" as a generic term for farmers serving extension functions within farmer-to-farmer programmes.

Background of Farmer-to-farmer Extension

Beginning in Guatemala in the 1970s, the farmer-to-farmer extension later moved to Nicaragua in the 1980s, Mexico, and Honduras. Many other nations in Latin America, Asia, and Africa currently use it widely and in various forms. The "Campesino a Campesino" (Farmer to Farmer movements) movement in Nicaragua is the most well-known and well-known farmer-to-farmer extension. A key component of this strategy is farmer trainers, who are recognised by various names in various nations and initiatives. The farmer teachers are referred to as promoters in Nicaragua and farmer teachers by the International Centre of Insect Physiology and Ecology (ICIPE) in Kenya. Farmer extension agents, or kamayog in the native language, are the names given to farmer trainers in Peru and Burkina Faso, respectively. Farmer trainers are people with little to no formal education who, through practise, experimentation, learning, and training, expand their knowledge and develop the skills necessary to serve as extension workers.

Farmers are frequently chosen by extension agencies to assist them in putting their programmes into action. Model, master, or lead farmers are terms used to describe the farmers who are chosen to lead "farmer-to-farmer" extension programmes. These farmers are chosen based on their level of agricultural competence. They are referred to as farmer promoters or trainers in other programmes to highlight their networking and training abilities. The community knowledge worker is another variation that can help farmers have better access to information and advisory services. These individuals occasionally have smartphones.

Strategies for Farmer-led Extension

1. Strengthening Farmers' led extension by promoting Farmers Interest Groups, Women Interest Groups, and Commodity Interest Groups.
2. Increasing these organised groups' capacity for cutting-edge agricultural production technology.
3. It is necessary to recreate farmers' forums, associations, etc. on a larger scale. In their social structure, these member farmers will act as para extension agents.
4. Supporting extension programmes and farmer participation in research for the creation, improvement, and spread of location-specific technologies
5. Farmer groups should have access to market information and market intelligence using information and communication technology (ICT).

Framework for the Farmer-to-Farmer Model

1. Lead farmers get training about the approach, the initiative (technology/tools/methods), and various extension methods. They are the first to test the strategy in their particular field.
2. Then the lead farmers impart their knowledge and expertise to other local farmers via modal farms, neighbourhood networks, hands-on training, etc.

Principles of Farmer-to-Farmer Extension Model

The term "Farmer-to-Farmer extension" method refers to the practise of educating farmers by other farmers, frequently by means of the establishing a structure of farmer-trainers. By allowing farmers to act as change agents for bettering the livelihoods in their communities, farmer-to-farmer extension can aid in the development of efficient, farmer-centered extension systems.

The following are key principles

1. Farmers and local institutions (such as producer organisations or village leaders) should play a significant role in choosing and assessing farmer-trainers. This makes the programmes more responsible to the people or organisations they serve.
2. Farmer-trainers are more sensitive to local cultures, mannerisms, farming techniques, and farmers' needs because they are part "of the community," speak the local languages, and communicate with them.
3. Rather than focusing just on their farming knowledge, farmer-trainers should be chosen for their talents and willingness to impart knowledge.

4. Extension agents whether public, private, or non-governmental organisations (NGO) who teach and support farmer-trainers need to have strong ties to them.
5. Farmer-trainers should typically work in convergence and collaboration with current extension systems rather than as a replacement for them.
6. To ensure that both men and women are able to become farmer-trainers, facilitating organisations and local institutions must take aggressive measures.
7. Farmer trainers should have access to straightforward and relevant reference materials.

Farmer-to-Farmer Extension Model Advantages and Limitations

In a large densely populated country like India with significant number of rural people, the ratio of extension workers to farmers is very high (1: 1000). The farmer-to-farmer extension approach can minimise the cost of extension and workload of extension functionaries.

Farmer to Farmer Extension Advantages

1. The low cost of the farmer-to-farmer extension strategy is valued.
2. It facilitates the reach of extension programmes and enhances community accountability.
3. Farmers' knowledge of regional languages and cultures facilitates and encourages the adoption of new methods.
4. Farmer-to-Farmer Extension programmes encourage input on new practises to research and extension and assist bolster communities' information access capabilities.
5. The strategy is generally sustainable since it is low-cost, with government extension workers or farmer organisations taking up the support of farmer-trainers after a project is over.
6. Farmer-to-Farmer Extension may enhance farmers' input to extension personnel.

Farmer-to-Farmer Extension Model Drawbacks

1. Without training and technical support, the farmer-trainers may not perform well.
2. Some programmes appear to hire more farmer-trainers than they can actually backstop, which lowers the program's total performance.
3. Conflicts between farmer-trainers and extension personnel may arise if the latter view farmer-trainers as a replacement for rather than an addition to their own services.

4. High drop-out rates in some programmes necessitate further training for new farmer trainers.
5. Farmer-to-Farmer Extension programmes might just be a component of a top-down, one-way technology transfer approach.
6. Lastly, even though Farmer-to-Farmer Extension is inexpensive, they might not be continued when a project is over if no local institution agrees to fund them.

Table 1: Paradigm shift from production-led to farmers-led extension system

Components	Production-led approach	Farmers-led extension approach
Purpose/ Objective	Transfer of production technologies	Capacity building (especially farmers extensionist), create para-professional extension workers, creating or strengthening local institutions
Goal	Food self-sufficiency	Livelihood security including food, nutrition, employment to alleviate poverty, sustainability and conserving bio-diversity
Approach	Top-down, commodity and supply driven	Participatory, bottom-up and demand driven
Actors	Mostly public institutions	Pluralistic with public, private, non-government and farmers organizations as a partner rather than competitors
Mode	Mostly interpersonal/ individual approach	Integration of clients oriented on-farm participatory/experiential learning methods supported by ICTs and media
Role of extension agents	Limited to delivery mode and feedback to research system	Facilitation of learning, building overall capacity of farmers and encouraging farmers experimentation
Linkages/liaison	Research-Extension-Farmers	Research- Extension-Farmers Organizations
Emphasis	Information management, Production "Seed to Seed"	Knowledge management and sharing
Nature of technology	Input intensive, crop based and general recommendations as per agro-climatic zone, fixed package of information	Knowledge intensive, broad based, farming system perspective and blending with ITKs
Critical areas	Improvement, production and protection	Decision support system, integrated farming system approach, natural resource management, clients group formation and community empowerment
Critical inputs	Money and material	Access to Information, building human and social capital
Accountability	Mostly government	To farmers rather than donors

Source: Kokate *et al.* (2016)

Information and Communication Technologies Icts

ICTs generally refer to an expanding assembly of technologies that are used to handle information and aid communication. These comprise the equipment, software, and media for gathering, storing, processing, transmitting, and presenting data in any form (such as speech, text, picture, and data) via computers, the Internet, CD-ROMs, email, telephone, radio, television, video, and digital cameras, among other devices. Earlier, radio, television, and print media were the main means of facilitating communication; today, these mediums are referred to as conventional/traditional ICTs. The term "evolving applications" or "new ICTs" refers to the technologies that rely on the Internet, communication networks, mobile phones, personal computers, and databases as well as other modern ICTs.

ICTs can broadly support agriculture and rural advisory services, farmers, and other innovation stakeholders and perform the following key tasks:

1. Knowledge and experience sharing and cross-learning;
2. Improving access to information, knowledge, and technologies;
3. Providing timely and relevant information and advisory services;
4. Establishing links to markets;
5. Improving links and networking to enhance collaboration and partnerships;
6. ICT is being used by industries outside of agriculture to spread information among its stakeholders.

The bulk of research findings do not reach farmers because there are limited and poor systems for transferring technology. To maximise benefits for agriculture in the sectors of cyber extension, the spirit of ICT can be implemented in the fields of Cyber extension (ICT-based initiatives), Remote sensing, Geographical Information System, E-Governance, Expert Systems

Cyber extension

The term "extension over cyber space" is used to describe cyber extension. To facilitate the spread of agricultural technology, it implies "using the strength of online computer networks with the assistance of communication channels to send content in the form of text, graphics, audio, and video either passively or interactively."

E-Governance

E-governance is the use of ICT applications to offer information and services to the public more quickly, affordably, easily, and effectively. E-government is the provision of public services that are more user-friendly, cost-effective, and customer-focused, as well as the dissemination of information through electronic media. In the context of the agricultural industry, e-governance is the use of ICTs to deliver governance services and products that are useful to the agricultural community, which includes farmers, livestock breeders, herders, dairy workers, agriculture extension workers, traders, scientists, middlemen, and employees of nongovernmental organisations who work in the field of agriculture and related industries.

Importance of e-governance

i. Quicker and simpler servicing
ii. Convenience, close to home, and a wide range of services
iii. Government offices should process information more quickly and have shorter lines.
iv. Fewer visits to government facilities
v. A better environment for interaction and no harassment
vi. Lower transportation costs
vii. Protects daily wage earners from wage loss
viii. Higher calibre services

Expert Systems

Expert systems are a typical use of artificial intelligence that are primarily based on a particular issue domain. With the aid of pre-set conditions in the software application, the expert system acts as if it were a human expert in order to solve the problem.

a) The creation of a *knowledge base*, which employs a formalism for knowledge representation to capture the knowledge of subject matter experts (SMEs), and
b) A process of gathering that knowledge from the SME and codifying it according to the formalism, which is called *knowledge engineering.*

Above are just two methods of the many techniques that can be used to simulate the performance of an expert.

Components of Expert Systems

a) User interface
b) Knowledgebase
c) Inference mechanism (IF-THEN-ELSE). For example, if the symptom of crop is X, then the nutrition deficiency is Y.

Advantages & Disadvantages of Expert Systems

Advantages

i. Ready to use by end user
ii. Provides consistent answers
iii. Holds and maintains significant levels of information
iv. Encourages human expert to clarify and finalize the logic of their decision-making
v. Never "forgets" to ask a question, as a human might

Disadvantages

i. Lacks common sense
ii. Cannot make creative responses
iii. Domain experts not always able to explain their logic and reasoning
iv. Cannot adopt to changing environments

Artificial Intelligence in Agriculture

Artificial Intelligence (AI) dwells on the idea that human intelligence can be described in a way that makes it simple for a computer to imitate it and carry out tasks of any complexity. Artificial intelligence has three main objectives: learning, reasoning, and perception. With the aid of artificial intelligence, farmers may automate their operations while also switching to precise cultivation for improved crop quality and production while consuming fewer resources.

AI start-ups in the agricultural sector are Prospera, Blue River Technology, Formbot, Harvest CROO Robotics, and others are.

Artificial Intelligence Applications in Agriculture

a) Making use of weather predictions
b) A technique to monitor the health of soil and crops
c) Using drones to evaluate crop health
d) Predictive analytics and precision agriculture
e) Agricultural Robots

Challenges in Adoption of AI in Agriculture

Although artificial intelligence has a wide range of potential applications in agriculture, most farms throughout the world are still unfamiliar with cutting-edge machine learning solutions. There is a lot of exposure of farming to environmental elements including weather, soil, and insect prevalence. Therefore, due to changes in external conditions, what can seem like a suitable answer during planning and the start of harvesting, may not be the best one.

To train computers and produce accurate predictions, AI systems also require a large amount of data. Though spatial data can be easily acquired in the case of huge agricultural area, temporal data is difficult to obtain. For instance, most crop-specific data can only be collected once a year, during the growing season. Building a reliable machine learning model involves a lot of effort since the data infrastructure takes time to develop.

Digital Divide

Over time, the idea of the digital divide has evolved. The fact that the digital divide is not just technological is becoming increasingly clear. There is a gender gap in the digital sphere between men and women in society as well as a societal split between information-rich and -poor civilizations (Huyer and Mitter, 2003). It was first thought to be an issue with connectivity or access, but in recent years, awareness of the idea has expanded to include the capacities and skills needed to use ICTs (Singh, 2010). The current definition of the digital divide includes four gaps: access to ICTs, capacity to use ICTs, actual use of ICTs, and impact of use.

Conclusion

In the last decades of the 20th century, the paradigm of development, particularly in agriculture, underwent a significant shift towards privatization, with enhanced roles for various stakeholders, including the private sector, NGOs, and ICT-based services. This transformation necessitated new skills and roles for those providing agricultural extension services to tackle challenges such as resource scarcity, market volatility, and the rapid adoption of ICTs. The impetus for change in agricultural extension has stemmed from several core issues: the changing nature of agriculture with its unique challenges, a more diverse array of service providers, innovative interactions between government and private sectors for advisory services, and insights from the digital revolution. Extension services have thus broadened their objectives to include market understanding, adaptation to market demands, and better integration of farmers into both local and global markets amidst increasing competition. Privatization in extension services doesn't aim to eliminate public services but rather introduce a competitive edge, driving efficiency and customer-focused service delivery. The concept involves a variety of players including commercial companies, financial institutions, farmer associations, and NGOs. The discussion extends to various forms of technological transfer connections—consultative, contractual, and collaborative—all of which have their unique functions and dynamics in the context of privatization. Additionally, market-led extension, a strategy for delivering quality information to farmers, shifts focus from production to profitability, from subsistence to commercial agriculture, and from local to global markets, embracing sustainable practices. The integration of farmers into markets is diverse, ranging from small local to large international enterprises, with various formal and informal linkages. Market orientation and market-led advisory services are highlighted as crucial for directing farmer's production decisions, emphasizing the need for market intelligence and value addition. The concept of farmer-led extension is discussed, where farmers themselves become trainers, creating a sustainable, cost-effective, and community-accountable model. While this approach has numerous advantages, including cultural sensitivity and community engagement, it also faces challenges like potential conflicts with traditional extension services and sustainability post-project completion. ICTs have supported this transition by enabling knowledge sharing, enhancing access to information, and establishing market linkages. Cyber extension, e-governance, and expert systems have become vital tools in disseminating agricultural technology and information. However, the adoption of AI in agriculture faces challenges like data scarcity and environmental variability, highlighting the complexity of bridging the digital divide.

Answer the Following Questions

1. Describe the role of Information and Communication Technologies (ICTs) in transforming agricultural extension services over the last decades of the 20th century. How have ICTs contributed to addressing the challenges faced by the agricultural sector
2. Explain how the privatization of extension services and the involvement of various stakeholders, such as NGOs, farmer groups, and private sector entities, have impacted the delivery and effectiveness of agricultural extension services.
3. Discuss how market-led extension strategies could enhance the profitability and market orientation of small-scale farmers. Include an explanation of how these strategies shift the focus from traditional production-led approaches.
4. Analyze the concept and implementation of farmer-led extension models, including their advantages and limitations. How do these models complement the traditional extension services provided by the public sector?

5. Critically evaluate the potential of artificial intelligence (AI) in agriculture, considering the challenges related to data availability and environmental variability. How can AI be effectively integrated into agricultural extension services to benefit farmers?

16

Communication

Pratick Mondal

Department of Agricultural Economics and Extension, Lovely Professional University Phagwara, Punjab

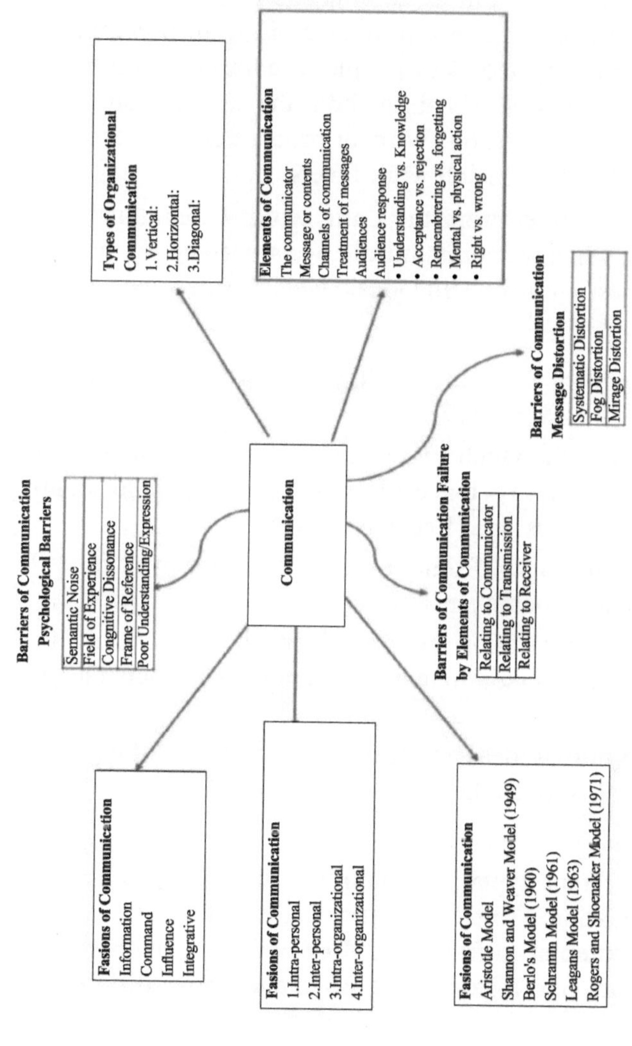

Figure 1: Overview of the chapter (Credit: Jarial, S)

Introduction

In the animal kingdom, there are many animals with a concrete social system in their ranks. Animals like lions, wolves, and apes have complex social systems in their lives. And what is the most important thing in a functional social system? It's communication! Communication is the most important function in any social system, which binds that system.

And what organism has the most complex social system? It's humans. Thus, the human social system requires a very complex communication system.

If you see from an agricultural point of view, considering the extension and rural development, communication becomes the key point for the transfer of technology and other extension activities. Nothing is more important than the transfer of useful ideas from one person to another. From improving the socio-economic circumstances of the rural people to educating and training them, extension workers work tirelessly throughout the season, and the key component they have is communication. Without proper communication, all kinds of rural development and extension work falters.

The word 'communication' comes from the Latin word 'Communis' which means Common. It means when we communicate, we are trying to establish a commonality through a message over some ideas, facts, feelings etc.

Definitions

Communication is anything that conveys meaning, that carries a message from one individual to another (Brooker, 1949).

Communication is a process by which two or more people exchange ideas, facts, feelings, or impressions in ways that each gains a common understanding of meaning, intent and use of message (Leagans, 1961).

The process of sending messages from a source to a receiver is called communication (Rogers and Shoemaker, 1971).

In extension education, communication refers to the process of transferring an idea, skill or attitude from one person to another accurately and satisfactorily. (Supe)

Communication is the sharing of ideas and feelings between or among human beings in a mood of mutuality. (Chaubey)

Communication Process

We have seen many different types of communication from the ancient times in the human civilization. From Rock Arts, Signs to Printing and Mass communication through internet, different kind of communication methods has been seen throughout our history. But no matter how different the communications are, their main goal is always the same – to transmit and share information, experiences and knowledge. And the process of communication is also almost same for every different kind of communication.

The process of communication has been always in debate for a long time. Many philosophers and social scientists established different ideologies and theories about the communication process.

Models of Communication

1. **Aristotle Model:** The famous Greek philosopher had his own model for communication process. It has three elements.

   a) Speaker: The person who speaks

   b) Speech: The message itself

   c) Audience: The person who listens.

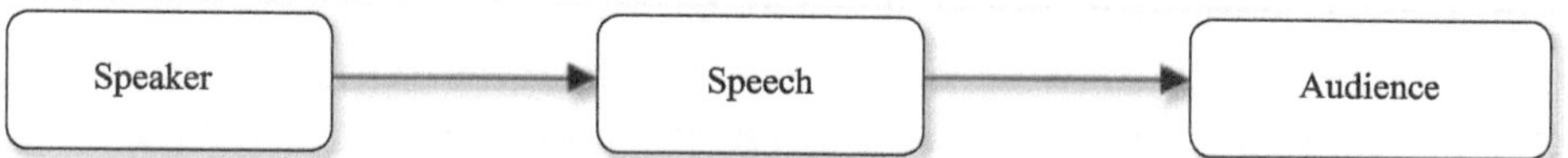

2. **Shannon and Weaver Model (1949):** This model also goes in line with Aristotle model. According to this model, the elements of communication are–

If we compare this to the Aristotle Model, we can see that the source is equivalent to the speaker, the signal is speech, and the destination is equivalent to the audience. With the two additional elements, the transmitter and receiver are the devices which send out the source's message and catch the message for the destination, respectively. For example, in a face-to-face conversation, the transmitter would be the speaker's mouth or vocal cord, and the receiver would be the ears of the audience.

3. **Berlo's Model (1960):** This model mainly focuses on coded messages. The elements of this model are – Encode means to put the message into a code. Channel is the medium through which the signal moves (like Radio or Morse Code), and the decoder means which converts the coded message into regular language, which may be easily understood by the receiver.

It can also be said that all human communication has some source, a person or a group of people with a purpose. The purpose of the source is basically the message that must be expressed. Then, the encoder is the one that takes the idea or purpose of the source and puts it into a message. The channel is the medium that carries the message to the intended destination. And for the communication to be successful, there must be someone at the other end to receive the message. The receiver also needs the help of the decoder to decode and convert the message from a coded one to an understandable one.

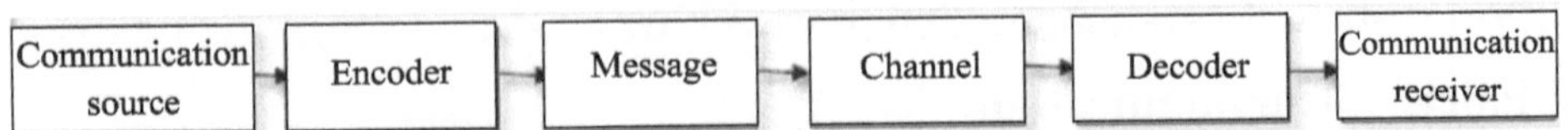

4. **Schramm Model (1961):** This model is focused on mass media communication. The elements of this models are-

This model is particularly relevant for the mass media like radio, television or internet. In human communication, it is extremely important whether people can properly encode or decode the message or not, i.e., sending a message and how interpret it for their own understanding.

In the mass media as well, communication happens through a particular process. Suppose you are watching live news on the television. Now, first, the news anchor will face the camera and voice any message. It will be recorded by the camera in a digital format, i.e., it is being encoded. Here the camera is the encoder. Then the encoded message will be sent through computers and satellites to your home television. This is a signal. Then your television will decode the digitalised message to video and audio for you to see. That makes your television the decoder and you the destination.

5. **Leagans Model (1963):** This model mainly focuses on the general communication. The elements of this model is as follows :

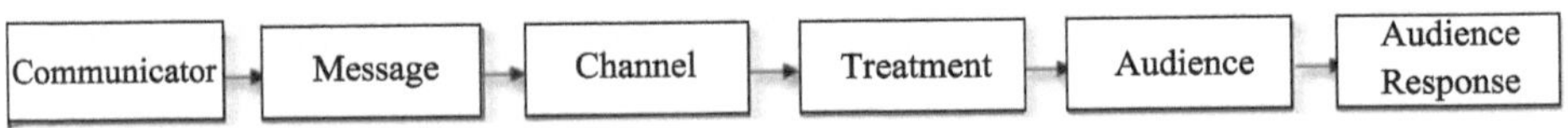

6. This model is the first model of the communication process, which includes feedback from the receiver of the message. According to him, the main purpose of communication is to provide powerful incentives for change from the receivers' side. Only by understanding all six elements of communication the success of the communication can be made. "A skilful communicator sending a useful message through proper channel, effectively treated, to an appropriate audience that responds as desired".
7. **Rogers and Shoemaker Model (1971):** This model is also called the SMCRE model. There are a total of five elements in this model which are –

According to this model, a source (S) sends a message (M) via certain channels (C) to the receiving individual (R), which cause some effects (E) i.e., changing the existing behaviour pattern of the receiver.

Communication in agricultural extension could also be two-way communication where necessary stimulus is provided by the communicator, the extension agent, in the form of a message that produces certain response on the audience or the farmers or vice-versa.

Functions of Communication

Communication has four basic functions

1. Information function: information plays a fundamental role in adaptation and adjustment to one's environment. Without information about what's happening around us, it becomes difficult to understand our surroundings, anticipate changes, and make informed decisions. Communication serves as the conduit for this vital information exchange. Whether it's directly sharing information or indirectly conveying it through cues and signals, communication enables individuals to stay connected to their environment and to each other, facilitating adaptation and adjustment.
2. Command or Instructive function: Individuals occupying higher positions within family structures, societal frameworks, or organizational hierarchies typically take the lead in communication, whether it's to convey information to their subordinates or provide guidance on tasks, methods, and timing. The directive and instructional aspects of communication are more prominently observed in formal organizational settings compared to informal ones.
3. Influence or persuasive function: A fundamental aim of communication involves exerting influence or persuasion upon others. This facet of communication holds particular significance in endeavours such as extension services, where the goal is to guide individuals towards adopting desirable behaviours. (Berlo, 1960)
4. Integrative function: Communication serves a crucial role in promoting integration and mitigating disintegration, whether it occurs at the interpersonal or organizational level. This function contributes significantly to preserving the stability and identity of individuals, societies, or organizations.

Elements of Communication

1. The Communicator

This individual initiates the communication process within an operation. They serve as the source or originator of messages, acting as the sender. Their role involves articulating messages intended to reach an audience, ensuring they are correctly interpreted and elicit a desirable response. The communicator could be an Agricultural Extension Officer, Village Development Officer, Principal or Instructor at a Training Centre, Mandal Agricultural Officer, villager, administrator, or any other relevant figure.

The following are the characteristics of a good communicator

He knows

a) The communicator should have clearly defined objectives for their communication efforts.
b) They must understand their audience, including their needs, interests, abilities, and predispositions.
c) Crafting a message entails considering its content, validity, usefulness, and importance to the audience.
d) Identifying effective channels to reach the audience and assessing their usefulness is crucial.
e) The communicator should determine how to organize and present their message in a manner that maximizes comprehension and engagement.
f) Being aware of their professional abilities and limitations is essential for effective communication.

He is interested in

a) Understanding the audience and prioritizing their welfare is paramount.
b) The communicator should focus on how their message can positively impact and assist people.
c) Evaluating the outcomes of communication is crucial to gauge effectiveness.
d) Having a grasp of the communication process enhances effectiveness in conveying messages.
e) Utilizing communication channels appropriately while recognizing their limitations is important.
f) Continuous improvement of communication skills is essential for enhanced effectiveness.

He prepares

a) Developing a communication plan, akin to a teaching plan, is essential for outlining objectives, content, methods, and timelines.
b) Procuring appropriate communication materials and equipment ensures effective delivery of messages and engagement with the audience.

c) Establishing a plan for evaluating results enables the assessment of communication effectiveness and the achievement of objectives.

He has skill in

a) Selecting messages
b) Treating messages
c) Expressing messages - verbal and written
d) The selection and use of channels
e) Uunderstanding his audience
f) Collecting evidence of results

2. Message or Content

A message embodies the information that a communicator intends for their audience to receive, comprehend, embrace, and respond to. These messages can encompass various forms, such as scientific facts related to agriculture, sanitation, or nutrition, descriptions of ongoing actions by individuals or groups, explanations for the necessity of certain actions, or guidelines outlining steps required for specific courses of action. The potential scope of messages is as vast as the content of the programs they accompany.

Messages related to programmes of change are, therefore, the relevant 'cargo' to be carried to people by the channels of communication. They are the important content, sometimes referred to as 'arguments' 'appeals' and 'stimuli'. Whether messages operate effectively as incentives to changed behaviour in any given situation depends on a wide range of influences. A successful communication is one in which the major factors influencing the message are controlled as far as possible. This is the responsibility of the communicator.

A good message must be

i. Aligned with the objective to be achieved;
ii. Easily comprehensible by the intended audience;
iii. Compatible with the mental, social, economic, and physical capacities of the audience;
iv. Meaningful and relevant to the economic, social, and aesthetic needs and values of the audience;
v. Specific, without including irrelevant material;
vi. Concisely expressed, addressing one point at a time;
vii. Accurate, grounded in scientific validity, factual information, and up-to-date knowledge;
viii. Timely, particularly considering seasonal factors and current issues;

ix. Supported by factual material presenting both sides of the argument;
x. Appropriate for the selected communication channel;
xi. Engaging and attractive to the audience, providing immediate utility;
xii. Applicable, enabling the audience to implement recommendations;
xiii. Comprehensive, balancing theory and practical application effectively.
xiv. Manageable – can be handled by the communicator with high professional skill and within the limits imposed by time.

3. Channels of Communication

The connection between message senders and receivers relies on communication channels, which act as physical pathways between them. These channels serve as avenues through which messages are transmitted to and from communicators and their audiences. Essentially, channels are the tools that communicators use to bridge the gap between themselves and their intended recipients. However, simply having channels available is not sufficient; they must be utilized carefully and appropriately. Effective communication requires channels to be directed and used correctly, at the right time, for the right purpose, and with the right audience, all in alignment with the intended message.

4. Treatment of Messages

Treatment refers to the way a message is handled to effectively convey information to an audience. It encompasses the techniques, procedures, and performance details necessary for adeptly presenting messages. Designing the treatment of messages does not pertain to message formulation or channel selection but rather focuses on the presentation technique within the context provided by the message and the channel.

The objective of treatment is to ensure that the message is clear, understandable, and relatable to the audience. Crafting treatment often demands originality, profound insight into human behaviour principles, and proficiency in employing sophisticated presentation techniques. This is where the distinction between an effective and a less effective communicator becomes apparent, and the art of communication truly shines. Exceptional communicators excel not only in their overall abilities but particularly in their capacity to skillfully "treat" messages.

5. The Audience

Certainly, the audience serves as the intended recipient of messages, essentially acting as the consumers of communication. They are the target respondents in message transmission, with the expectation that they will respond in ways that result in economic, social, or other benefits. Effective communication hinges on the communicator's ability to accurately identify the target audience. The success of communication efforts is contingent upon how the audience responds to the messages. Audiences can vary widely, ranging from individuals to groups, and may encompass diverse demographics such as men, women, youth groups, villagers, or leaders. They can also be categorized based on occupation groups, such as farmers or artisans, or professional groups like engineers, educators, or administrators.

Clearly identifying an audience is of utmost importance in communication. Homogeneity within an audience increases the likelihood of successful communication. Additionally, the more information a communicator possesses about their audience and their specific characteristics, the greater the potential impact of their message. Audience identification involves categorizing groups according to characteristics such as those mentioned previously.

In addition to knowing the identity of an audience and some of its general characteristics, there are other somewhat more specified aspects that help to clarify the exact nature of an audience and how to reach it. The following are some of these:

1. Communication channels established by the social organization play a significant role in facilitating the flow of information within a community or group.
2. The system of values held by the audience influences their perception of what is important, shaping their attitudes and responses to messages.
3. Forces such as custom and tradition can strongly influence group conformity, affecting how individuals within the group perceive and respond to messages.
4. Individual personality factors, such as susceptibility to change, vary among audience members and can impact their receptivity to new ideas or behaviors.
5. Both native abilities and acquired skills contribute to an individual's capacity to understand and engage with messages effectively.
6. Educational, economic, and social levels of the audience influence their level of comprehension and engagement with messages.
7. The pressure of occupational responsibility can affect how busy or concerned audience members are, impacting their attention and receptivity to communication efforts.
8. Understanding both the audience's perceived needs and the professional communicator's assessment of those needs is crucial for crafting relevant and impactful messages.

9. Recognizing why the audience is in need of changed ways of thinking, feeling, and doing provides valuable insights for tailoring messages to address those needs effectively.
10. Considering how the audience views the situation provides important context for crafting messages that resonate with their perspectives and experiences.

Understanding these and other audience traits is beneficial for a communicator when devising their communication strategy. Like a sharpshooter, unless a communicator sees his target clearly, he can shoot a thousand rounds, and yet accomplish nothing.

6. Audience Response

This serves as the concluding phase in communication within rural development programs. Audience response to received messages manifests as some form of action, whether mental or physical, to varying degrees. Thus, action should be regarded as an outcome rather than a process, emphasizing its significance as a final objective rather than merely a method. The actions taken by the intended audience, attributable to specific communicative acts by extension workers, serve as indicators of the effectiveness of these elements.

The potential range of responses to received messages is virtually limitless. The following provides an overview of the diverse responses that may occur when a valuable message is received by a typical village audience of Indian cultivators.

1. Understanding vs. Knowledge

Mere knowledge of facts is insufficient to achieve understanding; it merely marks the initial phase. True understanding emerges when one can assign significance to facts, perceive their interconnections, and comprehend their relevance to a proposition and its broader context. Additionally, understanding entails recognizing the correlation between the entirety of facts and the issue at hand. Typically, people do not act solely based on facts but rather upon the attainment of understanding. Therefore, effective communication endeavours must prioritize the promotion of understanding.

2. Acceptance vs. rejection

A liberated, attentive, and analytical human mind insists that comprehension precede the acceptance of facts and propositions. Similarly, it emphasizes the importance of mental acknowledgment before engaging in action. Ultimately, it is individuals' beliefs, rather than mere knowledge or understanding, that dictate their actions when they have the freedom to choose.

3. Remembering vs. forgetting

When the opportunity for immediate action is absent or action is postponed, the tendency to forget what was learned affects the nature and scope of future actions. This fundamental principle holds significant implications for timing within communication programs. Ensuring the timely transmission of the appropriate message to the appropriate audience frequently proves pivotal for achieving successful communication outcomes.

4. Mental vs. physical action

Alterations in human cognition invariably lead to corresponding modifications in behavioural patterns. In essence, a person's thoughts govern their outward actions. As a result, a message advocating physical engagement may elicit full mental consideration yet fall short of prompting the ultimate decision to act. This phenomenon is occasionally labelled as "lip service."

5. Right vs. wrong

The aim of communication is to encourage favourable actions from an audience, as determined by the communicator and outlined in their objectives. Consequently, actions aligned with the intended objectives are perceived as "correct" actions. However, the issue is more intricate. Unfortunately, "noise" frequently disrupts this process. Due to various factors, individuals often deviate from precise adherence to instructions, even if they comprehend and agree with them. For instance, consider a scenario where a message detailing five steps in seed treatment is conveyed to a group of cultivators. Individuals and groups inevitably harbor their own perspectives on how to proceed.

Levels of Communication

As per Thayer (1968), there are four levels of communication. They are –

1. **Intra-personal:** This is basically communicating with oneself.
2. **Inter-personal:** This is basically establishing a relationship with other person (personal or professional) through communication.
3. **Intra-organizational:** This is the communication among the members of an organization within the organization.
4. **Inter-organizational:** This is the system developed by any organization to communicate with other organizations.

Types of Organizational Communication

There are mainly 3 types of communication –

1. **Vertical:** This type of communication is also known as top-down communication. In this case, instruction from the higher authority of

the organization is being carry forward to the workers at the lower level through proper channel. Similarly, any feedback from the workers also flows through to the authorities in the same way.

2. **Horizontal:** This type of communication occurs within the same level of the organization. For example, communication between managers of the same level within the organization.
3. **Diagonal:** This happens when during communication, a level is skipped. For example, the CEO of the organization is directly communicating with the workers at the lower level, ignoring the mid-level managers.

Barriers in Communication- Barriers are all those hurdles which stop or interrupt the process of communication.

Category	Subcategory	Details
Types of Barriers	Physical Barriers	Problems in transmitting a message from its source to destination.
Types of Barriers	Psychological Barriers	Barriers related to internal problems of the receiver.
Psychological Barriers	Semantic Noise	Use of difficult, complex words outside the receiver's frame of reference.
	Field of Experience	Occurs when sender & receiver do not share a common field of experience.
	Cognitive Dissonance	Conflict in thinking; receiver accepts the message but fails to react as expected.
	Frame of Reference	Differences in perception and understanding between sender and receiver.
	Poor Understanding/ Expression	Mismatch between sender's expressions and the message tone.
Failure by Elements of Communication	Relating to Communicator	Issues like ineffective environment, unorganized communication efforts.
	Relating to Transmission	Problems like incorrect handling of channels, wrong selection, and physical distractions.
	Relating to Receiver	Issues like attention span, cooperation problems, and attitude towards the communicator.
Message Distortion	Systematic Distortion	Distortion due to displacement/mis-arrangement of the message.
	Fog Distortion	Message is fogged due to unwanted information.
	Mirage Distortion	Maximum loss of message occurs.

Conclusion

The study of communication, tracing back to ancient civilizations through various forms like rock arts and the internet, reveals its constant purpose: to transmit and share information, experiences, and knowledge. Through various models proposed by Aristotle, Shannon and Weaver, Berlo, Schramm, Leagans, and Rogers and Shoemaker, we understand communication as a multi-dimensional process involving elements like speaker, message, audience, encoding, channels, and decoding. These models collectively highlight the essentiality of clear, understandable, and effectively treated messages in achieving the desired response from the audience. The models and theories studied provide a framework for understanding how messages should be crafted, treated, and delivered to ensure maximum effectiveness. Furthermore, the elements of communication, such as the communicator, the message, channels, treatment of messages, the audience, and the audience response, are crucial in determining the success of any communication effort. The study of communication in various forms, from interpersonal to organizational, reveals its essence: to create a common understanding and induce change.

Answer the Following Questions

1. Define the concept of communication as presented by Rogers and Shoemaker (1971). How does this definition apply to agricultural extension?
2. Explain how the treatment of messages affects the communication process within the context of extension education. Why is it important to "treat" messages skillfully?
3. Discuss how the Leagans Model of communication, which incorporates feedback from the receiver, can enhance the effectiveness of extension workers in rural development programs.
4. Compare and contrast the Aristotle and Shannon and Weaver Models of communication. What are the similarities and differences, and how do these models facilitate understanding the communication process in extension services?
5. Critically evaluate the barriers to communication in the context of rural development and extension work. Which barriers do you consider most challenging, and what strategies could be employed to overcome them?

17

Diffusion of Innovations

Dangi Pooja Arun and Neelam Kumari

Department of Agricultural Economics and Extension, Lovely Professional University Phagwara, Punjab

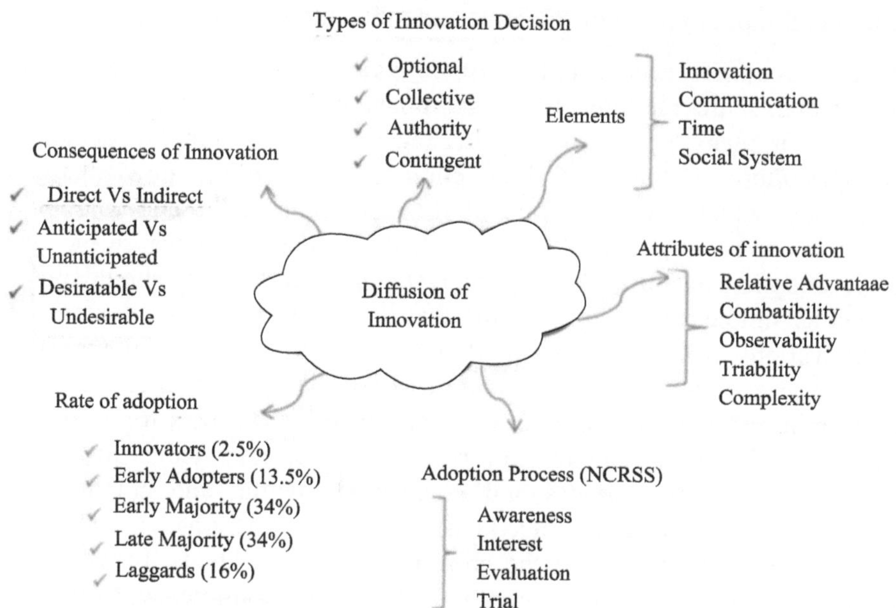

Figure 1: Overview of the chapter (Credit: Dangi, P.)

Introduction

Agriculture plays important role in boosting economic activity of farmers. Since it transfers new technologies within the knowledge and information system, it has special features related to knowledge, innovation, and those three. Agribusiness farming needs the diffusion of innovation. Many farmers were unable to boost their earnings. The development of the agribusiness and the welfare of the farmer were both significantly influenced by innovation. Diffusion includes three fairly distinct processes i.e. presentation of the new culture element or elements to the society, acceptance by the society, and the integration of the accepted element or elements into the pre-existing culture (Linton, 1936). Diffusion theory does not lead to the conclusion that one must wait for the diffusion of a new product or practice to reach the poorest people. In fact, one can accelerate the rate of adoption in any population segment through more intensive and more appropriate communication and outreach. (Green & Parcel, 1991). Improvement and development in any field are inseparable from technological advancement. The agricultural revolution is supported by the invention of new machinery and agriculture methods. The presence of technology has provided added value to the management of human activities in meeting their needs of life in agriculture, the concept of innovation and technology is implemented as a tool, way, or method used for processing agricultural input to produce effective and efficient output/agricultural yields

Rural communities, according to Petrovic *et al.* (2004), are a part of a global society and share its fate. They are, nonetheless, quite particular social organisms in many aspects, particularly regarding changes in the countryside and agriculture. Diffusion and adoption of innovation, knowledge, and technology, which are frequently at the core of social transformation in rural areas, are complicated and contradictory processes. Because the issue of the adoption and diffusion of innovations in agriculture should not be viewed as simple; one might assume that the diffusion and implementation of innovations will be successful if there are enough financial resources, agricultural experts, and adopters are aware of the innovations, with access etc. (Simin and Jankovic, 2014). Small and marginal farmers form complex systems of linkages, networking, resource base, knowledge acquisition pattern, perceptions, attitudes and associations within and among them. Hence extension mechanisms need customised refinement as per technology characteristics, physiology of the crop and farming systems. In homestead systems we can observe the apparent uniformity among farmers with regard to technology needs or knowledge/adoption potential. An area wide community approach in extension could play an effective role in situations that overlook the segmentation of adopter categories.

Concept of Diffusion

Diffusion of innovations refers to ideas, practices or objects that are disseminated via individuals. The primary responsibility of an extension worker in agricultural extension education is to communicate agricultural breakthroughs effectively, but this job description also includes ensuring that farmers implement these innovations into their daily operations. However, should not they point out the discrepancy between what is known and what farmers are actually doing? Why do some towns swiftly embrace new traditions while others adopt them more slowly?

By having a better understanding of the adoption and dissemination processes, extension personnel will be able to hasten the adoption of an invention in agriculture.

Definition

Diffusion is the process by which an innovation is communicated through specific channels over time among the members of a social system (Roger, 2003). It is a unique form of communication since the messages deal with novel concepts. To develop a shared understanding, participants in a communication process produce and exchange information.

Elements of diffusion of innovation

1. Innovation

Innovation is an idea, practice, or object that is perceived as new or an improvement over the existing one by the individual or members of a social system (Roger, 2003).

2. Communication channel

These are the channels via which information is transmitted from one person to another. For example, a source of one or a small number of people can reach a large audience through the use of mass media channels, which include radio, television, newspapers, and other mass media. Conversely, interpersonal channels are more successful in persuading someone to adopt a new thought, particularly if the interpersonal channel involves two or more people comparable to one another in terms of socioeconomic standing, level of education, or other significant factors. Face-to-face communication takes place through interpersonal channels between two or more people.

Most people rely mostly on subjective assessments provided to them by peers who have already embraced the advancements. This reliance on close peers' experiences suggests that dissemination is a social process, and the core of the diffusion process involves potential adopters mimicking and imitating their network partners who have already adopted. In organization when two or more people live or work close by and have similar interests, communication is more successful (*homophilous*). In *homophilous* conditions, communication is more successful. Therefore, communication is likely to benefit both parties involved when *homophily* is present.

i) **Interpersonal channels:** Those channels that allow for face-to-face interaction between two or more people.

ii) **Mass media outlets:** These help the communications reach a bigger, more varied audience all at once in a comparatively short amount of time. For example, Radio and Television.

iii) **Localite channels:** These come from the receiver's social structure. Neighbours, family members, public figures, etc.

iv) **Cosmopolite channels:** Theses are that come from outside of a specific social framework. For instance, a salesperson or an extension worker.

3. Time

Time is involved in diffusion in

1. The innovation - decision process
2. Innovations, and
3. And innovations rate of adoption.

The innovation-decision process is the mental cycle that a person or other decision-making unit goes through from first learning about an innovation to developing an attitude toward the innovation, to deciding whether to adopt or reject the innovation, to putting the new idea into practice, and to receiving confirmation of this decision.

Innovativeness is the extent to which a person or unit of an order adopts new concepts relative to other social system members. The adopters can be divided into five groups based on how innovative they are: (1) innovators, (2) early adopters, (3) early majority, (4) late majority, and (5) laggards.

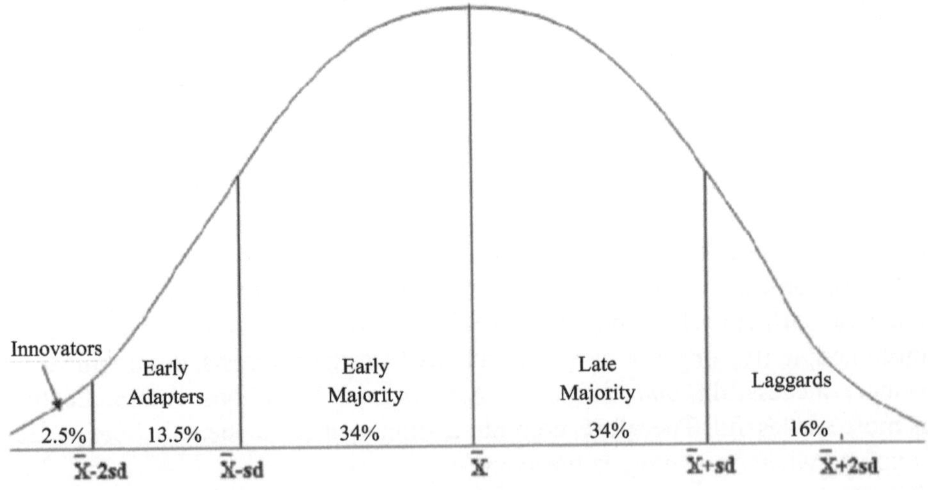

Figure 2: Adopter categories (*Source:* Roger, 2003)

Rate of adoption: This is the pace at which a social system's members scale up an innovation. The time it takes for a specific percentage of system members to accept an innovation is often how quickly an innovation gets adopted. Instead of using a single person as a unit of study, it takes a systems approach. The rate of adaptation to the same innovation varies depending on the social structure.

Innovators: Venturesome

Observers have remarked that inventors' impulsiveness borders on obsession. They want to test out novel concepts. They leave their local peer group due to this interest and form more cosmopolitan ties.

Early Adopter: Respectable

Early adopters are more integrated into the community's social system than innovators. Early adopters are localites, while innovators are cosmopolites. In most social systems, this adopter type possesses the highest level of opinion leadership compared to any other.

Early Majority: Deliberate

New concepts are adopted by the early majority immediately before the typical member of a social system. The early majority engage in frequent peer interaction, but rarely hold leadership positions.

Late Majority: Skeptical

Just after the typical member of a social system, the late majority adopts new concepts. Adoption might be the solution to mounting societal demands and an economic requirement.

Laggards: Traditional

The last to adopt a new idea are the laggards. They have very little influence on public opinion. Of all adopter categories, they have the most regional outlooks, and many live in remote areas. The laggard uses the past as a frame of reference. Decisions are frequently made in light of past generations' actions.

Social System

A social system is a collection of connected elements working together to solve problems for the benefit of everybody. Individuals, unorganized groups, organisations, or subsystems are all examples of members or units. The system is joined together by a shared goal. There is diffusion within a social system. The social structure of the system influences information dissemination methods and content. Therefore, when analysing dissemination, understanding social structure is crucial.

Attributes of Innovation

Relative Advantage

It is the degree to which an innovation is perceived as better than the idea it supersedes. It refers to how much innovation is considered superior to the concept it replaces. Economic metrics may be used to gauge the degree of relative advantage, but other relevant criteria frequently include convenience, satisfaction, and social prestige.

Rogers divided innovations into two categories: incremental (non-preventative) innovations and preventive innovations. "A preventative innovation is a new concept that a person adopts today to reduce the likelihood of some undesirable future event" (Rogers, 2003). Because preventive innovations typically take longer to spread, it is difficult to determine how advantageous they are in comparison. However, incremental advancements quickly have positive results.

Compatibility

It is the degree to which an innovation is perceived as consistent with the existing values, past experiences and needs of potential adopters.

Complexity

The degree to which an innovation is regarded as being challenging to comprehend and apply. In general, innovations that are easier to understand will be adopted faster than those that call for the adopter to acquire new knowledge and abilities. As Rogers noted, complexity negatively correlates with the adoption rate in contrast to the other qualities. Therefore, an innovation's excessive complexity is a significant barrier to its acceptance.

Trialability

It is the extent to which an innovation can be test-driven in a small-scale setting. A trial able invention reduces uncertainty for the person considering adoption since it allows for learning through experience. An innovation's adoption rate increases as more people try it. Re-invention occur during innovation trial, as was addressed in the implementation stage of the innovation-decision process. The potential adopter may then alter or modify the innovation. Faster acceptance of the innovation could result from increased re-invention. The vicarious trial is a crucial in accepting an invention and is especially useful for later adopters. According to Rogers, the trialability feature of inventions, is more significant to early adopters than too late adopters.

Observability

It refers to how people can see an innovation's consequences. Individuals are more inclined to adopt innovations if they can quickly see the benefits. The acceptance rate of of an innovation is positively connected with observability, similar to relative advantage, compatibility, and trialability.

Types of Innovation – decisions

Another significant type of effect on the dissemination of novel ideas comes from the social structure. An innovation may be accepted or rejected by a single system member, the entire social system, or both. Moreover, the decision to accept or reject an innovation may be made by a group of people or by a higher authority.

Optional innovation decisions: A person decides to adopt or reject an innovation without regard to the actions of other system participants.

Example: The spread of a new antibiotic drug among medical doctors.

Collective innovation decision: Decisions about whether to approve or reject an innovation are reached through consensus among system participants. Once the system has taken a decision, all of its units are required to abide by it.

Example: Co-operatives such as Farmer Producer Organizations, Farmer Producer Companies.

Authority innovation decision: A system's decision to approve or reject an innovation is typically made by few powerful, influential, or technically skilled individuals. The person merely carries out the decision; and has little to no influence.

Example: Decisions taken by the Board of Directors of a company.

Contingent innovation decision: Decisions about whether to adopt or reject an innovation can only be made in the wake of an earlier decision. For instance, only after his or her system has made a judgement regarding innovation may a particular member of a social system be free to adopt or not.

Adoption: Adoption is a decision to make full use of an innovation as the best course of action available

Stages of Adoption

Adoption's stages are not static but rather dynamic. Not all adopters experience the same five stages, and the order of all practices is not constant. A stage may occasionally appear more than once. Sometimes stages are so brief as to be undetectable, while other times, they appear to be skipped. Suppose the farmer trusts the extension worker's work and his advice. From the point of evaluation to adoption, they could skip forward. There are no apparent distinctions, occasionally, the entire procedure is packaged and appears to be a single act. Singh and Pink (1965) modelled adoption process in seven stages. Need, knowledge, interest, consideration, testing, assessment, and adoption.

The five steps that make up the process of an individual adopting an invention are as follows: (North Central Rural Sociology of Farm Practices, 1955).

a) **Awareness Stage:** The farmer learns of the new concept's existence but is not fully informed about it. The farmer is aware of the concept at this point but is not well-versed in it.

b) **Interest Stage:** The farmer becomes intrigued by the innovation and looks for further details. In other words, a farmer learns more about a new idea or invention by wanting to know what it is, how it operates, and what possibilities it offers.

c) **Evaluation stage**: The farmer considers the new concept considering current circumstances and predicted future developments before deciding whether to put it to use. He evaluates the innovation's usefulness, determines whether it applies to his position, and predicts the outcome if it were to be used.

d) **Trial Stage:** The farmer applies the new idea on a small scale to determine its utility or feasibility and applicability in their own situation. If, in the farmer's judgment, the innovation has some plus points i.e. applicable to own situation, and if applied shall in some way or other be of advantage, the person decides to try it.

e) **Adoption Stage:** The farmer consistently and extensively applies the new concept. The trial could be thought of as the practical assessment of an idea. His routine farming activities incorporate the innovation. It offers the benefit of innovation, so the farmer makes the ultimate decision and consistently implements it at a scale suited to his or her situation.

Before being adopted by humans, innovation goes through several stages, according to Rogers' model of innovation adoption. First, people learn how to create opinions, choose courses of action, carry them out, and decide whether or not to put innovations into effect.

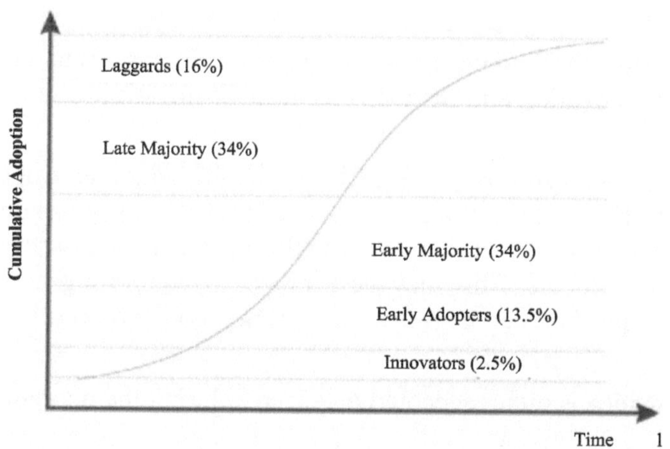

Figure 3: S shaped curve of Adoption (Source: Gabriel Tarde, 1903)

Stages in Innovation Decision Process

The Innovation Decision Process is an information -seeking and processing activity where individuals reduce uncertainty about the advantages or disadvantages of the innovation and decides to adopt or reject the innovation.

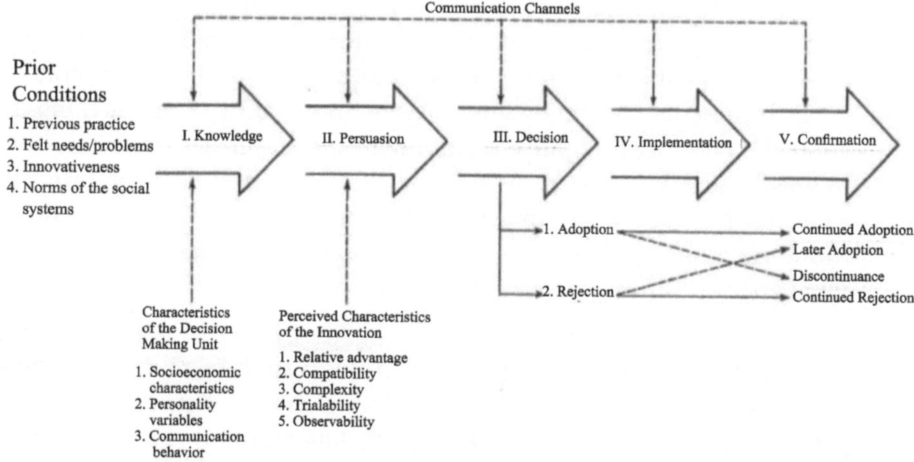

Figure 4: Stages in Innovation Decision Process (*Source:* Roger, 2003)

Everett Rogers investigates organisational dynamics and processes when a change is implemented within the Diffusion of Innovations paradigm. He outlines five stages in the adoption of change, each of which must be completed before the implementation may be successful.

There are Five Stages

1. **Knowledge:** During the knowledge stage, a person learns about the existence of the innovation and develops an interest in learning more about how it works.
2. **Persuasion:** When a person (or other decision-making units) develops a favourable or unfavourable attitude toward the innovation, persuasion occurs. It is crucial at this point that a potential user or beneficiary sees the innovation as valuable. This may be achieved by informing how the innovation in question can help them save time, money or perform better.
3. **Decision:** A new idea is either accepted or rejected during the decision stage.
4. **Implementation:** The steps involved in putting an idea into action are known as the implementation stage. The innovation-decision process has been a cerebral exercise until the execution. However, once the new concept is realised, implementation necessitates overt behaviour modification.
5. **Re-invention:** It frequently happens during the implementation phase. Re-invention is the degree to which a user alters or modifies an innovation during the adoption and implementation phases. The adopters of an idea frequently benefit from re-invention. It lessens errors and encourages adaptation of the innovation to suit local circumstances or shifting conditions better. An innovation may be more suitable in matching an adopter's current difficulties because of re-invention, and more sensitive to new issues that emerge throughout the innovation-decision process. More re-invention leads to a faster rate of adoption of an innovation. More re-invention leads to a higher degree of sustainability of an innovation. Re-invention can be beneficial to adopter of an innovation.
6. **Confirmation:** Confirmation happens when a person (or other decision-making units) looks for support for an innovation-related choice they have previously made. However, they may change their minds if they encounter contradictory information regarding the innovation. Following the choice to adopt or reject, the confirmation stage lasts indefinitely. At this point, the change agents also have the added duty of encouraging to those who have already adopted. "Discontinuance" as a sequential impact is a possibility. Discontinuance is the choice to stop using an innovation that was previously embraced.

There are two types of discontinuances

i) **Replacement discontinuance** - It is a decision to reject an idea to adopt a better one that supersedes it.

Example: Hybrid over Local variety, Mobile phones over Landlines

ii) **Disenchantment discontinuance** - It is a decision to reject an idea due to dissatisfaction with its performance.

Example: After a certain number of years, crop varieties typically degrade. If better kinds are not available, they are then either not farmed at all or replaced.

iii) **Forced Discontinuance:** This occurs when people are forced to make a shift due to government policies. Farmers are forced to stop using their current methods.

Example(s): The use of pesticides like DDT and BHC has been outlawed by the government, along with the usage of coal tar dyes and plastics by some groups.

Factors Affecting the Adoption of Innovation

According to studies, an individual's adoption of innovation is influenced by corporate policies, techniques, and behaviours in addition to their own opinions (Lewicka, 2011). Organizations must create enabling conditions, including the level and kind of assistance given to people who could impact on how they employ innovation. It is thought that the availability of training and the supply of assistance are among the facilitating factors. Training, management assistance, and incentives are examples of organisational variables. Employee adoption of an innovation may be motivated by organisational factors. Individual variables are one of the most significant predictors of accepting innovation, according to Lewis, Agarwal, and Sambamurthy (2003). It relates to how people understand innovations in their minds. Perceived utility, individual inventiveness, experience, perception, and pleasure of innovation are some of the elements that have a bigger impact on an individual's adoption of innovation.

The social environment influences innovation uptake by workers. Therefore, the adoption of innovation is likely to be significantly influenced by the innovation employed by others in the social context of the workforce. The degree to which members of a social group affect one another's conduct regarding adoption is known as social influence. Such influence is referred to as normative ideas about the acceptability of adopting innovation (Ajzen & Fishbein, 1980). This viewpoint contends that rather than because of an innovation's utility, workers may accept it because of perceived societal pressure. Such pressure may be viewed as coming from people, such as peers and members of social networks, whose thoughts and opinions are significant.

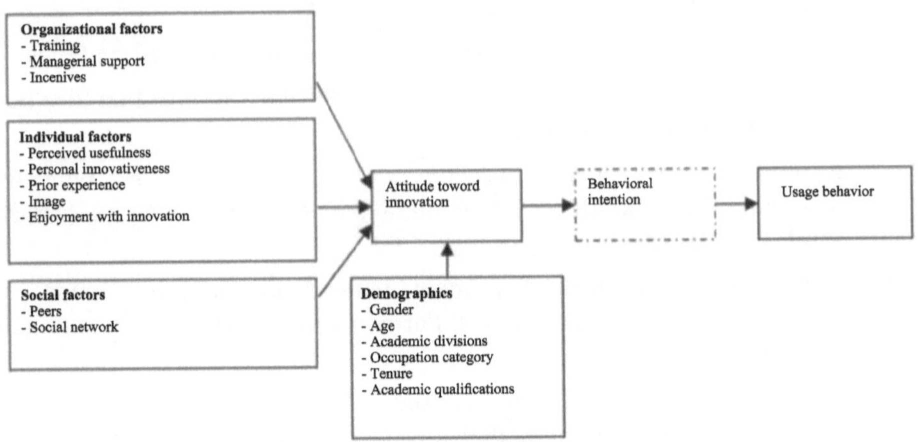

Figure 5: Factors affecting the adoption of innovation (*Source:* Talukder, 2012)

Consequences

The effects of an innovation's adoption or rejection on a person or a social system are known as consequences. These effects can be divided into three groups. First, change agents often bring innovations into a client system that they believe would result in changes that may be beneficial, direct, and anticipated. However, frequently innovations quickly have some unintended repercussions that are indirect and unfavourable for the members of the system.

Desirable Versus Undesirable Consequences

The practical effects of innovation are desirable outcomes for an individual or a social system. The dysfunctional repercussions of innovation on a person or a societal system are considered undesirable consequences. Whether consequences are functional or dysfunctional depends on how the innovation affects the adopters. An innovation can cause consequences for individuals other than its adopters.

Example: Internet, which advantages certain individuals and disadvantages others through the digital divide.

Direct Versus Indirect consequences

Direct effects are the adjustments made to a person or a social system as a direct result of the acceptance of an innovation. The modifications to a person or a social system brought on by an innovation's direct effects are known as its indirect consequences. These are the consequences of consequences.

Example- Wet Rice Farming in Madagascar - Direct versus Indirect Consequences

An anthropological study of the adoption of wet rice cultivation by a tribe in Madagascar serves as an example of an invention's direct and indirect effect. The nomadic group had grown rice using dryland techniques. They used a form of slash-and-burn agriculture, moving to a new place following each harvest. Then they started cultivating rice in wetlands using irrigation. As social status inequalities emerged, extensive clans were supplanted by nuclear families, and tribal governments evolved, a system of land ownership emerged. The effects of the technological advancement were both immediate and far-reaching since wet rice farming had several generations' worth of secondary effects that followed from the more immediate ones. (eGyankosh)

Anticipated Versus Unanticipated Consequences

Changes brought on by an innovation acknowledged and desired by the individuals inside a social system are referred to as anticipated effects. Changes resulting from an innovation that are neither intended nor acknowledged by the participants in a social system are known as unanticipated repercussions. No innovation comes without strings attached. The more technologically advanced innovation, the more likely its introduction will produce many consequences, both anticipated and latent.

Conclusion

Technology plays a significant role in developing the potency of agricultural resources. Technology created from research or study will be useful if it is applied in the field, especially in the efforts relating to farmer community empowerment. Therefore, it requires a concept considering innovation and technology diffusion in agricultural sector. Each innovation addresses and demonstrates an eagerness to set aside convention and adopt new practices by developing agribusiness. Proper training should be provided to the farmers which can led to an expansion of farmers communication networks and improve overall knowledge about the technology.

Answer the Following Questions

1. Define the concept of "diffusion of innovation" as described by Rogers (2003) and identify the key elements involved in the diffusion process within the agricultural sector.
2. Explain the role of communication channels in the diffusion of agricultural innovations. How do interpersonal channels differ from mass media outlets in their effectiveness for persuading farmers to adopt new practices?

3. Discuss the significance of an innovation's "trialability" attribute in agriculture. How does enabling farmers to test an innovation on a small scale influence its overall adoption rate?
4. Compare and contrast the different categories of adopters (innovators, early adopters, early majority, late majority, and laggards) as defined by Rogers. How might an extension worker customize their communication strategies to target each adopter category in a rural farming community effectively?
5. Critically evaluate the potential impact of the "social system" on the adoption of agricultural innovations. Consider factors such as social structure, norms, and existing practices. How can understanding the social system enhance the effectiveness of extension activities aimed at diffusing innovations among farmers?

18

Diffusion and Adoption

Haobijam James Watt and Devina Seram[1]

Department of Agricultural Economics and Extension, Lovely Professional University, Phagwara, Punjab

[1] Department of Entomology, Lovely Professional University, Phagwara, Punjab

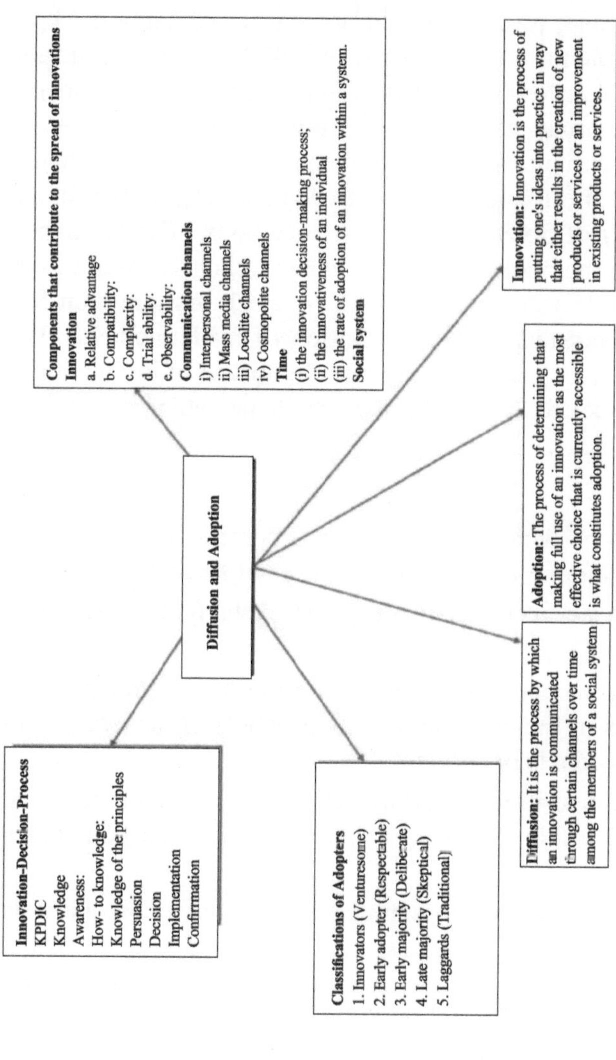

Figure 1: Overview of the chapter. (Credit: Jarial, S.)

Introduction

Diffusion is the process by which an innovation is transmitted to the members of a social system over some time and through channels in a specified manner. According to Rogers (1962), this is a unique form of communication in which the messages are focused on innovative concepts. The concepts can include (i) A new idea, (ii) An idea that is communicated via certain channels (iii) Among the members of a social system (iv) Overtime. On the other hand, the adoption process is the mental process through which an individual passes from first hearing about an innovation to final adoption, as defined by Rogers (1962). The concept of diffusion has been around for quite some time now; in fact, it was first investigated in the 19th century by Gabriel Tarde, a French Sociologist. On the other hand, researchers did not start conducting in-depth investigations on the phenomenon until the 1920s and 1930s. In 1943, Ryan and Gross carried out one of the earliest types of research that are now considered to be among the most important early studies. Previous study into the use of seeds in agricultural communities was strengthened because of this, and it offered a solid foundation for diffusion research to be conducted in the future. Everett Rogers, a Professor of Sociology, authored the book "Dissemination of Innovations" in 1962. In the book, he outlines a comprehensive framework for the process of invention dissemination, which is based on more than 500 investigations of the phenomena conducted in a variety of academic fields. The formal knowledge that involves modern study into the spread of innovation is founded on, can be traced back to Rogers's essay, which has remained relevant even today (Anonymous 1 n.a.).

Keywords

Diffusion: It is the process by which an innovation is communicated through certain channels over time among the members of a social system.

Communication: The process of understanding and exchanging meaning is defined as communication.

Innovation: Innovation is the process of putting one's ideas into practice in a way that either results in the creation of new products or services or an improvement in existing products or services.

Adoption: The process of determining that making full use of an innovation as the most effective choice that is currently accessible is what constitutes adoption.

The process by which an innovation is disseminated through certain channels over time among the participants of a social system is referred to as diffusion. It is a unique form of communication because the messages being sent are focused on novel concepts.

Components that Contribute to the Spread of Innovations

There are four main elements in the diffusion of innovations as described below:

1. Innovation
2. Communication channels
3. Time
4. Social system

1. Innovation

Innovation can be a concept, a practice, or a product, and it must be seen as a novel by a person or some other unit of adoption to be considered innovative. The degree to which an individual believes a concept to be novel is a significant factor in determining how they will respond to the notion. The "newness" of innovation can be represented in a variety of ways, including through information, persuasion, or a decision to adopt.

In this context, it would be useful to have some knowledge of the characteristics that are commonly associated with innovation. These characteristics are discussed in the paragraphs that follow.

a) Relative Advantage

It is the extent to which an innovation is seen as being superior to the concept that it replaces in some way. It is possible to quantify the degree of relative advantage in terms of economics, but elements relating to social prestige, convenience, and enjoyment are frequently also considered to be key components.

b) Compatibility

It is the extent to which potential adopters feel that an invention is compatible with the values they already hold, the experiences they have had in the past, and the requirements they currently have.

c) Complexity

It refers to the extent to which people believe a new idea is difficult to comprehend and utilize. In general, new concepts that are easier to comprehend will be accepted at a faster rate than innovations that need the adopter to gain new competencies and ways of thinking.

d) Trial ability

It refers to the extent to which a new idea can be tested out in a controlled environment on a restricted scale. An innovation that can be tested in the wild gives a person who is thinking about adopting it a lower level of uncertainty because it is possible to gain knowledge through experience.

e) Observability

It refers to the extent to which others can observe the effects that innovation has had. Individuals are more inclined to adopt an innovation when it is simpler for them to comprehend how the innovation will benefit them.

2. Communication channels

The process by which information is transmitted from one person to another is known as communication, and it takes place across a channel. The communicator could benefit from using the following categories of channels to make effective use of them:

i) **Interpersonal channels** – These refer to those that are utilized for communicating face-to-face amongst two or more individuals.

ii) **Mass media channels** - These make it possible for the messages to spread quickly and simultaneously to a wider audience. like radio and television.

iii) **Localite channels** - They have their roots within the social structure of the individual who receives them. for example, neighbours, family, influential people in the community, etc.

iv) **Cosmopolite channels** - They are not rooted in any particular social order or structure. eg: Extension worker, sales personnel, etc.

3. Time

The process of diffusion relies heavily on it as a crucial component. The passage of time is an unavoidable component of every communication procedure. Time is not something that exists apart from the occurrence of events; rather, it is an element that is present in every activity. The temporal dimension has a role in the following aspects of diffusion:

i) The innovation decision-making process;

ii) The innovativeness of an individual or other unit of adoption; and

iii) The rate of adoption of an innovation within a system.

4. Social Systems

It is described as a collection of interconnected units that collaborate on the solution of a common problem to achieve a shared objective. Individuals, informal groups, organizations, and/or subsystems can make up the components of a social system, also known as its members or units. Innovation will only spread so far within the confines of the social system it was introduced (Anonymous, 1 n.a.).

Innovation-Decision-Process

Due to recent developments in diffusion research, a new concept known as the "Innovation - Decision process" has been proposed. This concept sheds light on the sequential stages involved in the adoption decisions that are made by individuals or other units of adoption, and it is intended to serve as an alternative to the "Stages in the adoption process," which are defined as awareness, interest, evaluation, trial, and adoption. The process by which a person (or other decision-making unit) progresses from initial awareness of an invention to the construction of an attitude towards the innovation to the decision to adopt or reject the innovation, to the implementation of the new idea, and confirmation of this decision is referred to as the "Innovation-Decision Process." This procedure is characterized by a sequence of activities and decisions that are made over time, and it is how an individual or an organization analyses a novel concept and determines whether or not to implement the novel concept into ongoing practice Anonymous (2 n.a.). The five stages listed below make up the conception of the model of the innovation-decision process. (As illustrated in Fig.1).

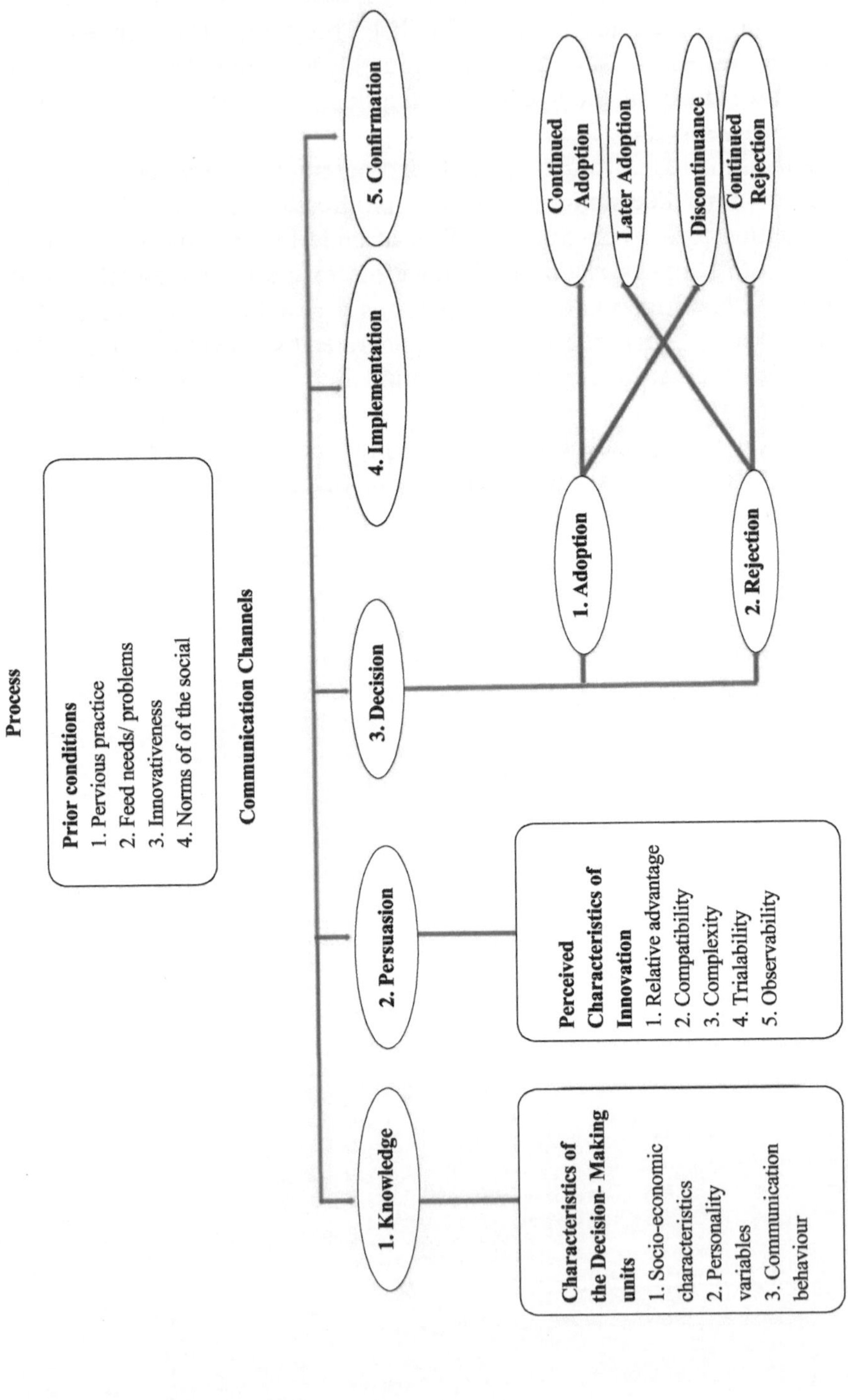

Figure 2. The five stages of Innovation Decision

1. Knowledge Stage

The knowledge stage begins when an individual (or the decision-making unit) is made aware of the existence of the invention and acquires some grasp of how it works. The decisions that an individual makes are heavily influenced by the following three sorts of knowledge that they possess:

i) **Awareness:** An individual who is aware of something is more likely to be motivated to pursue "how-to" information and principles understanding. This particular style of information-seeking is most prevalent during the knowledge stage of the innovation-choice process; however, it can take place throughout the persuasion and decision stages as well.

ii) **How-to knowledge**: It refers to the information that is required to make appropriate use of an innovation. If an acceptable amount of knowledge about how to do something is not gained before the trial and adoption of an innovation, then it is likely that the innovation will be rejected or discontinued. At the stage of testing and deliberation in the process, change agents could potentially play their unique role by focusing on "how-to knowledge."

iii) **Knowledge of the principles**: It underpins how the invention operates and comprises information dealing with the working principles underlying how the innovation operates. In most cases, it is possible to implement a new idea without first understanding its underlying principles; however, the risk of making inappropriate use of the innovative concept is significantly increased, which may lead to its abandonment. Knowledge of fundamental principles makes it easier for individuals to make accurate predictions about the development of new technologies in the future.

2. Persuasion Stage

When an individual (or any other decision-making unit) develops a favorable or unfavorable attitude towards the innovation, this is an example of the process of persuasion. While the majority of the thinking that occurred during the knowledge stage was of the cognitive, or knowing, variety, the majority of the thinking that occurs during the persuasion function is of the affective, or feeling, variety. At this point, an overarching impression of the innovation is being formed in people's minds. As a result of the individual's increased psychological involvement with the innovation, the individual will look for additional information regarding the novel concept.

3. The Point of Decision

A decision is made when an individual (or any other entity that makes decisions) participates in activities that lead to a choice about whether or not to accept the innovation. The decision to implement an innovation in its entirety and utilize its benefits to the fullest extent possible is an example of adoption. A choice to not embrace an innovation is an example of rejection. The choice to adopt an innovation will typically involve conducting a trial on a smaller scale first. This is an important step since it helps the adopter reduce the amount of uncertainty associated with the innovation.

4. Implementation Stage

The act of putting innovation into practice by an individual (or some other type of decision-making unit) is known as implementation. The innovation-decision process has been a purely mental activity up until this point when it will transition into the implementation stage. However, implementation necessitates overt behaviour modification because the new notion is part of the implementation process. It is more likely that more serious problems may arise throughout the implementation process when the adopter is an organization rather than an individual. The reason for this is that in a business or organizational context, a lot of people are typically involved in the process of deciding whether or not to execute an innovation, and the people who put the plan into action are frequently a separate group from those who make the decisions.

5. The Stage of Confirmation

It happens when an individual (or another decision-making unit) seeks reinforcement of an innovation choice that has already been taken. However, this individual may change this prior decision if they are exposed to competing messages regarding the innovation. After the decision has been made to either adopt or reject the proposal, the confirmation stage will continue for an unlimited amount of time. At this point, the change agents have the added role of providing words of support to persons who have already acquired the new perspective. There is a chance of "discontinuance" occurring as an outcome of successive events. A decision to stop utilizing a previously adopted innovation is known as discontinuation. This decision might come about for a variety of reasons. There are two categories of breaks in continuity:

i) The term "replacement discontinuance" refers to the choice to abandon one concept in favour of another, superior concept that succeeds and replaces it.

ii) Disenchantment, also known as discontinuation, is the act of choosing to abandon a concept because one feels unhappy with how well it has been implemented.

Classifications of Adopters

Innovation is not immediately adopted by every single member of a social system. This does not happen. They rather adopt in an orderly time sequence, and it is possible to classify them into adopter types based on the point in time at which they initially begin utilizing a new notion. It is of tremendous practical benefit for the extension agents participating in a technology transfer programme to identify the persons who are likely to accept innovations early and who may lag. When a bell-shaped curve is plotted over time on a frequency basis, the rate of adoption of an innovation over time tends to follow a normal distribution. A curve in the shape of an S can be obtained by plotting the total number of people who have adopted something. The S-shaped curve rises slowly initially when there are few adopters in a period, accelerates to a maximum when around half of the individuals in the system have adopted, and then grows at a steadily slower rate when the few individuals who are still lagging adopt eventually do so.

There are numerous sub-types of farmers to choose from. According to Rogers and Shoemaker (1971), farmers can be divided into five categories based on the degree to which they innovate.

1. Innovators (Venturesome)
2. Early adopter (Respectable)
3. Early majority (Deliberate)
4. Late majority (Skeptical)
5. Laggards (Traditional)

Characteristics of Farmer Innovators

Innovation is not immediately adopted by every single member of a social system. This does not happen. Rather, they adopt in a predetermined order over time, and we can divide them into different adopter types according to the point in time at which they initially implement a novel concept. In a technology transfer initiative, extension workers can identify those who are likely to absorb innovations quickly and others who are likely to lag behind. This allows the extension workers to target their efforts more effectively.

When a bell-shaped curve is plotted over time on a frequency basis, the rate of innovation adoption over time tends to follow a normal distribution. A curve in the shape of an S can be obtained by plotting the total number of people who have adopted something. The S-shaped curve rises slowly initially when there are few adopters in a period, accelerates to a maximum when approximately half of the individuals in the system have adopted, and then grows at a steadily slower rate when the few remaining individuals eventually adopt (Fig. 2). This pattern continues until all of the individuals in the system have adopted. The 'learning curve' that psychologists propose is very similar to the 'S-shaped curve' that they describe. Each instance of adoption within the social system can be thought of as being analogous to a learning experiment carried out by an individual.

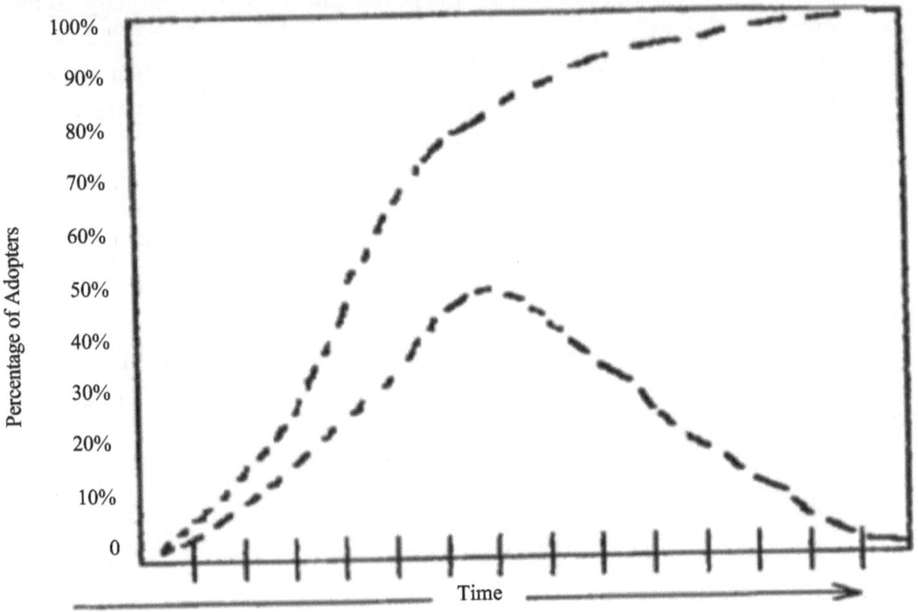

Figure 3. The bell-shaped frequency curve and the S-shaped cumulative curve

Both curves represent the same data, which is the gradual acceptance of innovation by the participants in a social system over time. The difference between the bell-shaped curve and the S-shaped curve is that the former displays the data in terms of the number of individuals who adopted each year, while the latter displays the data on a cumulative basis. The distribution of adopters over time comes very near to being normal, and this closeness can be described using a statistical notion called a normal curve. By calculating the mean (x) and the standard deviation of the adopters, it is possible to divide the distribution of the adopters into five distinct adopter categories. People who adopt innovations for the first time make up 2.5% of the population in the area that lies to the left of the meantime of adoption minus two standard deviations.

These people are referred to as innovators. Early adopters are the people who accept a new concept within the first 13.5% of the population, which falls between the mean minus one standard deviation and the mean minus two standard deviations. The early majority refers to the adopters who make up the next 34% of the population and whose dates of adoption fall between the mean and one standard deviation below the mean. The late majority, which consists of the next 34% of people to accept the new concept, can be found somewhere between the mean and one standard deviation to the right of the mean. The final 16% of people to the right of the mean plus one standard deviation are considered the laggards since they were the last to accept the innovation. The five different sorts of adopters are conceptualized as ideal types and are shown in Fig 3.

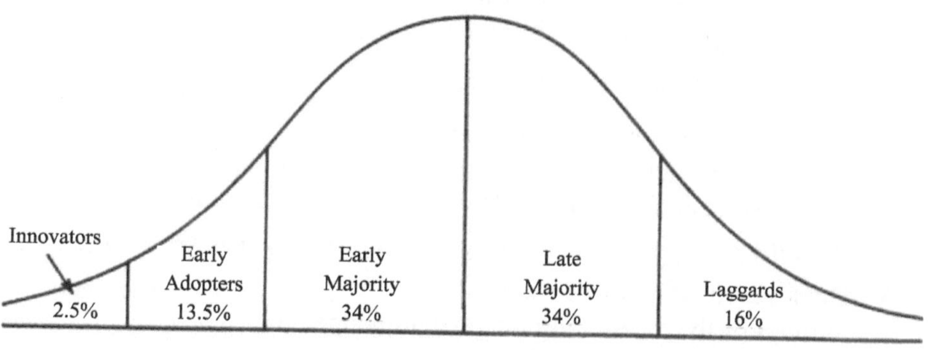

Figure 4. Classification of adopters according to their level of innovativeness

The innovativeness dimension can be thought of as a continuous process because it is measured by the rate at which an individual adopts an innovation. However, by subtracting standard deviations from the mean amount of time spent waiting to be adopted, it is possible to divide this variable into five distinct adopter categories (Anonymous, 2020). The information regarding the characteristics of the adopter categories is broken down into further details as mentioned below:

A. Innovators: Venturesome

Observers have seen that inventors tend to be risk-takers, even to the point of obsession. They are excited to test out novel concepts. Because of this curiosity, they find themselves moving beyond the confines of their immediate social group and into more globalized social connections. Even if there may be great geographical distance between the innovators, it is not uncommon for there to be established communication patterns and friendships among a group of innovators. Being an inventor requires fulfilling several conditions. Among these are the capabilities of controlling considerable financial resources to assimilate, understand, and apply intricate specialized information.

The ability to take risks is the most important quality of an inventor. He craves things that are reckless, risky, audacious, and hazardous to his health. The innovative person also needs to be willing to accept occasional failure, such as when one of the new ideas that they implement turns out to be unsuccessful Anonymous (2020). These are the pioneers who embrace novel concepts much in advance of other individuals in the world. They are extremely uncommon, and there are most likely no more than one or two in any given neighbourhood.

Characteristics of Innovators

1. Have larger farms
2. A high financial worth and a capacity for taking risks
3. Willing to take risks
4. Rarely after the age of middle age
5. To a large extent, highly educated
6. Respect and status in progressive communities, but neither in traditionalist communities nor traditionalist-type communities
7. Mentally engaged and constantly looking for new inspiration
8. Their realm of influence and activity frequently extends beyond the confines of the community in which they operate
9. They have a large number of contacts, both formal and informal, outside of the immediate neighbourhood
10. They frequently acquire information from the sources without going via the local extension worker, and as a result, they could find out about new developments even before he does. They are sometimes successful in acquiring samples of seeds or chemicals even before they are made available to the general public
11. They are subscribers to a wide variety of agricultural periodicals and specialized publications

Other farmers may keep an eye on the innovators and know what they are up to, but in most cases, these farmers do not name the innovators as "neighbours and friends" who they consult for advice.

B. Early Adopters: Respectable

In contrast to innovators, early adopters are already well-established members of the community in which they live. Early adopters are more like locations than innovators, who are more like cosmopolites. More than any other adopter's group, this adopter's category has the largest degree of opinion leadership in the majority of social systems. Early adopters are typically looked to by potential adopters for guidance and information regarding an innovation. Many people look to the early adopter as "the man to check with" before implementing a novel concept in their work. The members of this adopter type are typically sought after by agents of change to serve as local missionaries to accelerate the process of dissemination. Because early adopters are not far ahead of the average person in terms of innovativeness, they act as role models for a large number of other people who are part of a social system. Early adopters earn the respect of other participants in a social structure. The early adopter is held in high esteem by his contemporaries. He is the epitome of effectively integrating novel concepts while maintaining a low profile. In addition, the early adopter is aware of the fact that for him to keep his position in the social structure, he must continue to do things that will earn the respect of his peers.

Characteristics of Early Adopters

1. Younger than those who have a slower pace of adoption, but not necessarily younger than those who were the first to do something
2. They are not the people who test the ideas that have not been tested before, but they are the people who are the quickest to employ concepts that have been attempted in other contexts
3. Have large farms
4. Higher education compared to those that accept new technologies at a slower pace
5. Profitable endeavours
6. They are more active participants in the various community formats of activities
7. They are also more likely to participate in projects run by the government
8. In most cases, a disproportionate number of the formal leadership posts (elected positions) in the community are filled by members of this group
9. They keep up with the news by reading newspapers and agricultural journals, and they get more bulletins than people who adopt children later in life
10. They are potential leaders in the community when it comes to adoption

C. Early Majority: Deliberate (Local Adoption Leaders)

The early majority are the members of a social system that accept novel ideas immediately before the typical member of society. The early majority has frequent interactions with their contemporaries, although they rarely hold positions of leadership within the group. Because of their distinct position between those who were extremely early and those who were relatively late to adopt, the early majority serve as a vital link in the process of spread.

The early majority may take some time to mull over a new notion before fully embracing it. Their decision-making process about innovations takes significantly more time than those of innovators and early adopters. The early majority may have adopted as their motto, "Be not the last to lay the old aside, nor the first by which the new is tried" (do not be the person who tries anything new for the first time). They follow others with a determined eagerness to absorb ideas, but they rarely take the initiative themselves.

Characteristics of Early Majority

1. Age, education, and years of experience in farming are all slightly higher than normal
2. They subscribe to a greater number of agricultural periodicals and bulletins compared to the typical reader
3. They have a standing that is somewhere in the middle between economically and socially
4. They are more active than individuals who adopted the technology later on but are less active in formal groups than early adopters
5. In many instances, they do not hold official leadership positions within the association.
6. They also go to farm demos and sessions held by the extension service
7. They are much more likely to be informal resources than early adopters and pioneers, and as a result, they cannot afford to make decisions that are either hasty or poor
8. They primarily maintain relationships with members of their community
9. Because the opinions of their neighbours and friends are the primary source of their status and prestige, they place a great level of importance on these relationships
10. The majority of farmers seek information from their "neighbours and friends," and this is the most common way in which they are referred to.

D. Late Majority: Skeptical

The late majority are the members of a social system that embrace new beliefs shortly after the average member. It's possible that adopting a child is the solution to growing societal demands as well as a financial requirement. An attitude of skepticism and caution is taken towards innovations, and the late majority does not accept new practices until the majority of others in their social system have already done so. Before the late majority can be convinced, the innovation's weight in terms of system rules needs to be in its favour. They are open to being convinced of the usefulness of novel concepts, but the pressure of their contemporaries is required to inspire acceptance.

Characteristics of Late Majority

1. People who fall into this category have completed fewer years of schooling and are at an older age than the early majority
2. They make up the majority of formal organizational membership, even though that they are less active in formal groupings and still form the majority of the membership
3. They are less likely to take on leadership roles than early adopters
4. They subscribe to a smaller number of newspapers, magazines, and bulletins and read fewer of them than the early majority does
5. They do not take part in nearly as many activities outside their community as people who adopted children at an earlier age do

E. Laggards: Traditional

Laggards are the people who are always the last to adopt new technology. They are nearly completely devoid of opinion leadership. They have the most localized perspective of all the adopter categories, and many of them are quite close to being isolated. The laggard looks to the past as its primary point of reference. In most cases, choices are taken after considering what preceding generations have experienced and accomplished. This person spends most of their time interacting with those who share traditional ideals. It is possible that by the time laggards ultimately adopt an innovation, the idea will have been rendered obsolete by another, more recent concept that innovators are already implementing. Those who lag behind the times are typically openly hostile toward new ideas, pioneers, and agents of change. Their orientation towards tradition makes the decision-making process about innovation move at a snail's pace. Knowledge of the concept has significantly outpaced its adoption. A significant portion of the laggard's perspective reveals signs of alienation from a world that moves too quickly. The attention of laggards in a social system is focused on the rear-view mirror, whilst the majority of people in the system are looking forward to the path of change that lies ahead.

Characteristics of Laggards

1. The lowest level of schooling
2. Oldest
3. The least amount of participation in official institutions, cooperatives, and government activities
4. They do not spend much time reading farming journals and bulletins

Conclusion

The pattern and rate at which new ideas, practices, or goods spread through a population is referred to as the diffusion of innovations. There are five main types of people involved in the diffusion process: innovators, early users, early majority, late majority, and laggards. The concept of the dissemination of innovations is frequently utilized to better comprehend and encourage the use of newly introduced goods. People as members of a social system end up adopting a new idea, behaviour, or product as the ultimate consequence of this spread of information. A person is said to have adopted something when they do a thing differently than what they had been doing in the past. For example, when people buy or use a new product when they acquire or perform a new behaviour, etc.

Answer the Following Questions

1. Can you list the four main elements involved in the diffusion of innovations as described in the introduction, and briefly define what is meant by "innovation" in this context?
2. Explain in your own words how the concept of "trialability" can influence a farmer's decision to adopt a new agricultural practice or technology. Why is it significant for reducing uncertainty?
3. Given a scenario where a new drought-resistant crop variety is introduced in a rural community, how might an extension worker utilize the communication channels described to promote adoption among the different categories of farmers?
4. Compare and contrast the characteristics of "Early Adopters" and "Late Majority" in the context of adopting new agricultural technologies. How do their approaches to innovation and their influence within the social system differ?
5. Evaluate the potential impact of a social system's structure on the diffusion of a new farming technique. Consider the role of opinion leaders and the network of interpersonal relationships among farmers. How might these factors either facilitate or hinder the spread of innovation?

19

Agricultural Journalism

***Y.S. Bagal and Meenakshi Anand*[1]**

Department of Agricultural Economics and Extension, Lovely Professional University, Phagwara, Punjab

[1]Department of Home Science (Human Development), Lakshmibai College University of Delhi, Delhi

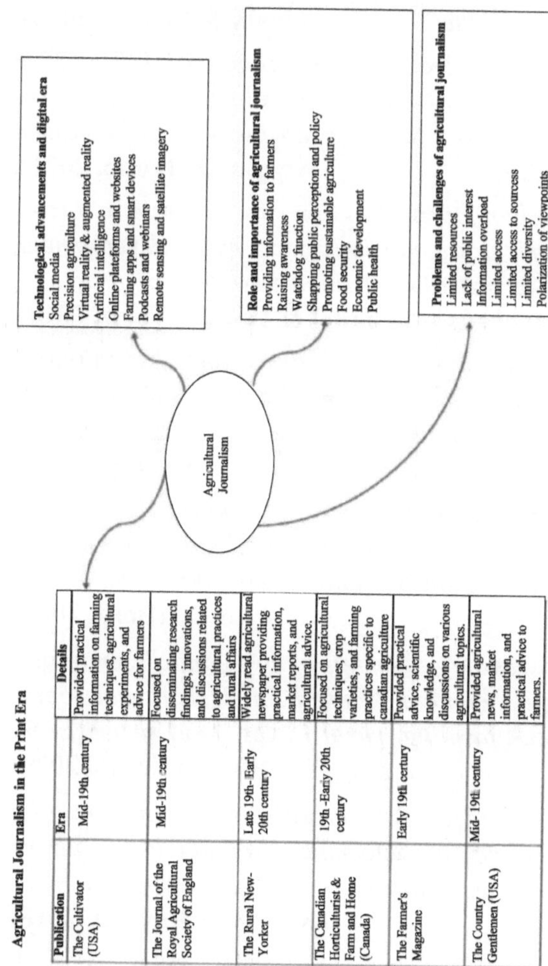

Publication	Era	Details
The Cultivator (USA)	Mid-19th century	Provided practical information on farming techniques, agricultural experiments, and advice for farmers
The Journal of the Royal Agricultural Society of England	Mid-19th century	Focused on disseminating research findings, innovations, and discussions related to agricultural practices and rural affairs
The Rural New-Yorker	Late 19th- Early 20th century	Widely read agricultural newspaper providing practical information, market reports, and agricultural advice.
The Canadian Horticulturist & Farm and Home (Canada)	19th -Early 20th century	Focused on agricultural techniques, crop varieties, and farming practices specific to canadian agriculture
The Farmer's Magazine	Early 19th century	Provided practical advice, scientific knowledge, and discussions on various agricultural topics.
The Country Gentlemen (USA)	Mid- 19th century	Provided agricultural news, market information, and practical advice to farmers.

Figure 1: Overview of the chapter (Credit: Jarial, S.)

Meaning and Definitions

Agricultural journalism refers to the specialized field of journalism focused on reporting, analyzing, and disseminating information related to agriculture, farming, rural development, and related topics. It plays a crucial role in educating and informing the public, policymakers, and stakeholders about the agricultural sector, its challenges, innovations, and contributions to society.

Here are a few definitions of agricultural journalism.

The Encyclopedia of Agricultural, Food, and Biological Engineering defines agricultural journalism as "a branch of journalism that focuses on reporting news and information related to agricultural and food production practices, policies, and issues. Agricultural journalists cover a range of topics, including crop and livestock production, agribusiness, agricultural policies, rural development, and environmental concerns" **(Joshi & Reaves, 2010).**

Agricultural journalism involves the collection, evaluation, and presentation of news, features, and other media content specifically related to agricultural issues, including crop production, livestock farming, agribusiness, agricultural policies, and environmental concerns **(Wiggins & Tropp, 2021).**

Agricultural journalism is a branch of journalism that specializes in reporting news and information about agriculture, agribusiness, rural development, and agricultural policies, as well as providing insights into farming practices, innovations, and challenges **(Poudel & Van der Vorst, 2019).**

Agricultural journalism refers to the reporting, analysis, and dissemination of news and information specifically related to agriculture, including farming practices, agricultural policies, agribusiness, rural development, and environmental issues **(Thorsøe et al., 2019).**

Agricultural journalism involves the communication of agricultural information through various media channels, aimed at informing and educating diverse audiences about the agricultural sector, its challenges, innovations, and societal impacts **(Berg, 2020).**

Agricultural journalism encompasses the gathering, analysis, and dissemination of news, features, and multimedia content focused on agricultural topics, such as crop production, livestock farming, rural issues, food security, and sustainable agriculture **(Rutsaert et al., 2020).**

Agricultural journalism is a specialized form of journalism that concentrates on reporting, interpreting, and communicating information about the agricultural sector, including farming practices, agricultural policies, technology adoption, and agricultural markets **(Barton & Hayden, 2018).**

These definitions emphasize the utilization of journalistic practices, such as news gathering, verification, storytelling, and audience engagement, within the context of agriculture. It highlights the scope of agricultural journalism, which encompasses a wide range of topics related to farming, rural communities, and agricultural policies.

History of Agricultural Journalism

History of agricultural journalism trace back to the early stages of human civilization. Throughout time, the methods, mediums, and purposes of agricultural journalism have evolved alongside advancements in technology and the changing needs of society.

Early forms of Agricultural Journalism

Early forms of agricultural journalism can be traced back to ancient civilizations, where various means of disseminating agricultural information existed. Although the concept of journalism as we know it today did not exist in those times, agricultural writings and documents provided valuable information about farming practices, land management, and agricultural knowledge.

History of Agricultural Journalism in Ancient Times

Period	Event
Ancient Civilizations	Early forms of agricultural journalism with writings and documents about farming practices, land management, and agricultural knowledge.
Ancient Egypt	Knowledge documented in texts such as the 'Kahun Papyrus' and the 'Ebers Papyrus', containing information on agricultural practices, irrigation techniques, and crop cultivation methods.
8th century BCE	Hesiod, a Greek poet, wrote 'Works and Days', providing agricultural advice on planting, plowing techniques, and observing natural phenomena for agricultural planning.
Middle Ages	Almanacs became popular, providing calendars, weather predictions, planting guides, and other practical agricultural information.

(*Source:* Coser & Rimanelli, 2004)

Agricultural Journalism in the Print Era

During the print era, agricultural journalism saw significant developments with the establishment of newspapers, magazines, and other printed publications that focused specifically on agricultural topics. These print publications played a crucial role in disseminating agricultural information and connecting farmers with the latest developments in the field. "The Cultivator" in the

United States was a prominent agricultural newspaper published in the mid-19th century. It provided practical information on farming techniques, agricultural experiments, and advice for farmers. This publication helped establish agricultural journalism as a distinct field (Gates, 2016). "The Journal of the Royal Agricultural Society of England" was an influential agricultural publication that started in the mid-19th century. It focused on disseminating research findings, innovations, and discussions related to agricultural practices and rural affairs (Black, 1997). "The Rural New-Yorker" was a widely read agricultural newspaper published in the late 19th and early 20th centuries. It provided farmers with practical information, market reports, and advice on agricultural practices. The newspaper played a crucial role in disseminating agricultural knowledge to rural communities (Horowitz, 1989).

In Canada, several agricultural magazines emerged in the 19th and early 20th centuries, such as "The Canadian Horticulturist" and "Farm and Home." These magazines focused on providing information on agricultural techniques, crop varieties, and farming practices specific to Canadian agriculture (Hugill, 2007).

"The Farmer's Magazine" was a significant agricultural publication that originated in the early 19th century. It provided practical advice, scientific knowledge, and discussions on various agricultural topics. The magazine played a crucial role in disseminating agricultural information and promoting improvements in farming practices (Bennett, 2006). "The Country Gentleman" was a prominent agricultural newspaper that emerged in the mid-19th century. It focused on providing agricultural news, market information, and practical advice to farmers. The newspaper helped connect farmers across different regions and contributed to the development of agricultural knowledge (Clark, 1983).

Agricultural Journalism in the Print Era

Publication	Era	Details
The Cultivator (USA)	Mid-19th century	Provided practical information on farming techniques, agricultural experiments, and advice for farmers.
The Journal of the Royal Agricultural Society of England	Mid-19th century	Focused on disseminating research findings, innovations, and discussions related to agricultural practices and rural affairs.
The Rural New-Yorker	Late 19th - Early 20th century	Widely read agricultural newspaper providing practical information, market reports, and agricultural advice.
The Canadian Horticulturist & Farm and Home (Canada)	19th - Early 20th century	Focused on agricultural techniques, crop varieties, and farming practices specific to Canadian agriculture.

The Farmer's Magazine	Early 19th century	Provided practical advice, scientific knowledge, and discussions on various agricultural topics.
The Country Gentleman (USA)	Mid-19th century	Provided agricultural news, market information, and practical advice to farmers.

Technological Advancements and Digital Era

Technological advancements and the digital era have significantly impacted agricultural journalism, enabling journalists to reach a broader audience, deliver news faster, and provide more engaging content.

Social media: Social media platforms such as Twitter, Facebook, and Instagram have become crucial tools for agricultural journalists to communicate with their audience and share information. Farmers, agribusinesses, and industry experts use social media to discuss agricultural topics, share news, and provide updates on farming practices (Lowenberg-DeBoer *et al.*, 2017). Agricultural journalists can leverage social media analytics tools to monitor and analyze trends, conversations, and public sentiment related to agricultural topics. These insights can inform journalists about popular issues, emerging trends, and public concerns, helping them shape their reporting and engage with their audience more effectively (Budzinski *et al.*, 2019).

Precision agriculture: Precision agriculture technologies such as drones, GPS mapping, and sensors have revolutionized farming practices, enabling farmers to increase efficiency, reduce costs, and improve yields. Agricultural journalists can report on these technological advancements, providing insights on how they work and their potential benefits (Kloppenburg, 2017).

Virtual reality and augmented reality: Virtual reality (VR) and augmented reality (AR) technologies are increasingly being used in agricultural journalism to provide immersive experiences for readers. Journalists can use VR and AR to showcase new technologies, simulate farming practices, and visualize complex concepts (Barr, 2019).

Artificial intelligence: The use of artificial intelligence (AI) in agriculture is becoming more widespread, with AI-enabled machines being used for tasks such as planting, harvesting, and monitoring crop growth. Agricultural journalists can report on these developments, providing insights on the potential benefits and risks of using AI in agriculture (Kloppenburg, 2017).

Online platforms and websites: The digital era has witnessed the rise of online platforms and websites dedicated to agricultural journalism. These platforms provide a centralized hub for agricultural news, articles, blogs, and resources, allowing farmers and industry professionals to access information conveniently (Barton & Hayden, 2018). The digital era has given rise to online forums and communities where farmers can connect, exchange ideas, seek advice, and share experiences. These platforms foster knowledge-sharing, networking, and community building among farmers, enabling them to learn from each other and stay updated on the latest agricultural practices (Guthman, 2018). The digital era has seen the development of online data platforms that provide comprehensive agricultural data, statistics, and research findings. Agricultural journalists can access these platforms to gather accurate and up-to-date information, enhancing the credibility and depth of their reporting (Kromrey *et al.*, 2019).

Farming apps and smart devices: The development of mobile applications specific to agriculture has facilitated access to agricultural information on smartphones and tablets. These applications offer features such as weather forecasts, market prices, pest management strategies, and farm management tools, empowering farmers with real-time information (Nwokeji *et al.*, 2020). The proliferation of farming apps and smart devices has transformed agricultural practices and information sharing. These apps and devices offer functionalities such as soil testing, crop management, irrigation control, and livestock monitoring, empowering farmers and enabling agricultural journalists to report on emerging technologies and their impact (Beukes *et al.*, 2020).

Podcasts and webinars: Technological advancements have made it easier for agricultural journalists to create and distribute audio content through podcasts and conduct webinars on agricultural topics. These mediums provide an interactive and convenient way for farmers to access expert insights, industry trends, and educational resources (Barton & Hayden, 2018).

Remote sensing and satellite imagery: Technological advancements in remote sensing and satellite imagery have revolutionized the way agricultural journalists gather data and monitor crop conditions. These tools provide high-resolution images and data on crop health, vegetation indices, and land use patterns, enabling journalists to report on agricultural practices and environmental changes (Huang *et al.*, 2018).

Role and Importance of Agricultural Journalism

Agricultural journalism plays a crucial role in providing information and knowledge to farmers, policymakers, and the general public regarding the agricultural sector. It helps in raising awareness about the latest agricultural technologies, practices, and innovations, which can enhance agricultural productivity and sustainability. Agricultural journalists also serve as watchdogs, providing critical analysis and information about the challenges faced by farmers and the industry.

Providing information to farmers: Agricultural journalism provides information to farmers about the latest agricultural technologies, practices, and innovations, which can enhance agricultural productivity and sustainability. It also helps farmers access information about market trends, prices, and new opportunities, enabling them to make informed decisions and stay competitive.

Raising awareness: Agricultural journalism raises awareness about the challenges and opportunities in the agricultural sector. It informs the public about the importance of agriculture in society, including its role in providing food, fuel, and fiber.

Watchdog function: Agricultural journalists serve as watchdogs, providing critical analysis and information about the challenges faced by farmers and the industry. They report on issues such as food safety, agricultural policies, and regulations, and hold policymakers and industry leaders accountable for their actions.

Shaping public perception and policy: Agricultural journalism can influence public opinion and policymakers' decisions, particularly in areas such as genetically modified crops and food safety. It can also shape public perception and policy on agriculture by providing accurate and unbiased information about the industry.

Promoting sustainable agriculture: Agricultural journalism plays a vital role in promoting sustainable agriculture and reducing environmental degradation. It informs the public about sustainable agricultural practices and the importance of conservation and environmental stewardship.

Food security: Agricultural journalism plays a crucial role in ensuring food security by providing information about the latest farming technologies, practices, and innovations. Farmers can make informed decisions about what crops to grow, how to manage pests and diseases, and how to improve productivity, which can help meet the growing demand for food.

Economic development: Agriculture is a critical sector in many countries, and agricultural journalism can contribute to economic development by promoting agricultural entrepreneurship, facilitating access to markets, and providing information about investment opportunities in the sector.

Public health: Agricultural journalism can play a crucial role in promoting public health by providing information about food safety, food labeling, and other issues related to public health.

Problems and Challenges of Agricultural Journalism

Agricultural journalism faces several challenges that can limit its effectiveness and impact.

Limited resources: Agricultural journalism often operates on limited budgets, which can limit the amount and quality of reporting. This can result in a lack of coverage of important issues, and the inability to investigate and report on complex topics.

Lack of public interest: Agricultural issues may not always be considered newsworthy or interesting to the general public, which can result in a lack of interest in agricultural journalism. This can make it difficult for journalists to attract and maintain an audience.

Information overload: With the abundance of information available online, it can be challenging for readers to find accurate and reliable information. This can lead to confusion and mistrust of agricultural journalism.

Limited access: In some regions, access to information and resources may be limited, making it difficult for agricultural journalists to report on important issues. This can result in a lack of coverage of rural areas and smaller agricultural sectors.

Limited access to sources: Agricultural journalism may face challenges in accessing sources and experts, especially in remote or rural areas. This can limit the depth and quality of reporting, as well as limit the diversity of voices represented in agricultural journalism.

Limited diversity: Agricultural journalism may lack diversity in terms of gender, ethnicity, and perspectives. This can limit the range of stories and viewpoints covered by agricultural journalists, resulting in a narrow perspective on agricultural issues.

Polarization of viewpoints: Agriculture is often a highly politicized industry, with different viewpoints and agendas competing for attention. This can lead to polarization of perspectives, making it difficult for journalists to report objectively and accurately on issues related to agriculture.

Lack of trust: Like many areas of journalism, agricultural journalism may suffer from a lack of public trust, which can be exacerbated by misinformation and polarization. This can make it difficult for agricultural journalists to gain the trust of their audience and to report on issues in a way that is seen as fair and balanced.

Pressure to serve industry interests: Some agricultural journalists may face pressure to serve the interests of industry groups or advertisers, which can compromise their objectivity and independence. This can be especially challenging for agricultural journalists who work for trade publications or other specialized media.

Overall, agricultural journalism faces several challenges that can limit its ability to inform and engage the public on important agricultural issues. Addressing these challenges will require a sustained effort to invest in agricultural journalism, greater public interest in agricultural issues, and a commitment to promoting diversity and to uphold the values of accuracy, objectivity, and independence in reporting.

Answer the Following Questions

1. What role does agricultural journalism play in ensuring that advancements in agriculture reach the intended audience effectively?
2. Consider the evolution of agricultural journalism from its early forms in ancient civilizations to the digital era's impact. How have technological advancements and the rise of digital media transformed the way agricultural information is disseminated and accessed by farmers and the general public? Analyze the benefits and potential challenges introduced by this evolution.
3. Reflecting on the problems and challenges faced by agricultural journalism, such as limited resources, lack of public interest, and the pressure to serve industry interests, evaluate the potential strategies agricultural journalists could employ to overcome these obstacles. How can agricultural journalism maintain its integrity, objectivity, and relevance in the face of these challenges while still effectively serving its audience?

20

Agriculture Journalism

Yanglem Lakshimai Devi, Sapna Jarial, Sharad Sachan and Roop Kumar

Department of Agricultural Economics and Extension, Lovely Professional University Phagwara, Punjab

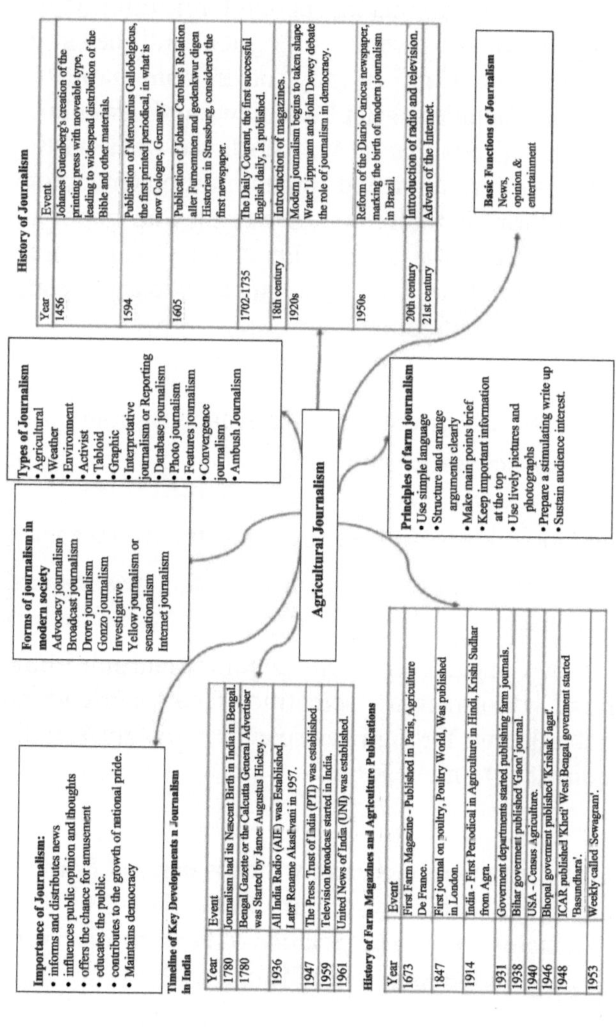

Figure 1: Overview of the chapter (Credit: Jarial, S)

Introduction

The emergence of the green revolution highlighted the significance of agricultural communication. Its strategy and attitude were modified to reflect the priorities of contemporary agriculture. Earlier attempts at agricultural journalism drew their power mostly from agricultural extension rather than journalism or mass communication. The primary objective was to provide farmers with a collection of techniques authored by scientists or subject matter experts about a variety of crops. Due to the lack of synergy between journalism and extension, agricultural journalism stalled for many years..

Journalism is the profession of writing for or editing newspapers, magazines, and other publications, whereas agricultural journalism is the task of gathering, writing, editing, publishing, and disseminating agricultural information, scientific facts, agricultural technology, events, or agricultural news via newspapers, magazines, radio, television, or any other communication medium. Common farm literature includes agricultural news and agricultural feature articles. There are specific criteria that must be observed when writing farm literature. Even in this era of information and communication technology advancements, print media and farm literature continue to play an important role in the transfer of technology to rural areas. This chapter will instruct students on how to integrate journalism into agricultural extension using various approaches for preparing farm literature.

Key terms

Agricultural news: A timely report of agricultural events, facts or opinions.

Agricultural feature story: An accurate, unbiased account of facts to be published in periodicals.

Communication: The mutual interchange of ideas by any effective means.

Journalism: Journalism is a profession of writing for or editing newspapers, magazines and other publications.

Agricultural Journalism: the task of gathering, writing, editing and publishing or disseminating agricultural information, scientific facts, agricultural technology, events or agricultural news through newspapers, magazines, radio and television or by any media of communication

Journalism: Concept

Journalism is derived from the French term journal, which is derived from the Latin word diurnal, meaning daily. Originally, a diary was a record of daily events. The word “journey” denotes a day. The practice of keeping diaries or daily accounts gradually gave rise to the term journalism.

Journalism: Definition

According to Webster's Dictionary: Journalism means business of managing, editing or writing for journals or news paper and also collectively.

According to Wolsley (1969): Journalism as the systematic and reliable gathering, writing, interpreting, processing and disseminating of public opinion, public information and public entertainment for publication in news papers, magazines and telecast.

According to Wikipedia Journalism: Journalism is the activity or product of journalists or others engaged in the preparation of written, visual, or audio material intended for dissemination through public media with reference to factual, ongoing events of public concern Journalism is the craft of conveying news, opinion via widening spectrum of media.

According to Leslie Stephens: "Journalism consists of writing for pay on matters of which you are ignorant".

According to Eric Hodgins of Time Magazine: "Journalism is the conveying of information from here to there with accuracy, insight and dispatch and in such a manner that the truth is served and the rightness of things is made slowly, even if not immediately, more evident".

According to Websters third International Dictionary Journalism define as "The collection and editing of material of current interest for presentation, publication or broadcast".

Table 1: History of Journalism

Year	Event
1400	Businessmen in Italian and German cities were compiling hand written chronicles of important news events
1456	Johannes Gutenberg's creation of the printing press with moveable type, leading to widespread distribution of the Bible and other materials.
1594	Publication of Mercurius Gallobelgicus, the first printed periodical, in what is now Cologne, Germany.
1605	Publication of Johann Carolus's 'Relation aller Fürnemmen und gedenkwürdigen' historian in Strassburg, considered the first newspaper.
1702-1735	The Daily Courant, the first successful English daily, was published.
18th century	Introduction of magazines.
1920s	Modern journalism begins to take shape; Walter Lippmann and John Dewey debate the role of journalism in democracy.
1950s	Reform of the Diario Carioca newspaper, marking the birth of modern journalism in Brazil.
20th century	Introduction of radio and television.
21st century	Advent of the Internet.

Table 2: Timeline of Key Developments in Journalism in India

Year	Event
1780	Journalism had its nascent birth in India in Bengal.
1780	Bengal Gazette or the Calcutta General Advertiser was started by James Augustus Hickey.
1936	All India Radio (AIR) was established, later renamed Akashvani in 1957.
1947	The Press Trust of India (PTI) was established.
1959	Television broadcast started in India.
1961	United News of India (UNI) was established.

Importance of Journalism

Journalism helps to an understanding of the publishing and editing of newspapers, magazines, and other publications. Thus, it is one of the most studied careers in modern times. Its significance resides in the following points.

1. It informs and distributes news

It is fundamentally the transmission of information. The everyday happenings are transmitted in a few words, sounds, images, etc. to fulfil people's curiosity about the environment and globe. Daily, the news informs the public on a variety of topics, including politics, history, laws, science, geography, socioeconomic issues, sex, crime, violence, and racial strife, among others. The media, such as radio, television, newspapers, magazines, and journals, can utilise satellite and other technologies to disseminate important and timely information.

2. It influences public opinion and thought by communicating social or commercial messages

It provides knowledge on past, current, and future happenings by detailing many aspects of past, present, and future facts. It leads people's minds by explaining the truth, difficulties, possible solutions, and potential repercussions of a given event or thing, etc. It acts as a custodian of the people's ideas and speech, i.e., they can freely express their opinions through various journalism media.

3. It offers the chance for amusement

By publishing features, comedy, comics, and fictions, as well as by broadcasting or televising music, songs, and dances, etc., the various journalism media provide entertainment to the public.

4. It educates the public

Journalism's many media have a crucial role in disseminating information on a wide range of topics, including health and sanitation, laws, cultural aspects such as conventions, traditions, and norms, and other human activities. In

India, a developing country with a 23 percent illiterate population, journalism plays a crucial role in educating the uneducated through the use of audiovisual aids. These media assist in altering the people's knowledge, abilities, attitudes, values, norms, understandings, and beliefs in the desired direction.

5. It contributes to maintaining democracy

Journalism disseminates the news and relevant information of the parliament and legislature throughout the nation. At election time and for other related matters, the public can communicate with the government through the various media outlets. It also aids in the battle against injustice towards a specific group, community, or strain. In addition, it facilitates voting and other decisions.

6. It contributes to the growth of national pride.

These media disseminate news and non-news regarding national and international topics across the nation. The sharing of ideas, facts, and scientific knowledge in various sectors contributes to the growth of national pride. It also contributes to the development of national unity and integrity by disseminating the facts to all segments of the community and nation.

7. It functions as an agent in the collecting, preservation, and presentation of news and reading materials to journalistic outlets.

Today, stock market news is accessible by computer from a data bank. The electronic or word processing typewriter eliminates the need to retype letters and draughts. The evolution of electronic and computer technology has improved the dissemination and utilization of information. In addition to current events, it provides information on every aspect, including underground news.

8. It encourages the use of new agricultural methods by the populace.

Agriculture, dairy, poultry, horticulture, forestry, and other enhanced technology and packages of practices are regularly disseminated to the farming community via the many forms of journalism. It also gives the farmers with information pertaining to cost, price, market, weather records, etc.

Forms of journalism in modern society

'Prestige' journalism is believed to serve as a 'fourth estate', acting as watchdogs over the government's operations.

Other forms of journalism feature different formats and cater to different intended audiences.

- **Advocacy journalism** — writing to promote specific perspectives or sway the opinions of the public. Initiated by the United States in the early 19th century Advocacy journalism is a kind of journalism that adopts a non-objective position intentionally and openly, typically for a social or political cause. Since it is intended to be factual, it differs from propaganda. public relations orientated Here, journalists advocate for any public topic. In this form of journalism, journalists might be openly biased toward a specific individual or group of individuals. This form of journalism disapproves of one-sided viewpoints.

- **Broadcast journalism** – writing or speech meant for radio or television broadcasting, as opposed to written form for readers alone.
- **Drone journalism** entails the use of unmanned aerial vehicles to obtain journalistic footage. In this form of journalism, drones are used to collect news, as the term suggests. Using these drones, images, videos, and news are gathered. In the event of war, natural disasters, etc., drones are the most effective means of gathering intelligence.
- **Gonzo journalism** — pioneered by journalist Hunter S. Thompson, gonzo journalism is a "very personal reporting approach."
- **Investigative journalism** is writing that aims to provide additional facts to explain or better characterize the people and events of a specific issue.
- **Tabloid journalism** - work that contains subjective or outlandish statements
- **Yellow journalism** (or sensationalism) refers to writing that focuses on exaggerated claims or rumors.
- **Internet Journalism-** refers to the practice of journalism conducted over the Internet. It is a broad term that encompasses various forms of news and information dissemination that utilize the unique capabilities of the web. Here are some key aspects of Internet Journalism:
  - **Digital Platforms**: Unlike traditional journalism, which relies on print, television, or radio, Internet Journalism uses websites, social media, podcasts, and other digital platforms to distribute news and information.
  - **Interactivity and Engagement**: One of the defining features is the ability for readers or viewers to interact with the content and the content creators. This can include commenting on articles, sharing content on social media, or even contributing to the news process through citizen journalism initiatives.
  - **Multimedia Content**: Internet Journalism often combines various forms of media – text, video, audio, and interactive graphics – to tell stories in a more dynamic and engaging way.

- **Real-time Reporting**: The Internet allows for immediate publication and update of news, leading to real-time reporting. This immediacy is particularly crucial for breaking news situations.
- **Global Reach**: The Internet's global nature means that journalism conducted on this medium can reach a worldwide audience, transcending geographical and political boundaries.
- **Diverse Voices and Decentralization**: The Internet has lowered the barriers to entry for journalism, allowing more voices to be heard. Independent journalists, bloggers, and citizen journalists can now contribute to the news ecosystem.
- **Adaptation of Traditional Media**: Traditional news organizations have adapted to the Internet age by establishing online presences and incorporating digital strategies into their reporting and distribution.

Elements of Journalism

1. The primary commitment of journalism is to the truth.

   Our primary obligation is to obtain accurate information. News is the stuff that people use to study and reflect on the world beyond themselves; therefore, it must be usable and trustworthy. For the truth to triumph, journalists must make clear to whom they owe their primary allegiance.

2. Journalism's first obligation is to citizens.

   As a result, the term "journalistic independence" was coined. Consumers are aware that the restaurant review they are reading was not impacted by the business's print, web, or broadcast advertisement. Therefore, journalists must adhere to ethical norms by refusing gifts.

3. Journalism is essentially a study of verification.

   Verify the content of reports and other media sources. Absence of personal bias

4. Journalists must retain their impartiality toward people they cover.

   We inhabit their world, but it is not ours. Conflict of interest: when a journalist covers an event, venue, or person in which he or she has a personal stake.

5. Journalists must serve as an independent monitor of power.

   Watergate – 1972 – President Nixon is caught resigns as president. More than just government, it extends to all powerful institutions in society. Journalism gives voice to the voiceless.

6. Journalism must provide a forum for public criticism and comment.

Journalism serves as a public forum, a place for the sharing of information, ideas and the debate of those ideas. This comes in the form of letters to the editor, phone forums, guest columnists, etc.

7. Journalists must make the news significant, relevant & interesting.

   There is no such thing as a boring story, there are only boring reporters. Journalists are storytellers, with a purpose.

8. Journalists should keep the news in proportion and make it comprehensive. Consumers should ask

   a) Can we see the whole community in the coverage?

   b) Do I see myself?

   c) Does the report include a fair mix of what most people would consider either interesting or significant.

9. Journalists have an obligation to personal conscience.

   Every journalist must have a sense of personal ethics and responsibility–a moral compass. They must recognize a personal obligation to disagree with editors, owners, advertisers, and even citizens.

Basic Functions of Journalism

1. News purpose

The basic purpose of the media is to inform. Examining the abundance of public events, ideas, and situations, newspaper editors must select which would pique the public's interest. In addition to the factual presentation of news, analysis and explanation are required for complex situations.

2. The function of opinion

The modern man usually finds himself in a state of perplexity regarding which thing to buy. What choice should be made? Whom to vote? Because of logical reasoning, he requires a medium of six communications to help him comprehend the good and negative aspects of the situations. Consequently, the modern press must serve as both a daily educator and a daily tribute. Therefore, editorials are the only way to shape public opinion.

3. The entertainment purpose

Public amusement is both the function and business of the organisation. Since the task is too large for the local team, the newspaper relies on syndicated content. Entertainment can be found anywhere. It appears in stories of human interest and news segments. Sometimes, the selection of a newspaper is influenced by the level of public interest in specific elements, particularly comics.

Other Functions of Journalism

- Journalism is the "voice of the voiceless," conveying the perspectives of all members of society. It serves as a link between the government and the people. Consequently, its principal objective is to ensure that all citizens are informed of their rights.
- Information dissemination is journalism's primary duty. Information dissemination is an integral aspect of the democratic decision-making process, as it promotes openness in society and ensures that decisions reflect the people's sense of justice.
- Journalism is the examination and dissemination of information about events, issues, and trends to a broad audience for various purposes.
- Journalism's function at the time was to serve as a mediator or interpreter between the public and policy-making elites.
- The journalist became an intermediary. When elites spoke, journalists listened, took notes, and disseminated the knowledge to the people.
- Additionally, journalism serves as a two-way conduit between the public and government. The significance of journalism stems from the right of the people to opinion and expression.
- In the modern world, the press plays a crucial function as a vehicle of mass communication.
- The press attempts to inform its audience honestly about events in their town, nation, and the world.

Types of Journalism

Agricultural Journalism

Agricultural journalism is the profession of gathering information about technologies, issues, and accomplishments in agriculture and allied fields, and then writing, reporting, editing, publishing, and disseminating it for the intended audience (i.e. farmers in rural areas) using various print, electronic, and computer-added media.

Weather Journalism

People rely on journalism for climate and environment-related information, particularly those who live in places frequently affected by natural disasters such as tornadoes, cyclones, volcanoes, etc. In such instances, weather journalism saves lives by alerting individuals to potential threats.

Environment Journalism

Environmental safety is a major concern that has grown in significance in the current context. Journalism devoted to the environment sector informs the public on changes, variations, and developments in the environment, allowing the public to make ecologically savvy decisions.

Activist Journalism

The journalist provides his own view on the subject of current interest.

Tabloid Journalism

This is sensationalized news; significant portions of the news are effectively twisted. This sort of journalism is also known as "yellow journalism" since the information it contains is not entirely trustworthy.

Graphic Journalism

This is the piece of news that is presented in comic strip format. The content is normally serious yet given with a hint of satire.

Interpretative Journalism or Reporting

Interpretative or explanation oriented reporting is the farm reporters explain Why, How, What, etc. Here, farm reporter is not only writer of news but he is also orator. He publishes news in such a way the readers are motivated and enthusiastic to adopt any new technology that he writes about separate school of thought which increases the sense of people focuses on protection of farming community and their development and creates sense of improvement in the people for their own development.

Database Journalism

In this sort of journalism, the news is presented as a compilation of data in the form of statistics, charts, and maps, among other formats.

Photojournalism

In this genre, images are utilized to tell a story. Occasionally the photographs serve as whole narratives, and sometimes they are used to supplement the written narratives.

Features Journalism

A featured story is typically of a less immediate nature than normal stories. The compilation of a feature requires significantly more investigation and data acquisition.

Convergence Journalism

Convergence journalism is a type of journalism that mixes several types of media, such as print, photography, and video, into a single or collection of articles. This type of journalism mixes several types of journalism, such as print, photography, and video, into a single article or collection of pieces. CNN and a large number of other news websites feature convergence journalism.

Ambush Journalism

Refers to the aggressive tactics employed by journalists to confront and interrogate individuals who do not wish to speak with them. This is especially prevalent among television journalists. Refers to the aggressive tactics employed by journalists to confront and interrogate individuals who do not wish to speak with them. This is especially prevalent among television journalists.

Agricultural Journalism: Concept

In the age of information, intensive agriculture farmers want localized and timely information regarding their farming practices. Farm journalism can play a vital role in the collecting, processing, and dissemination of information tailored to farmers' needs. The agricultural journalism should be based on scientific research, timely, regionally specialized, and tailored to farmers' requirements.

Agricultural Journalism: Definition

Agricultural Journalism is the application of journalism to the dissemination of farm-related information.

Agricultural journalism is the profession of gathering information about technologies, issues, and achievements in agriculture and allied fields, and then writing, reporting, editing, publishing, and disseminating it for the target audience (i.e. farmers in rural areas) using various print, electronic, and computer-added media.

Farm journalism is another name for agricultural journalism. Farm journalism plays a significant role in communicating with farmers, housewives, etc. The extension team increasingly writes and distributes newspaper articles, magazine articles, booklets, pamphlets, bulletins, circular letters, wall newspapers, and radio scripts, which are increasingly read and listened to. The written work is enhancing the interest of advising work with farmers.

It evaluates all processes, including agricultural research and production, as well as processing, marketing, consumption, nutrition, and health.

It is obvious from the term that specialized journalism concentrates on specific topics. Agriculture Journalism refers to the eleven articles on agricultural topics. A journalist in the field of agriculture is required to have awareness for the agriculture industry and to pose pertinent, insightful inquiries.

Complex enterprises relating to food, feed, fiber, renewable energy, natural resource management, and rural development are among the topic areas.

Nature of Agricultural Journalism

- It expands the scope of this area by examining communication and human dimension issues in relation to agriculture.
- It evaluates a vast array of subject areas, including agricultural research and production, as well as processing, marketing, consumption, nutrition, and health.

Importance of Agricultural Journalism

The following points highlight the importance of Agricultural Journalism

1. To convey knowledge regarding fast evolving farm technologies.
2. More trustworthy than competing media
3. The pen is stronger than the sword
4. It is retrievable at any time.
5. Information dissemination is faster and less expensive.
6. Useful for agriculture because it is based on the season
7. Additional examples can be provided.

Scope of Agricultural Journalism

1. There is lot of scope for agricultural Journalism, since more than 70 % population depends on Agriculture and Allied activities for their livelihood.
2. Literacy percentage in rural areas, lead to readership among the farmers.
3. Farmers realized the importance of adopting latest production technologies.
4. More number of magazines on agriculture and allied aspects are published both at regional, state and national level.
5. Devoting time or space for agriculture subjects
6. Agricultural journalism serves purposes of carrying information to the farming community and to get genuine problems of the farmers as feedback to researchers.

Table 3: History of Newspaper in India

Year	Event
1780	The history of newspapers in India began. James Augustus is considered the 'father of Indian press', published Bengal Gazette from Calcutta.
1789	The first newspaper from Bombay, the 'Bombay Herald', appeared, followed by the 'Bombay Courier' the next year.
1818	The first newspaper published in an Indian language was the Samachar Darpan in Bengali on May 23.
1854	The first Hindi newspaper, the Samachar Sudha, started its circulation.
2005	The total number of newspapers and periodicals published in India was around 41,705, including 4,720 dailies and 14,743 weeklies.
2008	India consumed 99 million newspaper copies, making it the second largest market in the world for newspapers.

Table 4: History of Agricultural Journalism

Year	Event
1763	The first attempt at agricultural journalism.
1842	"American Agriculturist and Rural New Yorker" was founded, the nation's first farmer publication.
1940	The United States Government published the magazine Census of Agriculture.
Mid-19th Century	Emergence of hundreds of farm periodicals in the United Kingdom, the United States, France, and other European countries, covering topics like dairying, poultry, livestock, and other agricultural disciplines.

Table 5: Beginning of Agricultural Journalism in India

Year	Event
1873	Indian Forestry
1905	The Imperial Department of Agriculture released the first Indian agricultural publication.
1914	The first Hindi journal, 'Krishi Sudhar', was launched in Agra.
1928	Andhra Pradesh's 'Zamin Ryot', the first farm journal in India, was established.
1931	'Agriculture and Livestock in India', published by the Imperial Council of Agricultural Research, marked the beginning of agricultural journalism in India.
1938	Goan (Bihar govt)
1938	Ryot (Maharastra)
1940	Indian Farming
1946	Basundhara (W.B.)
1946	Krishi Jagat (Bhopal)
1947	Indian Livestock, Pashudhan, Indian Horticulture, Animal Science
1954	First Communication workshop

Mid-1960s	Establishment of the 'Indian Farm Journalist Association' by a group of agricultural writers and reporters.
1970	Indian Farm Journalist Association (IFJA) held exhibitions of farm journals and compiled a world dictionary of farm journals in New Delhi.
1993	'Indian Journal of Agricultural Sciences' was published.

Table 6: History of Farm Magazines and Agriculture Publications

Year	Event
1673	First Farm Magazine - Published in Paris, Agriculture De France.
1847	First journal on poultry, 'Poultry World', was published in London.
1914	India - First Periodical in Agriculture in Hindi, 'Krishi Sudhar', from Agra.
1931	Government departments started publishing farm journals.
1938	Bihar government published 'Gaon' journal.
1940	USA - Census Agriculture.
1946	Bhopal government published 'Krishak Jagat'.
1948	ICAR published 'Kheti'. West Bengal government started 'Basundhara'.
1953	Weekly called 'Sewagram'.

- The Maharashtra government started farm magazine called 'Shetkan' (Marathi) has a circulation over 1,20,000 copies.
- Krishi Vigyan – published by University of Agricultural Sciences (UAS), Bangalore
- Krishi Munnade – by University of Agricultural Sciences (UAS), Dharwad
- Adike Patrike – by Arecanut Growers Association,
- Siri Samruddhi – Bhartiya Agro Industries Foundation(BAIF) Pune

After Independence

Kurukshetra and Yojana are published from government of India on rural aspects the following agricultural universities are also publishing farm journals.

- Kisan Bharat - Pantnagar
- Farm digest – Pantnagar
- Apna Patra – Rajasthan
- Sugi – Rahuri (Maharashtra)
- Er ushavan – Coimbatore (TN)
- Krishi vignana – Karnataka
- Haryana Kheti – HAU ,hissar
- Krishi Sansar – Orissa

Table 7: Journal & Magazines Published in Agricultural Extension

Indian Journal of Extension Education	Indian Agricultural Research Institute , New Delhi
Indian Research Journal of Extension Education	Agra
Journal of Extension Education	Tamil Nadu Agricultural University , Coimbatore
Extension Digest	MANAGE, Hyderabad
Journal of Extension	USA
Media Asia	Singapore
Rural India	Indian Institute of Mass Communication (New Delhi)
Communicator	Pune
Agriculture and Livestock	ICAR (1930)
Zamindoot	1928
Krishi Chayanika	ICAR
Indian Farming	ICAR
Journal of Rural Development	National Institute of Rural Development
Kurukshetra	Ministry of Rural development
Yojana	Ministry of information & broadcasting
Rural Youth and Gram Yuvak	Young Farmer Association
Goan	Bihar government
Kisan Bharti	Pantnagar
Indian Farmers Digest	Pantnagar
Intensive Agriculture (English)	Ministry of Agriculture
Agriculture Extension Review (English)	Ministry of Agriculture
Krishi Vistar Samiksha (Hindi)	Ministry of Agriculture
Agriculture Situation in India	Ministry of Agriculture
Annals of Agricultural Research	Indian Society of Agricultural Sciences
First Farm Periodicals	Krishi - Sudhar (1914)
The first farm magazine in India is	Kheti

ICAR Publications

Journals (English) Monthly

- The Indian Journal of Agricultural Sciences
- The Indian Journal of Animal Sciences

Semi-technical Journals (English) Quarterly

- Indian Farming
- Indian Horticulture

Semi-technical Journals (Hindi) Quarterly

- Phal Phool
- Krishi Chayanika

Semi-technical Journals (Hindi) Monthly

- Kheti

ICAR News: A science and technology newsletter (every three month)

ICAR Reporter: House journal (every three month)

Table 8: Efforts of ICAR

Year	Publication
1940	Indian Farming
1956	Indian Horticulture
1970	ICAR News
1979	Phal Phool
1979	Krishi Chayanika, ICAR Reporter
1996	Establishment of Directorate of Information and Public Awareness
1998	Agriculture Research Information System (ARIS) News
2002	Indian Agricultural Science Abstract
2002	Indian Animal Science Abstract
2011	Renaming of Knowledge Management in Agriculture {D-KMA} & Agricultural Knowledge Management Units (AKMU) in place of Directorate of Publication & Information of Agriculture (DIPA) and (ARIS).

Functions of Agricultural Journalism

1. **News function** - It will carry recent farm information to farmers
2. **Opinion function** - It will give opinion / feedback of farmers on new farm information.
3. **Persuasion function** - Newspapers on farm journals not only tell farmers about what is happening but also persuade them to act.
4. **Economic functions** - It will give ways and means for improving their farm income and provide information on market prices.
5. **Education function** - These farm journals overall increase the knowledge level of farming community by providing farm information.
6. **Entertainment**
7. **Advertisement**

Advantages of Agricultural Journalism

1. Coverage - Farm publications reach large number of farmers within short period.
2. They increase the knowledge level of farmer
3. They can be stored and read at leisure time and can be preserved for future use.
4. Publications play a vital role in formation and changing attitude of farmers.
5. Farm publications increase the rate of adoption of agriculture technologies
6. Illiterates can also use these publications by taking help of educated counter parts.
7. Provides scope for advertisements and also entertainment to readers.

Disadvantages

1. Illiterates cannot read them
2. People have less time for reading

Principles of Farm Journalism

- **Use simple language**: Explain the technical terms in short and simple sentence, using common words which have concrete meaning.
- **Structure and arrange arguments clearly**: Present ideas in a logical order, clearly distinguishing between the main and the side issues.
- **Make main points brief**: Restrict arguments to the main issues clearly directed towards achieving stated goals without unnecessary use of words.
- **Keep important information at the top**: Organize the write-up like an inverted pyramid, keeping the most important information at the top.
- **Use lively pictures and photographs**: The pictures and photographs should be simple, bold, with good composition.
- **Prepare a stimulating write-up**: The presentation should be interesting, inspiring, personal and sufficiently diversified to be simple
- **Sustain audience interest**.
- Information should be timely, be precise, should be need based, should be based on language, should be interesting to the end users facts/ scientific research

ABC of Journalism: Accuracy, Brevity and Clarity which are fundamentals of good writing.

Role of Agricultural Journalism in Agricultural Development

1. In contemporary agriculture, the need for the exchange of agricultural ideas amongst individuals has become apparent. In this communication process, agricultural journalism plays a crucial role in raising awareness and overcoming ignorance.
2. In India, emphasis is placed on effective communication through agricultural journalism in order to bridge the gap between the level of research findings available at agricultural research stations and their actual adoption and use by farmers.
3. Continual dissemination of superior scientific technology from agricultural research stations to the farming community through a variety of media in the shortest time possible is a current necessity. This is achievable via agricultural journalism.
4. The journalist's function is viewed as a link between the effective communication between the research scientists and the farmers' demand for rapid feedback to bridge the gap. Effective conveyance of fresh knowledge from its source to its users through agricultural journalism facilitates the involvement and active participation of technology creators and users.
5. The duty of the agricultural journalist include aiding the successful communication of new agricultural knowledge in a manner that leads to its effective application and adoption.
6. The primary objective of agricultural extension education is to bring about beneficial changes in the farmers' and rural peoples' knowledge, skill, attitude, comprehension, activeness, involvement in developmental efforts, participation, and psychology; this can only be accomplished through communication. Communication is contact between the journalist as communicator and the public.

Conclusion

Agricultural journalism is one of the communication interventions through print and electronic media to scientists/extension workers/agriculturalists/ farmers to "speak" or "write" directly about their work in order to increase synergy and cooperation between the two groups. Be more sensitive to 'gender' in broadcasting and journalism, as rural women are frequently invisible or sidelined in the media despite their vital role in rural development. It establishes 'agricultural information centres' at the village level, where "people can chronicle their knowledge, listen, and learn together'. The media should be included in more networks, collaborations, and multi-stakeholder platforms. To foster more participation media such as participatory radio and video, development organisations should make greater efforts to transport journalists to project sites in exchange for increased coverage of agriculture. Innovative methods for the dissemination of agricultural knowledge to farmers. Few farm periodicals and other mass media are equipped with and controlled by farm journalism-trained individuals, and farm periodical circulation in India is relatively low compared to other circulation due to price and other factors. We must pay close attention to the problem facing agricultural journalism today by increasing their circulation in consideration of the growth of our farmers.

Answer the Following Questions

1. Define agricultural journalism and explain how it differs from general journalism. What are the key components that make up agricultural journalism?
2. Discuss the significance of the green revolution in the context of agricultural journalism's evolution. How did the approach and strategy of agricultural journalism change with the advent of the green revolution?
3. How can the principles of farm journalism, such as using simple language and keeping important information at the top, be applied to create effective agricultural communication for farmers?
4. Examine the role of agricultural journalism in agricultural extension and education. What are the challenges faced in integrating journalism into agricultural extension, and how do these challenges affect the transfer of technology to rural areas?
5. Consider the various forms of journalism mentioned in the text, such as advocacy journalism, broadcast journalism, and investigative journalism. Evaluate the potential impact of these different forms on promoting agricultural development and education among rural communities.

References

—. (2014). Key indicators of situation of agricultural households in India (70th Round January-December 2013). New Delhi, India: National Sample Survey Organisation, Ministry of Statistics and Programme Implementation.

—. (2019a). Basic animal husbandry statistics 2019. New Delhi, India: Department of Animal Husbandry and Dairying, Government of India.

—. (2019b). Report of the high-level committee on corporate social responsibility. New Delhi, India: Ministry of Corporate Affairs, Government of India.

A New Model and Measurement of Spirituality Bachelor's of ... CORE. Retrieved from https://core.ac.uk/download/pdf/215279504.pdf

A Research Project of IIIT, Hyderabad & Media Lab Asia. Retrieved from http://www.esagu.in

A SAGE White Paper Illustrating the dogmas in rural development and how .... Retrieved from https://in.sagepub.com/sites/default/files/rural_development_whitepaper.pdf

Abdullai, A. (2002). Motivating farmers for Action. How a strategic Multi-media campaign can help. Frankfurt: GTZ p125-126.

Adhiguru, P., Birthal, P.S. & Kumar, G.P. (2009). Strengthening pluralistic agricultural information delivery systems in India. Agricultural Economics Research Review, 22(1), 71-79.

AEXT392: Lecture 04: Extension Program Planning and Evaluation. Retrieved from http://agridr.in/tnauEAgri/eagri50/AEXT392/lec02.html

Agrawal, S. (2016). Pre- post rural development. International Journal of Socio – Legal Analysis and Rural Development, 2(1), 97-106.

Ahmed, A. (1982). The role of the information system in development (Studies Series No. 314). Baghdad, Iraq: Ministry of Culture and Information.

Ajzen, I., & Fishbein, M. (1980). Understanding attitudes and predicting social behavior. Englewood Cliffs, NJ: Prentice-Hall.

Alex, G., & Rivera, W. (2004). Demand-driven approaches to agriculture extension: Case studies of international initiatives (Vol. 3).

Alice, C., & Eliana, M. (2021). Servant leadership: a systematic literature review and network analysis. Employee Responsibilities and Rights Journal, 34, 267-289. https://doi.org/10.1007/s10672-021-09381-3

Amanchukwu, R., Stanley, G., & Ololube, N. (2015). A review of leadership theories, principles and styles and their relevance to educational management. Management, 5(1), 6-14. doi:10.5923/j.mm.20150501.02

Anandajayasekeram, P., Puskur, R., Sindu Workneh, & Hoekstra, D. (2008). Concepts and practices in agricultural extension in developing countries: A source book. Washington, DC, USA: IFPRI; Nairobi, Kenya: ILRI.

Anonymous (2020). Adoption and diffusion of innovations, adoption and diffusion process, adopter categories & barriers in diffusion of fisheries innovations. Retrieved May 11, 2023, from https://www.basu.org.in/wp-content/uploads/2020/06/6.-Adoption-and-diffusion-of-innovations-adoption-and-diffusion-process-adopter-categories-and-barriers-in-diffusion-of-fisheries-innovations.pdf

Anonymous (n.d.). Diffusion and adoption of innovation. Retrieved May 10, 2023, from http://eagri.org/eagri50/AEXT392/lec11.html

Anonymous (n.d.). The diffusion of innovation - Strategies for adoption of products. Retrieved May 12, 2023, from https://www.interaction-design.org/literature/article/the-diffusion-of-innovation-strategies-for-adoption-of-products

Anonymous. (2022). Demands for grants (2020-21). Report No. 4. Department of Rural Development, Standing Committee on Rural Development.

Anonymous. (2022). Expansive social security programmes a top priority. Economic and Political Weekly, 57(37), 20-26.

Arasingham, S.R. (1981). Agricultural extension in Sri Lanka. Tropical Agriculturist, 137,41-54.

Arnon, I. (1989). Agricultural research and technology transfer. Springer Dordrecht. Essex, England.

Azad, A.K. and Singh, K. (2017). A basic book on Fundamentals of Agricultural Extension. Kalyani Publishers, New Delhi.

Bamberger, M., & Hewitt, E. (1986). Monitoring and evaluating urban development programs: A handbook for program managers and researchers (Technical Paper No. 53). Washington, D.C.: World Bank.

Barber, B. (n.d.). History of Indian press essay on history of Indian. Retrieved from https://benjaminbarber.org/history-of-indian-press/

Barr, T. (2019). Virtual reality and the future of agricultural journalism. Agricultural Journalism, 10(1), 28-33.

Barton, L., & Hayden, G. (2018). Agricultural journalism in the 21st century: Concepts, methods, and challenges. Journal of Agricultural Communications, 5(1), 58-77.

Basic Elements of Rural Development - Agriculture. Retrieved from https://imp.center/agri/basic-elements-of-rural-development/

Bass, B. M. (1990). Bass and Stogdill's handbook of leadership: Theory, research, and managerial applications. New York, NY: Free Press.

Basu, A. K. (2013). Impact of rural employment guarantee schemes on seasonal labor markets: Optimum compensation and workers' welfare. The Journal of Economic Inequality, 11(1), 1-34.

Bathla, S., Joshi, P. K., & Kumar, A. (2019). Targeting agricultural investments and input subsidies in low-income lagging regions of India. European Journal of Developmental Research, 31(1), 1197-1226.

Beevi, A. C. N., Wason, M., Padaria, R. N., & Singh, P. (2018). Gender sensitivity in agricultural extension. Current Science, 115(6), 1035-1036.

Benin, S., Nkonya, E., Okecho, G., Randriamamonjy, J., Kato, E., Lubade, G., & Kyotalimye, M. (2011). Returns to spending on agricultural extension: The case of the National Agricultural Advisory Services (NAADS) programme of Uganda. Agricultural Economics, 42(2), 249-267.

Bennett, M. K. (2006). The farmer's magazine and the discourse of improvement in early-nineteenth-century England. Rural History, 17(1), 23-42.

Benor, D., Harrison, J. O., & Baxter, M. (1984). Agricultural extension: The training and visit system. Washington, D.C.: The World Bank.

Berg, M.E. (2020). The changing landscape of agricultural journalism: A study of the use of digital media by agricultural journalists. Journal of Applied Communications, 104(2), 8-21.

Beukes, P., Fischer, G., & Laubscher, R. (2020). Smart farming: Investigating smart device adoption and the digital divide in South African agriculture. Information Technology for Development, 26(1), 90-120.

Bhaskaran, C., Kumar, N. K., & Prakash, R. (2008). Farm journalism and media management. Agrotech Publishing Academy, Udaipur.

Birner, R., & Anderson, J. R. (2007). How to make agricultural extension demand-driven? The case of India's agricultural extension. IFPRI Discussion Paper 729. Washington, DC: International Food Policy Research Institute.

Birthal, P. S., & Joshi, P. K. (2007). Smallholder farmers' access to markets for high-value agricultural commodities in India. Food Policy for Developing Countries: The Role of Government in the Global Food System, Case Study No 6–4. Retrieved from http://faculty.apec.umn.edu/kolson/documents/4103_cases/case_6-4.pdf

Birthal, P. S., Kumar, S., Negi, D. S., & Roy, D. (2015). The impacts of information on returns from farming: Evidence from a nationally representative farm survey in India. Agricultural Economics, 46(4), 549-561.

Black, A. W. (1976). Organizational genesis and development: A study of Australian agricultural colleges. St. Lucia, Australia: University of Queensland Press.

Black, J. (1997). A new approach to agricultural journalism: The Journal of the Royal Agricultural Society of England 1840-1914. Journal of Historical Geography, 23(1), 34-48.

Blackburn, D. J., & Vist, D. L. (1984). Historical roots and philosophy of extension. In D. J. Blackburn (Ed.), Extension handbook (1st ed.). Guelph, Ontario, Canada: University of Guelph.

Blum, M. L., Cofini, F., & Sulaiman, R. V. (2020). Agricultural extension in transition worldwide: Policies and strategies for reform. Rome, Italy: FAO.

Bne Saad, M. H. A. Al-h. (1990). An analysis of the needs and problems of Iraqi farm women: Implications for agricultural extension services. Unpublished doctoral thesis, University College, Dublin.

Boudreau, J. W. (1996). Human resources and organization success (CAHRS Working Paper #96-03). Ithaca, NY: Cornell University, School of Industrial and Labor Relations, Center for Advanced Human Resource Studies.

Boulet, M. (n.d.). Un type original d'enseignant: Le professeur departmental d'agriculture. Unpublished paper.

Bray, P. (1984). Joseph Needham's science and civilization in China: Vol. 6. Biology and biological technology. Pt. II: Agriculture. Cambridge, UK: Cambridge University Press.

Brewminate. (n.d.). A brief history of journalism in America. Retrieved from https://brewminate.com/a-brief-history-of-journalism-in-america/

Bscagristudy.online. (n.d.). ELE EXTN-244. Retrieved from https://bscagristudy.online/wp-content/uploads/2021/06/ELE-EXTN-244-PRINTED-NOTES1.pdf

Budzinski, O., Hook, H., & Shankar, R. (2019). Big data, social media analytics, and agricultural policy-making: Insights from twitter analytics of Brexit. Journal of Agricultural and Environmental Ethics, 32(6), 1027-1048.

Burman, R. R. (2008). ICT led agricultural extension in India: issues and opportunities. Journal of Global Communication, 1(1), 91-100.

Businessline. (2017). Spending on agri R&D alleviates poverty substantially: Study. Retrieved from https://www.thehindubusinessline.com/economy/agri-business/spending-on-agri-rampdalleviates-poverty-substantially-study/article9992439.ece

CAG. (Various Years). Combined finance and revenue accounts–Union and states. New Delhi, India: Comptroller and Auditor General of India.

Campbell, D., Pyett, P., & McCarthy, L. (2007). Community development interventions to improve Aboriginal health: Building an evidence base. Health Sociology Review, 16, 304-314.

Chambers, R. (1993). Challenging the professions: Frontiers for rural development. London, UK: IT Publications.

Chand, R., Kumar, P., & Kumar, S. (2011). Total factor productivity and contribution of research investment to agricultural growth in India. Policy Paper, 25. New Delhi, India: National Centre for Agricultural Economics and Policy Research.

Clark, S. V. (1983). The Country Gentleman: Catalyst of agricultural improvement. Agricultural History, 57(4), 492-503.

CLVS. (1845). Wiesenbewasserung. Wochenblatt für Land-und Hauswirthschaft, Gewerbe und Handel (Centralstelle des Landwirthschaftlichen Vereins zu Stuttgart), 24, 133.

Cohen, W. A. (1990). The art of a leader. Englewood Cliffs, NJ: Prentice Hall.

Coletti, F. ([1900] 1985). Le associazioni agrarie in Italia della meta del secolo XVIII al XIX. Reprinted in Il Dottore in Science Agrarie e Forestali, 15(1985, October), 17-30.

Collins Dictionary. (n.d.). First-hand report definition and meaning. Retrieved from https://www.collinsdictionary.com/dictionary/english/first-hand-report

Common Sense and Ramblings. (2021, May 11). Journalism, its past, present and future. Retrieved from https://common-sense-in-america.com/2021/05/11/journalism-its-past-present-and-future/

Concept of Rural Development - SocialWorkin. Retrieved from https://www.socialworkin.com/2022/08/concept-of-rural-development.html

Coombs, P. H., & Ahmed, M. (1974). Attacking rural poverty: How non-formal education can help. Baltimore, MD: The Johns Hopkins University Press.

Coser, L. A., & Rimanelli, M. (2004). Communication and agriculture: An overview of the past 100 years. In L. A. Coser & M. Rimanelli (Eds.), Communication and agriculture: Approaches, issues, and applications (pp. 1-12). New York, NY: Hampton Press.

Cote, R. (2017). A comparison of leadership theories in an organizational environment. International Journal of Business Administration, 8(5), 28. doi:10.5430/ijba.v8n5p28

Cristovao, A., Kochen, T., & Portela, J. (1997). Developing and delivering extension programmes. In B.E. Swanson, R.P. Bentz, & A.J. Sofranko (Eds.), FAO.

Cuban, L. (1988). The managerial imperative and the practice of leadership in schools. Albany, NY: SUNY Press.

DAC&FW. (2015). All India report on agriculture census 2010–11. New Delhi, India: Agriculture Census Division, Department of Agriculture, Cooperation and Farmers' Welfare, Ministry of Agriculture and Farmers' Welfare.

DAC. (2014). Guidelines for the centrally sponsored scheme 'National Mission on Agricultural Extension and Technology (NMAET)' to be implemented during the XII Plan. New Delhi, India: Department of Agriculture and Cooperation, Ministry of Agriculture.

Dahama, O.P. and Bhatnagar, O.P. (2007). Education and Communication for Development. Oxford and IBH Publishing Co. Pvt, Ltd., New Delhi.

de Failly, D. (1970). Histoire de l'enseignement agricole au Congo (Pt. 1). Cahiers Congolais, 13(1), 100-133.

Delman, J. (1991). Agricultural extension in Renshou County, China: A case-study of bureaucratic intervention for agricultural innovation and change. Aarhus, Denmark: Institute of East Asian Studies.

Dev, S. M. (1995). India's (Maharashtra) employment guarantee scheme: Lessons from long experience. Employment for poverty reduction and food security, 90, 108-143.

Dhama, O. P., & Bhatnagar, O. P. (1991). Education and communication for development. New Delhi, India: Oxford IBH Publishing Co.

Dooris, M., & Heritage, Z. (2013). Healthy cities: Facilitating the active participation and empowerment of local people. Journal of Urban Health, 90(1), 74-91.

Drucker, P. F. (2008). Management – Revised edition. New York, NY: Collins Business.

Eaton, C. & Shepherd, A.W. (2001). Contract farming: Partnerships for growth. FAO Agricultural Services Bulletin 145. Rome, Italy: Food and Agriculture Organization.

Education Today News. (2012, June 7). Agricultural journalism. Retrieved from https://www.indiatoday.in/education-today/plan-your-career/story/agricultural-journalism-institutes-104856-2012-06-07

Elvin, M. (1973). The pattern of the Chinese past. London, UK: Methuen.

Ensminger, D. (1957). A guide to community development. New Delhi, India: Ministry of Community Development and Cooperation, Government of India.

Evenson, R. (2001). Economic impacts of agricultural research and extension. In Gardner, B., & Rausser, G. (Eds.), Handbook of agricultural economics, Vol. 1A (pp. 573–628). Amsterdam, Netherlands: Elsevier Science.

Extension Education Institute. (n.d.). Concept and principles of journalism with special reference to farm. Retrieved from http://www.eei-ner.org/wp-content/uploads/2019/09/Handout-farm-journalism-mass-media-production-in-agricultural-extension.pdf

Extension Education Meaning. (n.d.). Retrieved from https://www.agrostudy.in/2021/10/extension-education-meaning-definition.html

Extension teaching methods. (n.d.). Retrieved from http://ecoursesonline.iasri.res.in/mod/resource/view.php?id=4374

Extension Teaching Methods. Retrieved from https://www.researchgate.net/deref/http%3A%2F%2Fwww.textbooksonline.tn.nic.in%2Fbooks%2F11%2Fstd11-homesci-em.pdf

FAO. (1993). The potentials of microcomputers in support of agricultural extension, education and training. Rome, Italy: FAO.

Fayol, H. (1949). General and industrial management. London, UK: Sir Isaac Pitman & Sons.

Feder, G., Willet, A., & Zijp, W. (1999). Generic challenges to agricultural extension and some ingredients for solution. The World Bank Rural Development Department.

Ferroni, M., & Zhou, Y. (2011). Review of agricultural extension in India. Syngenta Foundation for Sustainable Agriculture.

Fox, E. (2012). Defining social and behavior change communication (SBCC) and other essential health communication terms. Washington, DC: The Manoff Group.

Francis, S. (2011). A sectoral impact analysis of the ASEAN-India free trade agreement. Economic & Political Weekly, 46(2), 46-55.

Freeman, R. E., Wicks, A. C., & Parmar, B. (2004). Stakeholder theory and "the corporate objective revisited". Organization Science, 15(3), 364-369. doi: 10.1287/orsc.1040.0066

Gandhian Approach of Rural Development - Aligarh Muslim University. Retrieved from https://old.amu.ac.in/emp/studym/6561.pdf

Garforth, C. (1986). Mass media and communications technology. In G.E. Jones (Ed.), Investing in rural extension: Strategies and goals (p. 185-192). London, UK; New York, NY: Elsevier Applied Science Publishers.

Garforth, C. (1993). Seeing the people for the trees: Training for social forestry in Karnataka, India. Rural Extension Bulletin, 2, 33-39.

Gates, P. (2016). American farmers and the rise of agricultural journalism. Journalism and Communication Monographs, 18(3), 153-199.

GFRAS. (2012). Fact sheet on extension services, position paper. Global Forum for Rural Advisory Services.

Gledenning, S., Babu, S., & Asenso-Okere. (2010). Review of agricultural extension in India. IFPRI Working Paper. Rome, Italy: IFPRI.

Glendenning, J.C. Babu, S. & Asenso-Okyere, K. (2010). Review of agricultural extension in India: Are farmers information needs being met? Discussion Paper 01048. Washington, DC

GoI. (2017). Empowering the farmers through extension and knowledge dissemination. Report of the Committee on Doubling Farmers' Income, Vol 11. New Delhi, India: Ministry of Agriculture and Farmers Welfare.

Google Drive. (n.d.). [Link to document]. Retrieved from https://drive.google.com/file/d/1oldLn4NQLphlfA-EcHZOo-

Gray, E. M. (1952). The educational work of Philipp Emanuel von Fellenberg (1771-1844). Unpublished master's thesis, The Queen's University, Belfast.

Green, L. W., & Parcel, G. S. (1991). Diffusion theory extended. In W. B. Ward & F. M. Lewis (Eds.), Advances in health education and promotion (p. 114). London: Jessica Kingsley.

Grobel, M. (1933). The Society for the Diffusion of Useful Knowledge, 1826-1846, and its relation to adult education in the first half of the nineteenth century. Unpublished master's thesis. University of London.

Gross National Product: Definition, Formula, Importance - BYJUS. Retrieved from https://byjus.com/commerce/gross-national-product/

Groves, K. S., & LaRocca, M. A. (2011). An empirical study of leader ethical values, transformational and transactional leadership, and follower attitudes toward corporate social responsibility. Journal of Business Ethics, 103, 511. doi:10.1007/s10551-011-0877-y.

Guggisberg, K. (1953). Philipp Emanuel von Fellenberg und sein Erziehungsstaat (2 vols.). Bern, Switzerland: Verlag Herbert Lang.

Gulati, A., Sharma, P., Samantara, A., & Terway, P. (2018). Agriculture extension system in India: Review of current status, trends and the way forward. New Delhi, India: Indian Council for Research on International Economic Relations.

Gulati, R., Nohria, N., & Wohlgezogen, F. (2010). Roaring out of recession. Harvard Business Review, 88, 62-69.

Gulick, L. H. (1937). Notes on the theory of organization. In L. Gulick & L. Urwick (Eds.), Papers on the science of administration (pp. 3–45). New York, NY: Institute of Public Administration.

Gunnar Myrdal's development state theory – article1000.com. Retrieved from https://article1000.com/gunnar-myrdals-development-state-theory/

Guthman, J. (2018). Agrarian dreams and digital farms: Technological imaginaries and farming futures. Journal of Rural Studies, 59, 19-28.

Hanrahan, T. (n.d.). Journalism notes. Blogger. Retrieved from https://thomashanrahan.blogspot.com/

Haque, T. (2012). MGNREGS and its effects on agriculture exploring linkages. Right to Work and Rural India: Working of the Mahatma Gandhi National Rural Employment Guarantee Scheme (MGNREGS), 226.

Hayward, J. (1990). Agricultural extension: The World Bank's experience and approaches. In FAO Report of the Global Consultation on Agricultural Extension (p. 115-134). Rome, Italy: FAO.

Hicks, G. H., & Gullet, C. R. (1975). Organizations: Theory and behavior. New York, NY: McGraw-Hill.

Higgins, J. M. (1991). The management challenge: An introduction to management. New York, NY: Macmillan.

Hilaveli. (n.d.). Week 1 definition and forms of journalism. SlideShare. Retrieved from https://www.slideshare.net/hilaveli/week-1-definition-and-forms-of-journalism

Hodgson, P., & White, R. (2003). Leadership, learning, ambiguity and uncertainty and their significance to dynamic organizations. In R. Peterson & E. Mannix (Eds.), Leading and managing people in the dynamic organization. Hillsdale, NJ: Lawrence Erlbaum.

Home Science. Higher Secondary First Year. (2005). Tamil Nadu Textbook Corporation. Retrieved July 12, 2017, from [URL].

Horowitz, H. L. (1989). Newspapers and the shaping of modern rural society. In Seeds of Concern: The Genetic Manipulation of Plants (pp. 35-58). University of California Press.

Horton, M. (1952). Extension philosophy. In R. K. Bliss *et al.* (Eds.), The spirit and philosophy of extension work. Washington, DC: Graduate School, USDA.

Huang, X., Cao, J., Zhu, T., & Gong, W. (2018). Using remote sensing technology in the agricultural information service system: A case study of rice information services in Zhejiang Province, China. Remote Sensing, 10(6), 936.

Hudson, K. (1972). Patriotism with profit: British agricultural societies in the eighteenth and nineteenth centuries. London, UK: Hugh Evelyn.

Hugill, P. J. (2007). Moving beyond Farm and Home: Women's Magazines, the Farm Press, and Canadian Farm Women, 1890-1920. Journal of Women's History, 19(1), 70-95.

Human Development Index | Human Development Reports. Retrieved from https://hdr.undp.org/data-center/human-development-index

Ife, J. (2016). Community development in an uncertain world: Vision, analysis and practice (2nd ed.). Port Melbourne, Australia: Cambridge University Press.

Igbaria, M., Parasuraman, S., & Baroudi, J. (1996). A motivational model of microcomputer usage. Journal of Management Information Systems, 13(1), 127-143.

ILoveIndia. (n.d.). Different types of journalism. Retrieved from https://lifestyle.iloveindia.com/lounge/types-of-journalism-14037.html

India | Encyclopedia.com. Retrieved from https://www.encyclopedia.com/places/asia/indian-political-geography/india

Introduction to Agricultural Extension. (n.d.). Retrieved from https://www.rafflesuniversity.edu.in/pdf/agri/Agri_II_Sem_Introduction%20to%20Agriculture%20Extension.pdf

Jayanta, K., & Ratnaprava, B. (n.d.). Administrative theory: Principles and approaches. Political Science Paper- II. Retrieved from https://ddceutkal.ac.in/Syllabus/MA_Pol_Science/PAPER-2.pdf

Jenkins, H. M. (1884). Report on agricultural education in north Germany, France, Denmark, Belgium, Holland, and the United Kingdom (C.3981-1). London, UK: Eyre and Spottiswoode.

Jones, G. E. (1979). The original agricultural advisory service: Lord Clarendon's practical instructors in mid-nineteenth century Ireland. In Proceedings of the 4th International Seminar on Extension Education. Dublin, Ireland: University College, Department of Agricultural Extension.

Jones, G. E. (1981). The origins of agricultural advisory services in the nineteenth century. Social Biology and Human Affairs, 46(2), 89-106.

Jones, G. E. (1982). The Clarendon letter. In G. E. Jones & M. J. Rolls (Eds.), Progress in rural extension and community development: Vol. 1. Extension and relative advantage in rural development (pp. 11-19). Chichester, UK: John Wiley & Sons.

Jones, G. E. (1994). Agricultural advisory work in England and Wales: The beginnings. Agricultural Progress, 69, 55-69. Journal d'Agriculture Pratique. (1874). 38th year, Vol. 2.

Kelsey, L. D., & Hearne, C. C. (1967). Cooperative extension work. Ithaca, NY: Cornell University Press.

Kenny, S. (2007). Developing communities for the future (3rd ed.). South Melbourne, Australia: Thompson.

Kesley, L. D., & Hearne, C. C. (1966). Cooperative extension work. Ithaca, NY: Constock Publishing Associates.

Khan, M.S., Khan, I., Qureshi, Q.A., Ismail, H.M., Rauf, H., Latif, A., & Tahir, M. (2015). The styles of leadership: A critical review. Public Policy and Administrative Research, 5(3), 87-92.

Khan, Z. A., Nawaz, A., & Khan, I. U. (2016). Leadership theories and styles: A literature review. Journal of Resources Development and Management, 16, 1-7.

Kile, O. M. (1921). The farm bureau movement. New York, NY: Macmillan.

Kloppenburg, S. (2017). The digital transformation of agriculture: Potential impacts and pitfalls. Journal of Agricultural and Environmental Ethics, 30(4), 441-462.

Kokate, K. D., Kharde, P. B., Patil, S. S., & Deshmukh, B. A. (2016). Farmers'-led extension: experiences & road ahead. Indian Research Journal of Extension Education, 9(2), 18-21.

Kothari, C. R. (1996). Research methodology: Methods and techniques (2nd ed.). New Delhi, India: New Age International Publishers.

Kouzes, J. M., & Posner, B. Z. (1995). The leadership challenge. San Francisco, CA: Jossey-Bass.

Kreitner, R. (1989). Management (4th ed.). Boston, MA: Houghton Mifflin.

Kromrey, D., Haag, S., Peters, L., & Rössel, J. (2019). The role of agricultural data platforms in Germany: Perspectives of providers and users. Agricultural Systems, 170, 13-21.

Kumar, B., & Hansra, B. S. (2000). Extension education for human resource development. New Delhi, India: Concept Publishing Company.

Kumar, U., Singh, D. K., Bhatt, B. P., Sarkar, B., Koley, T. K., & Gupta, S. (2017). Market led agricultural extension-concept & practices. Training Manual ICAR Research Complex for Eastern Region, Patna.

Laogu, E. A. (2005). Extension Teaching/Learning Process and Methods. In: S.

Leagans, J. P. (1967). A concept of the extension education process. In L. D. Kelsey & C. C. Hearne (Eds.), Cooperative extension work. Ithaca, NY: Cornell University Press.

Leagans, J.P. (1961). Characteristics of Teaching and Learning in Extension Education. In: Extension Education in Community Development, Directorate of Extension, Ministry of Food and Agriculture, Government of India, New Delhi.

Leeuwis, C. (1993). Of computers, myths and modelling: The social construction of diversity, knowledge, information, and communication technologies in Dutch horticulture and agricultural extension. Wageningen Studies in Sociology, 36. Wageningen, Netherlands: Agricultural University.

Lewicka, D. (2011). Creating innovative attitudes in an organisation – Comparative analysis of tools applied in IBM Poland and ZPAS Group. Vol. 1, No. 1, 1-12.

Lewis, W., Agarwal, R., & Sambamurthy, V. (2003). Sources of influence on beliefs about information technology use: An empirical study of knowledge workers. MIS Quarterly, 27(4), 657-678.

Linton, R. (1936). The study of man. New York, NY: Appleton-Century-Crofts.

Logan, G. N. (1984). Man and the land in Queensland education 1874-1905: Agricultural education as a solution to man-physiography dissonance in colonist Queensland. Unpublished M.Ed. thesis, University of Queensland.

Lovely Professional University. (n.d.). Agricultural journalism AEE 314 unit 1- Reading material. Retrieved from [URL not provided]

Lowenberg-DeBoer, J., Bickel, M., & Bröring, S. (2017). Big data in agriculture: A challenge for the future. Agricultural and Food Economics, 5(1), 1-4.

Lucas, C. P. (1913). A historical geography of the British colonies: Vol. III, West Africa (3rd ed.). Oxford, UK: Clarendon Press.

Maier-Bode, F. (1910). Die Organization und die Erfolge des landwirtschaftlichen Wanderunterrichts im Königreich Bayern. Landsberg am Lech, Germany: Georg Verza.

Masefield, G. B. (1950). A short history of agriculture in the British colonies. Oxford, UK: Clarendon Press.

McCaffery James A. (1986). Independent effectiveness: A reconsideration of cross-cultural orientation and training. International Journal of Intercultural Relations, 10(2): 159–78.

Meena, B. S. (2018). Dairy Extension Education.

Meena, M. S., Kale, R. B., Singh, S. K., & Gupta, S. (2016). Farmer-to-farmer extension model: Issues of sustainability & scalability in Indian perspective.

Miller, R. L. (2015). Rogers' innovation diffusion theory (1962, 1995). In Information seeking behavior and technology adoption: Theories and trends (pp. 261-274). IGI Global.

Ministère de l'Agriculture. (1882). Bulletin, 1st year, Vol. 1.

Ministry of Agriculture. (1993). Outline of cooperative agricultural extension service in Japan. Tokyo, Japan: Ministry of Agriculture, Forestry and Fisheries (Extension and Education Division).

Ministry of Rural Development, Government of India. (2021). 75 Inspirational stories of Aatmanirbhar rural women.

Misra, D. C. (1990). New directions in extension training: A conceptual framework. New Delhi, India: Directorate of Extension, Ministry of Agriculture.

Mitra, K. P., & Jana, B. L. (2010). Farm journalism. Agrotech Publishing Academy, Udaipur.

Module 6: Rural Development: Conceptual Discussions - Inflibnet Centre. Retrieved from https://epgp.inflibnet.ac.in/epgpdata/uploads/epgp_content/S000032SW/P001729/M021629/ET/1501587312Module-6_e-Text.pdf

Mohanty, A. K., Sanjeev, M. V., & Sajev, V. K. (2020). Innovative extension approaches for sustainable technology dissemination in fisheries. In Pluralistic extension for upscaling secondary fisheries (pp. 17-24). 17–24 January, ICAR-Central Institute of Fisheries Technology.

Mohanty, A. K., Suresh, A., & Sajesh, V. K. (2020). Novel extension approaches for technology dissemination in fisheries. Training Manual on ICAR Winter School, Responsible Fishing: Recent Advances in Resource and Energy Conservation, 21 November 2019–11 December 2019.

Mondal, A. (2010). Farmer's producer company (FPC): Concept, practice and learning—A case from Action For Social Advancement. Financing Agriculture, 42(7), 29–33.

Mondal, S. (2016). Textbook of agricultural extension with global innovations. ISBN 978-93-272-2877-9.

Mondal, S. (2021). Fundamentals of agricultural extension education. New Delhi, India: Kalyani Publishers.

Mook, B. T. (1982). The world of the Indian field administrator. New Delhi, India: Vikas Publishing House.

MoRD. (2014). MGNREGA, 2005: Report to the people. Ministry of Rural Development, Government of India.

Moreno, J. L. (1953). Who shall survive? Foundations of sociometry, group psychotherapy and sociodrama (2nd ed.). Beacon, NY: Beacon House.

Moris, J. (1991). Extension alternatives in tropical Africa. London, UK: Overseas Development Institute.

Muhammad, A. M., & Sameen, A. (2019). Leader and leadership: Historical development of the terms and critical review of literature. Annals of the University of Craiova for Journalism, Communication and Management, 5, 16-32.

Nandeshwar, V. (n.d.). ELE extension notes [Autosaved]. SlideShare. Retrieved from https://www.slideshare.net/VikkiNandeshwar/ele-extension-notes-autosavedpptx

Napier, R. W., & Gershenfeld, M. K. (1999). Groups: Theory and experience (6th ed.). Boston, MA: Houghton Mifflin.

National Commission on Agriculture. (1976). Report, Part I, Review and Progress, and Part XI, Research, Education and Extension. New Delhi, India: Ministry of Agriculture and Irrigation, Government of India.

Navbharat Times. (n.d.). Urdu Journalism. Retrieved from https://navbharattimes.indiatimes.com/career/alternate-career/urdu-journalism/articleshow/52278112.cms

Newman, W. H. (1950). Administrative action: The technique of organization and management. Prentice-Hall.

Nieman Reports. (n.d.). The news has become the news. Retrieved from https://niemanreports.org/articles/the-news-has-become-the-news/

NITI Aayog. (2018). Demand and supply projections towards 2033: Crops, livestock, fisheries and inputs. New Delhi, India: Government of India.

Northouse, P. G. (2010). Leadership: Theory and practice (6th ed.). Thousand Oaks, CA: Sage Publications.

NSSO. (2005). Situation assessment survey of farmers: Access to modern technology for farming (59th Round, January–December 2003, Report No 499[59/33/2]). New Delhi, India: National Sample Survey Organisation, Ministry of Statistics and Programme Implementation.

Nwokeji, V. C., Onwumere, J. I., & Ugbogu, A. E. (2020). Assessment of agricultural mobile applications as an innovation in agricultural extension service delivery in Nigeria. Journal of Agricultural Extension, 24(1), 161-174.

O'Farrell, C., Norrish, P., & Scott, A. (1999). ICTs for sustainable livelihoods: Preliminary study, April-November.

Oakley, P., & Garforth, C. (1985). Guide to extension training. Rome: Food and Agriculture Organisation of the United Nations.

Padilla, A., Hogan, R., & Kaiser, R. B. (2007). The toxic triangle: Destructive leaders, susceptible followers, and conducive environments. The Leadership Quarterly, 18(3), 176. doi: 10.1016/j.leaqua.2007.03.00

Pal, S. (2017). Strengthening delivery of agricultural extension services in India: Experiences and contemporary issues. In Agricultural R&D Policy in India: The funding, institutions and impact. New Delhi, India: National Institute of Agricultural Economics and Policy Research.

Peansupap, V., & Walker, D. (2005). Exploratory factors influencing information and communication technology diffusion and adoption within Australian construction organizations: A micro analysis. Construction Innovation, 5(3), 135-157.

Perkins, D. H. (1969). Agricultural development in China, 1368-1968. Chicago, IL: Aldine Publishing; Edinburgh, UK: Edinburgh University Press.

Pfiffner, J. M., & Presthus, R. V. (1967). Public administration (5th ed.). New York, NY: The Ronald Press Company.

Phi Sigma Pi National Honor Fraternity. (n.d.). Elements of journalism. SlideShare. Retrieved from https://www.slideshare.net/leviphisig/elements-of-journalism

Physical Quality of Life Index (PQLI) - Indian Economy. Retrieved from https://lms.indianeconomy.net/glossary/physical-quality-of-life-index-pqli/

Pindur, W., Rogers, S. E., & Kim, P. S. (1995). The history of management: a global perspective. Journal of Management History, 1(1), 59-77.

Pingali, P., Aiyar, A., Abraham, M., & Rahman, A. (2019). Linking farms to markets: Reducing transaction costs and enhancing bargaining power. In Transforming food systems for a rising India (pp. 193-214). Cham, Switzerland: Palgrave Macmillan.

Planning Commission. (2012). Report of the working group on animal husbandry and dairying, Twelfth Five Year Plan (2012–17). New Delhi, India: Government of India.

Plunkett, H. (1901-1902). Agricultural education for Ireland. Department of Agriculture and Technical Instruction for Ireland, Journal, 2(1), 18-41.

Poudel, K. C., & Van der Vorst, J. G. (2019). The role of agricultural journalism in empowering smallholder farmers: A case study from Nepal. Agricultural Systems, 172, 1-10.

Prasad, G. N. R., & Babu, A. V. (2008). A study on various expert systems in agriculture. In N. Anandaraj (Ed.), Extension of technologies - from labs to farms. New Delhi, India: New India Publishing Agency.

Prasad, R. M. (2001). Private extension system: Options and issues. In Private extension in India: Myths, realities, apprehensions and approaches (Chandrasekhara, P., Ed.). Hyderabad, India: National Institute of Agricultural Extension Management.

Price-Robertson, R. (2011). What is community disadvantage? Understanding the issues, overcoming the problem. Melbourne, Australia: Australian Institute of Family Studies.

Province of Ontario. (1900). Report of the superintendent of farmers' institutes of the Province of Ontario, 1899-1900. Toronto, Canada: L. K. Cameron.

Quazi, A., & Talukder, M. (2011). Demographic determinants of employees' perception and adoption of technological innovation. Journal of Computer Information Systems, 51(3), 38-46.

Rama Rao, T. P. (2010). Dairy information services kiosk and dairy portal. Working Papers id:3269, eSocialSciences.

Ranjan, R. (n.d.). A study of relevance of print media in. SlideShare. Retrieved from https://www.slideshare.net/RohitRanjan48/a-study-of-relevance-of-print-media-in

Rao, M. V. (1994). Issue paper on National Agriculture Technology Project. Hyderabad, Andhra Pradesh: Agricultural University.

Rath, N. (1985). Garibi Hatao: Can IRDP do it?. Economic and Political Weekly, 20(6), 131-140.

Ray, G. L. (2006). Extension communication and management (6th ed.). Ludhiana, India: Kalyani Publishers.

Reddy, Y.N. (1998). Audio-Visual Aids in Teaching Training and Education. Haritha Publishing House, Hyderabad.

Reiter-Palmon, R., & Illies, J. J. (2004). Leadership & creativity: Understanding leadership from a creative problem-solving perspective. The Leadership Quarterly, 15(1), 55-77.

Renaissance College of Commerce. (n.d.). Class B.A. (Hons.) mass communication. Retrieved from https://rccmindore.com/wp-content/uploads/2020/12/History-of-Media-Paper-01.pdf

Report of the Recess Committee on the establishment of a Department of Agriculture and Industries for Ireland. (1896). Dublin, Ireland: Browne and Nolan.

Rhoades, R. E., & Booth, R. H. (1982). Farmer-Backto-Farmer: A model for generating acceptable agricultural technology. Agricultural Administration, 11, 127-137.

Rivera, W. M., & Gustafson, D. J. (Eds.). (1991). Agricultural extension: Worldwide institutional evolution and forces for change. Amsterdam, Netherlands; New York, NY: Elsevier.

Robert, K. (1955). Skills of an effective administrator. Harvard Business Review, 33(1), 33-42.

Robert, L., & Aho, W. (n.d.). The four functions of management. Retrieved from https://fhsu.pressbooks.pub/management/chapter/the-history-of-management/#:~:text=The%20concept%20of%20management%20has,recorded%20by%20Middle%20Eastern%20priests.

Rogers, E. (2003). Diffusion of innovations. New York, NY: The Free Press.

Rogers, E.M. & Shoemaker, F.F. (1971). Communication of innovations: A cross-cultural approach.

Roling, N. (1988). Extension science - Information systems in agricultural development. Cambridge, UK: Cambridge University Press.

RURAL DEVELOPMENT - IDC-Online. Retrieved from https://www.idc-online.com/technical_references/pdfs/civil_engineering/Rural_development.pdf

Rural Development - SlideShare. Retrieved from https://www.slideshare.net/jobitonio/rural-development-109551216

Rural development and livelihood - slideshare.net. Retrieved from https://www.slideshare.net/TAMIRE345/rural-development-and-livelihood

Rural Development and Research Ethics |authorSTREAM. Retrieved from https://www.authorstream.com/Presentation/sagarjadav2-2335786-rural-development-research-ethics/

Rural Development. Retrieved from https://d2cyt36b7wnvt9.cloudfront.net/exams/wp-content/uploads/2021/01/17232344/keec106.pdf

Russell, E. J. (1966). A history of agricultural science in Great Britain, 1620-1954. London, UK: George Allen and Unwin.

Rutsaert, P., *et al.* (2020). Agricultural journalists' role in bridging the gap between science and consumers: Insights from a cross-national survey. Journal of Science Communication, 19(01), A03.

Sajesh, V. K., & Suresh, A. (2016). Public-sector agricultural extension in India: A note. Review of Agrarian Studies, 6(1), 116-131.

Sajesh, V. K., Suresh, A., Mohanty, A. K., Sajeev, M. V., Ashaletha, S., Rejula, K., & Ravishankar, C. N. (2018). Trend and pattern of expenditure on fisheries extension in India: Implications for policy. Indian Journal of Extension Education, 54(2), 32-40.

Saraswath, V. K., Priya, P., & Ghosh, A. (2019). A note on free trade agreements and their costs. New Delhi, India: NITI Aayog. Retrieved from https://niti.gov.in/writereaddata/files/document_publication/FTA-NITI-FINAL.pdf

Sawant, P. A. (n.d.). Course no.: ELE. EXTN 244 credits: 3 (2+1). Retrieved from https://bscagristudy.online/wp-content/uploads/2021/03/ELE-EXTN-244-PRINTED-FULL-NOTES.pdf

School of Economics | Leibenstein Critical Minimum Theory. Retrieved from https://www.schoolofeconomics.net/leibenstein-critical-minimum-theory/

Sen, A. K. (1975). Employment, technology, and development. Oxford: Clarendon Press.

Simin, M. T., & Janković, D. (2014). Applicability of diffusion of innovation theory in organic agriculture. Economics of Agriculture, 61(2), 517-529.

Simpson, B. M., Franzel, S., Degrande, A., Kundhlande, G., & Tsafack, S. (2015). Farmer-to-farmer extension: Issues in planning and implementation. University of Illinois, Modernizing Extension and Advisory Services (MEAS) Technical Note, USA.

Singh, A. K. (2014). Agricultural Extension and Farm Journalism. Agrobios Publishing.

Singh, K. K., & Ali, S. (2001). Role of Panchayati Raj Institutions for rural development. New Delhi, India: Sarup & Sons.

Sinha, R. S. (2022). Poverty in India has declined over the last decade but not as much as previously thought. Policy Research Working Paper. Washington, DC: World Bank.

Slade, R. H., & Feder, G. (1985). Training and visit extension: A manual of instruction (mimeo). Washington, DC: World Bank.

SlideShare. (n.d.). Week 1 Definition and Forms of Journalism. Retrieved from https://www.slideshare.net/hilaveli/week-1-definition-and-forms-of-journalism

Smith, H. (1972). The Society for the Diffusion of Useful Knowledge, 1826-1846. London, UK: Vine Press.

Smith, V. (1994, Summer). A learner centered approach to social skills for technical foresters. In From the field. Rural Development Forestry Network Paper 17e (p. 12-20). London, UK: Overseas Development Institute.

Society for the Diffusion of Useful Knowledge. (1827). Rules of the Society for the Diffusion of Useful Knowledge. London, UK: William Clowes.

Stogdill, R. M. (1950). Leadership, membership and organization. Psychological Bulletin, 47, 1-14.

Suchman, E. (1976). Evaluative research. New York, NY: Russell Sage Foundation.

Sulaiman, R. V., & Davis, K. (2012). The 'New Extensionist': Roles, strategies, and capacities to strengthen extension and advisory services. Global Forum for Rural Advisory Services, Lindau.

Sulaiman, R. V., Hall, A., Kalaivani, N. J., Dorai, K., & Reddy, T. S. V. (2012). Necessary, but not sufficient: Critiquing the role of information and communication technology in putting knowledge into use. Journal of Agricultural Education and Extension, 18(4), 331-346.

Swami, P. (2012). Figures bust myth India's bureaucracy is "bloated." The Hindu. Retrieved from https://www.thehindu.com/news/national/Figures-bust-myth-Indias-bureaucracy-is-%E2%80%9Cbloated%E2%80%9D/article13386342.ece

Swanson, B. E., & Claar, J. B. (1984). The history and development of agricultural extension. Urbana, IL: Illinois University, International Programs for Agricultural Knowledge Systems.

Swanson, B., & Samy, M. (2006). Extension strategies for poverty alleviation: Lessons from China, India and Egypt. Journal of Agriculture.

Tajima, S. (1991). Processes of development of agricultural extension in Japan. In Agricultural extension in Asia and the Pacific (pp. 19-36). Tokyo, Japan: Agricultural Productivity Organization.

Taylor, C. C., Ensminger, D., Johnson, H., & Joyce, J. (1965). India's roots of democracy. Bombay, India: Orient Longmans.

Tead, O. (1936). The art of leadership. New York, NY: McGraw-Hill.

TermPaper Warehouse. (n.d.). Farm journalism. Retrieved from https://www.termpaperwarehouse.com/essay-on/Farm-Journalism/507975

The planning and evaluation of extension programmes. Retrieved from http://www.fao.org/docrep/t0060e/T0060E09.htm

Thorndike, E. (1932). The Fundamentals of Learning. New York: Teachers College Press.

Thorsøe, M. H., *et al.* (2019). Strategies for engaging stakeholders through agricultural journalism: Insights from Denmark. Journal of Rural Studies, 68, 57-68.

True, A. C. (1895). Education and research in agriculture in the United States. In Yearbook of the U.S. Department of Agriculture, 1894 (pp. 81-116). Washington, DC: U.S. Government Printing Office.

True, A. C. (1900). Agricultural education in the United States. In Yearbook of the U.S. Department of Agriculture, 1899 (pp.157-190). Washington, DC: U.S. Government Printing Office.

True, A. C. (1928). A history of agricultural extension work in the United States, 1785-1923 (USDA, Miscellaneous Publication No.15). Washington, DC: U.S. Government Printing Office.

Tusser, T. ([1580] 1984). Five hundred points of good husbandry. Oxford, UK: Oxford University Press.

University of Agricultural Sciences Dharwad. (n.d.). Agricultural extension AEE 311 e-courses. Retrieved from [URL not provided]

University of Journalism. (n.d.). Journalism - Journalism 101. Retrieved from https://sites.google.com/site/mojouniversityofjournalism/journalism

Urwick, L. (1933). Organization as a Technical Problem. In L. Gulick & L. Urwick (Eds.), Papers on the science of Administration (pp. 49–88). New York, NY: Institute of Public Administration.

Van den Ban, A. W., & Hawkins, H. S. (2002). Agricultural extension. New Delhi, India: CBS Publishers.

Venkatesh, V., & Davis, F. (2000). A theoretical extension of the technology acceptance model: Four longitudinal field studies. Management Science, 46(2), 186-204.

Wallerstein, N. (2006). What is the evidence on effectiveness of empowerment to improve health? Copenhagen, Denmark: World Health Organization.

War Child. (2006). Planning, monitoring and evaluation. Retrieved from http://www.toolkitsportdevelopment.org/casab~anca2007/html/resources/86/86C76D76-2A25-4C32-BC8F-2B241F064176/Monitoring%20and%20evaluation.pdf

White, K. D. (1970). Roman farming. London, UK: Thames and Hudson.

White, K. D. (1977). Country life in classical times. London, UK: Elek Books.

White, L. D. (1955). Introduction to the study of public administration. Macmillan.

Wiggins, S., & Tropp, D. (2021). Agriculture journalism: Challenges and opportunities in a digital world. Choices, 36(1), 1-7.

Wikipedia. (n.d.). History of journalism. Retrieved from https://en.wikipedia.org/wiki/History_of_journalism

Willis, J. C. (1922). Agriculture in the tropics: An elementary treatise (3rd ed.). Cambridge, UK: Cambridge University Press.

Wilson, M.C. and Gallup, G. (1955). Extension Teaching Methods. Extension Service Circular 495, USDA, Washington, D.C.

World Bank. (1986). Project monitoring and evaluation. In World Bank technical paper: Monitoring and evaluating urban development programs: A handbook for program managers and researchers. Washington, DC: World Bank.

World Bank. (2004). Monitoring & evaluation: Some tools, methods, and approaches. Washington, DC: World Bank.

World Development Report. (2007). Cape Town: World Bank.

Yahaya, M. K. (2003). Development Communication. Lesson from Change and Social Engineering Projects. Pp 197-198.

Yukl, G. (2006). Leadership in organizations (6th ed.). Upper Saddle River, NJ: Pearson-Prentice Hall.

Zijp, W. (1994). Improving the transfer and use of agricultural information: A guide to information technology (World Bank Discussion Paper 247). Washington, DC: The World Bank.

Index